D1545218

487.3
M

MASTERING NEW TESTAMENT GREEK

A Beginning Greek Grammar, Including Lesson Plans for Intermediate and Advanced Greek Students

Monastic Library
Holy Cross Monastery
West Park, NY 12493

W. Harold Mare

BAKER BOOK HOUSE
Grand Rapids, Michigan

To

BETTY,

my loving and steadfast wife,

who has supported me in all my

scholarly and ministerial

endeavors

Copyright 1975, 1977
by W. Harold Mare

Reprinted 1979 by
Baker Book House

ISBN: 0-8010-6064-8

Third printing, August 1985

Printed in the United States of America

TABLE OF CONTENTS

PART I: BEGINNING GREEK GRAMMAR AND READING LESSONS

Lesson 1: Introduction – Alphabet, Breathing and Accents   1
Lesson 2: Present Active Indicative of λύω   5
Lesson 3: Second Declension O Stems; Meaning of the
           Cases   8

Types of First and Second Declension Endings   11

Lesson 4: Future Active Indicative of λύω   12
Lesson 5: Present Middle-Passive and Future Middle and
           Passive Indicative of λύω   13
Lesson 6: First Declension in α and η   17
Lesson 7: The Article, and First Declension Masculine
           and Second Declension Feminine Nouns   19
Lesson 8: Personal Pronouns   21
Lesson 9: Explanation of the Demonstrative and Relative
           Pronouns   23
Lesson 10: Perfect Active, Middle-Passive of λύω   26
Lesson 11: Imperfect Active, Middle-Passive of λύω   28
Lesson 12: Aorist Active, Middle, and Passive of λύω   30
Lesson 13: Pluperfect Active, Middle-Passive of λύω, and the
           Verb εἰμί   32
Lesson 14: Proclitics, Enclitics; Second Aorist Verbs   35
Lesson 15: Third Declension   37
Lesson 16: Third Declension Continued   39
Lesson 17: The Greek Moods Explained   41
Lesson 18: Third Declension Continued; Interrogative
           and Indefinite Pronouns   43
Lesson 19: The Present Active Participle   45
Lesson 20: The Participle Explained; Principal Parts
           of the Verb   47
Lesson 21: The Aorist Active Participle   50
Lesson 22: The Present Middle-Passive and Aorist Middle
           Participles   52
Lesson 23: The Aorist Passive Participle; the Genitive
           Absolute; Second Aorist Middle Participle   55
Lesson 24: The Perfect Active Participle   57
Lesson 25: The Perfect Middle-Passive Participle   59
Lesson 26: The Subjunctive   61
Lesson 27: Uses of the Subjunctive   63
Lesson 28: The Infinitive; Using the Lexicon   66

Lesson 29: The Imperative   69
Lesson 30: The Contract Verbs   71
Lesson 31: The Contract Verbs Continued; The Liquid Verbs   75
Lesson 32: The μι Verbs   79
Lesson 33: The μι Verbs Continued   83
Lesson 34: The μι Verbs Continued; Aorist of γινώσκω; Forms
            of εἰμί; Second Aorist of ἔρχομαι   85
Lesson 35: Use of the Relative and Syntax of the Cases   88
Lesson 36: Syntax of the Cases Continued; Parsing Exercises   91
Lesson 37: The Verb οἶδα; The ἵνα Object Clause; Conditional
            Sentences; and The New Testament Optative Paradigm   94
Lesson 38: The Greek Comparative and Superlative; Articular
            Infinitive of Purpose; Two-ending Third Declension
            Adjectives   98
Lesson 39: Greek Numerals, and Coordinate and Subordinate
            Clauses   101

Supplemental List of Greek Verbs for Parsing   103

Supplemental Sentences for Practice in Translating
English to Greek   105

The Greek Reader on The Gospel of John   110

The Greek Reader Notes   123

PART II: LESSON PLANS FOR THE INTERMEDIATE GREEK STUDENT   160

PART III: LESSON PLANS FOR THE ADVANCED GREEK STUDENT   162

APPENDIX

Greek Verbal Prefixes and Suffixes   168
Greek Parsing Number System   170
Greek First and Second Declension Charts   171
Greek Third Declension Chart   172

Principles of the NT Greek Verb: Contract, Liquid
and μι Verbs   175

Greek Tenses Chart   177
The Greek Optative Chart   178

Chart of Suffixes for Substantives   179
Chart of Suffixes for Adjectives   180
Chart on Compound Words   181

Greek Word Formation Analysis   182

Examples of Diagramming of Greek Sentences   185

New Testament Greek Syntax Chart:

    Case Chart   191

Case Chart	191
The Verb	194
The Moods	198
New Testament Greek Conditional Sentences	203
Types of Subordinate Clauses and Phrases	205
Prepositions Chart	207
Chart on the Use of the Greek Article	213
Chart on Coordinating Conjunctions	215
Chart on Intensive Particles	219
Pronunciation of the Alphabet in Modern Greek	221
Common Expressions in Modern Greek	222
Greek to English Vocabulary	226
English to Greek Vocabulary	237
Paradigms of the Omega Verb λύω	248

PREFACE

This beginning Greek Grammar results from many years of teaching Greek on the seminary level. The various parts of this grammar have been tested in the classroom for several years and the composite edition which appeared in 1975 has been used in a number of beginning, intermediate and advanced Greek classes.

In the last three years I have made a number of changes for the improvement of this revised edition. My thanks goes out to my colleagues in the New Testament Department of Covenant Theological Seminary, Dr. Wilber B. Wallis and Dr. George W. Knight, III, for their wise counsel and valuable suggestions which have contributed to the improvement of the book. I greatly appreciate their help and encouragement. I also express my sincere appreciation to our faculty secretary, Mrs. June Dare, for her valuable assistance in helping me with proofreading and correcting the manuscript in preparing it for final publication.

The approach to the study of beginning Greek in this volume, Mastering New Testament Greek, is neither inductive nor deductive. Rather it is a combination of both. Right from the beginning the student is given the necessary principles of grammar which are substantially added to from lesson to lesson and combined with word frequency vocabularies, analytical charts and paradigms, all to help the student see and understand various grammatical principles of the Greek language. Then also, from the beginning the student is presented with translation exercises similar in content to the Greek text of John, through which he can put his grammar into practice.

In considering a suitable method of teaching beginning Greek, I have felt that the exclusively inductive approach to the language in which the student on the first day begins to translate some portion of the New Testament text itself with exposure to only minute and sometimes disconnected segments of grammar makes him face too many linguistic problems all at once and involves him in an excessively laborious activity.

On the other hand, the deductive approach which starts the student translating Greek sentences that have no connection with the Biblical text and content can make the study dull and frustrating for him. Therefore, I have developed a simplified Greek Reader Text based on the Greek text of John 1 to 5, which, while presenting the substance of the Biblical account given by John, does so in simplified Greek sentences. As the material in the Reader Text progresses, the sentences become more complex in construction. These reading lessons are synchronized with the grammar lessons, so that near the end of the course of the lessons the student is able to move quite easily into translating the actual Greek text of John 6.

The students who have studied under this system have appreciated the fact that, while they have been learning the basics of Greek grammar and have been applying these principles in translation, their interest has been kept alive through reading a narrative that is quite similar to the Greek text of John 1 to 5.

The Greek Reader Notes, which accompany the Greek Reader Text, enable the student to translate the Greek Reader Text more easily and accurately without having to look up every word in the vocabulary list given in this book.

As an additional feature, I have included in the book a series of lesson plans for Intermediate Greek which leads the student through the lessons of this text in a review of the basic Greek grammar principles and then brings him on to translation of further material in the Greek text of the Gospel of John. The book also contains lesson plans for Advanced Greek that include the study of advanced Greek syntax through the use of my New Testament Greek Syntax Chart found in this book. In these advanced Greek lessons extensive translation is done in the Gospel of Luke.

It is the author's hope that this text will enable beginning students to facilitate their progress in learning the basic principles of Koine Greek and that it will aid them, as well as the intermediate and advanced Greek students, in their understanding of the language and thought of the Greek New Testament.

W. Harold Mare
Covenant Theological Seminary
September, 1977
St. Louis, Missouri

PART I

BEGINNING GREEK GRAMMAR

AND

READING LESSONS

Introduction - Alphabet, Breathing and Accents

INTRODUCTION

The following text is not intended to be an exhaustive grammar of the Greek New Testament, but in it are compiled the necessary essentials needed by the beginning Greek student. The student will observe that the forms found in the New Testament have been classified to enable the beginner to grasp the elementary principles as quickly and easily as possible.

The syntactical principles presented are those that are most common in the New Testament. If desired, this book may be supplemented with New Testament Greek for Beginners by J. Gresham Machen. The vocabulary word lists are based upon the frequency with which words occur in the New Testament, those most frequently used being given to the student first.

ALPHABET

Form[1]	Name	Transliteration	Sound
A α	alpha	a	father
B β	beta	b	Bible
Γ γ	gamma	g, ng[2]	gate, angel
Δ δ	delta	d	date
E ε	epsilon	e	elephant
Z ζ	zeta	z	adze
H η	eta	e	they
θ ϑ	theta	th	theist
I ι	iota	i (short/long)	intrigue
K κ	kappa	k, c (hard)	capital, kangaroo
Λ λ	lambda	l	lemon
M μ	mu	m	motor
N ν	nu	n	never
Ξ ξ	xi	x	axiom
O ο	omicron	o	office
Π π	pi	p	picnic
P ρ	rho	r, rh[3]	swimmer, catarrh
Σ σ (ς)[4]	sigma	s	silent
T τ	tau	t	take
Y υ	upsilon	u	French "u" or German "ü"
Φ φ	phi	ph	Philip
X χ	chi	ch	character
Ψ ψ	psi	ps	apse
Ω ω	omega	o	over

---

[1]"For centuries capital letters were used by the Greeks. Though the small letters that later came into use are less like the Latin-English, we can easily trace their development from the capitals. The difference between the two types is no greater than that between capitals and small letters in English." H. L. Crosby and J. N. Schaeffer, An Introduction to Greek (Boston: Allyn and Bacon, 1928), p. xxiii, footnote.

[2]Before another γ, κ or χ, γ is pronounced ng.

[3]At the beginning of a word it is ῥ.

[4]ς is written at the end of a word, σ elsewhere.

VOWELS

The vowels α, ι, υ, can be either long or short, while ε and o are always short, and η and ω are always long.

DIPHTHONGS

The diphthongs, a combination of two vowels in one syllable, the second of which is always an ι or υ, are as follows:

αι as in <u>ai</u>sle
ει as in w<u>ei</u>ght
οι as in f<u>oi</u>l
υι as in sq<u>ue</u>ak
αυ as in c<u>ow</u>
ευ as in <u>eh</u>-oo
ηυ as in <u>ēh</u>-oo
ου as in gr<u>ou</u>p

Greek diphthongs are to be considered long, for accenting purposes, except αι and οι when they are the final letters of a word.

CONSONANTS

The following is a classification of consonants:

Liquids: λ, μ, ν, ρ

Sibilants: σ, ς

Double consonants: ζ, ξ, ψ

Stops (or mutes):

	Labial:	dental:	velar:
Voiceless	π	τ	κ
Voiced	β	δ	γ
Fricatives	φ	θ	χ

NOTE: Memorize this chart. It will be extremely useful in the study of the verb.

BREATHING

Every Greek word beginning with a vowel has either a smooth (') or a rough (') breathing. E.g., ἄγω, εὑρίσκω. The rough breathing indicates that a blowing or <u>h</u> sound should be pronounced before the initial vowel, e.g., ὑπό, hupo. The initial υ vowel always has the rough breathing. Breathings are written over the small vowels, over the second vowel of a diphthong (υἱ), and before a capital letter ('Ελλάς).

PROCLITICS AND ENCLITICS

A proclitic is a monosyllable which has no accent of its own and is pronounced with the following word; e.g., ὁ βίος, "the life."

An enclitic is a one or two syllable word, usually with no accent of its own, which is pronounced with the preceding word; e.g., καλοί εἰσιν, "They are beautiful."

PUNCTUATION

The period is indicated by (.) and the comma by (,). The question mark is indicated by (;) and the colon or semi-colon by (·).

ACCENTS[1]

Primary rules:

1. The verb accent is recessive, while the noun accent remains on the same syllable on which it occurs in the nominative singular form, if possible. Examples of:

   The recessive verb accent: λύω, ἔλυον;
   The constant noun accent: υἱός, υἱόν; λόγος, λόγον;
   ἄνθρωπος, ἄνθρωπον.

2. The acute accent (´) may occur on any one of the last three syllables, the circumflex (~) on the last two syllables, and the grave (`) only on the last syllable. Examples of:

   The acute accent: υἱός, λόγος, ἄνθρωπος;
   The circumflex accent: υἱῶν, δοῦλος;
   The grave accent: υἱὸν καὶ.....

3. A long ultima (i.e., the last syllable of the word) will keep the accent from going farther back than the penult (i.e., the next to the last syllable). A short ultima will allow the accent in certain words to go back to the antepenult (the third syllable from the end of the word).

---

[1]For further elaboration see A. J. Koster, <u>The Greek Accents</u> (Leiden: E. J. Brill, 1962).

(The student may work from left to right or vice versa)

If there occurs on the:

Antepenult, an acute	Penult, an		Ultima, an			The word has
	acute	circumfl.	acute	circumfl.	grave	
X						a short ultima, ἄνθρωπος
	X					The word has 1) a short penult and a long or short ultima, θανάτου, λίθος, or 2) a long penult and long ultima, δούλου, προφήτης.
		X				A long penult and a short ultima, οἶκος δοῦλος
			X			Either a long or short ultima, ἀδελφός ἀδελφούς
				X		A long ultima, ἀδελφοῦ υἱοῦ υἱῷ
					X	The word is followed by other words without intervening punctuation, πιστὴ καὶ ἀμὴν λέγω ἀδελφὸς δοῦλος.

EXERCISES

1. Practice writing the letters of the Greek alphabet and the diphthongs and sound them out loud.

2. Accent the following forms:
    <u>Verbs</u>: λυω, λυουσι(ν), λυει, λυομεν, ἐχω, ἐχομεν, ἐχετε, εἰπον, βλεπει, ἠγον, ἠγομεν, λυομεθα.
    <u>Nouns</u> (vocabulary forms, ἄνθρωπος and θεός): ἀνθρωπος, θεος, ἀνθρωπου, ἀνθρωπου, θεου, ἀνθρωπους, θεοις, θεων, ἀνθρωπε, ἀνθρωπων, θεῳ.

Present Active Indicative of λύω

VOCABULARY[1]

ἄνθρωπος, ου, ὁ	– man	εἶπον	– I said (epic)
γάρ	– for	ἔχω	– I have, hold
δέ	– but, and	θεός, οῦ, ὁ	– God (theology)
ἐγώ	– I (ego)	ἵνα	– in order that, that
εἰμί	– I am	λύω[2]	– I loose

EXPLANATIONS

The Greek verb has tense, voice and mood. The <u>tenses</u> are seven and have to do with time (past, present and future) and/or kind of action (linear or continuous, ———; punctiliar or definite, ● ; or a combination of both linear and punctiliar, ●———, or ———●).

<u>Voice</u> has to do with the relationship of the subject to the action expressed in the verb: <u>active</u> voice in the verb represents the subject as acting (John <u>hits</u> the ball); <u>passive</u> voice indicates that the subject is acted upon (John <u>is hit</u> by the ball); and <u>middle</u> voice in the verb represents the subject as acting on himself or for himself (John hit himself or John hit for himself).

<u>Mood</u> in the form of the verb has to do with the way the statement is made, whether as fact, probability, possibility, command, wish, etc. That with which we are concerned for the present is the <u>indicative</u> mood in which the verb makes an assertion as a fact (John hits the ball). Whether it is actually a fact is determined by the context.

Greek verbs, as in English, are used in both the singular and plural, with first, second and third persons in each case.

The present tense (continuous or punctiliar action), active voice, and indicative mood of λύω is as follows:

<u>Singular</u>

1.	λύω	– I loose (●), I am loosing (———).
2.	λύεις	– You loose, you are loosing.
3.	λύει	– He, she, it looses, or is loosing.

<u>Plural</u>

1.	λύομεν	– We loose, we are loosing.
2.	λύετε	– You loose, you are loosing.
3.	λύουσι(ν)[3]	– They loose, they are loosing.

---

[1]The vocabulary section in these lessons gives first those words in the New Testament which occur with more and more frequency. See Bruce M. Metzger, <u>Lexical Aids for Students of New Testament Greek</u> (Princeton, N.J., 1958).

[2]λύω is used only 42–45 times in the <u>New Testament</u>, but because of its regular structure in the formation of all of its tenses, we insert it here and use it as a verbal model.

[3]This ν is simply orthographical and has no meaning. It is added when the next word begins with a vowel, before a punctuation mark, and sometimes (in the New Testament) even when the next word begins with a consonant.

In analyzing these present active indicative forms of λύω, it will be observed that the forms are composed of three parts: the base or stem, λυ; certain vowels added to the stem called the variable or thematic vowels (ω, ο, ε) and in some cases an additional personal ending (either a single letter as σ, or several letters as μεν, τε, σι).

These present tense personal endings, called primary[4], are then as follows:

–ω	–μεν
–ς	–τε
–ει	–σι

The variable vowel, when separate from the personal ending itself, precedes that personal ending and is something like a verbal connective or cushion between the stem and the ending.

The variable vowel varies with the tense, mood, person, and number of the verb. This vowel sometimes occurs at the end of a verb with no further ending following it. In connection with many verbs, the following generalizations apply regarding the variable vowels:

1. ω, ο, ε, ει are generally the variable vowels for:

> The present tense (active, middle, and passive voice) in the indicative, imperative, infinitive, and participial moods.
> The imperfect tense (active, middle, and passive voice) in the indicative mood.
> The future tense (active, middle, and passive voice) in the indicative mood.
> The second aorist tense (active and middle voice) in the indicative mood.
> The pluperfect tense (active voice) in the indicative mood.

2. α is generally the variable vowel for:

> The first aorist tense (active and middle voice) in the indicative, imperative, infinitive, and participle.
> The perfect tense (active voice) in the indicative.

3. ω, η, ῃ are generally the variable vowels for:

> The present tense (active, middle, and passive voice) in the subjunctive mood.
> The aorist tense (active, middle, and passive voice) in the subjunctive mood.

GREEK PARSING NUMBER SYSTEM

TENSE		VOICE	MOOD	PERSON		NUMBER	
	I–Present	a–active	Indic.	1–1st sing.		4–1st plur.	
	II–Imperfect	m–middle		2–2nd sing.		5–2nd plur.	
1&2	III–Future	p–passive		3–3rd sing.		6–3rd plur.	
1&2	IV–Aorist						
1&2	V–Perfect		Subj.	11–1st sing.		14–1st plur.	
	VI–Pluperfect			12–2nd sing.		15–2nd plur.	
	VII–Future Perfect			13–3rd sing.		16–3rd plur.	

[4]Those endings in the present, future, perfect, and future perfect tenses are called primary tense endings, while those of the imperfect, aorist, and pluperfect (or past perfect) are called secondary.

MOOD	PERSON	NUMBER
Impv.	22–2nd sing.	25–2nd plur.
	23–3rd sing.	26–3rd plur.
Infin.	31	
Participles	33–sing.	36–plur.
Opt.	41–1st sing.	44–1st plur.
	42–2nd sing.	45–2nd plur.
	43–3rd sing.	46–3rd plur.

For example:

λύεται	– I, mp., 3	
λύων	– I, a., 33 nom. masc.	
λύσετε	– III, a., 5	
λύοι	– I, a., 43	
λῦσον	– 1–IV, a., 22	
λελυκέναι	– V, a., 31	
λυθῶμεν	– 1–IV, p., 14	

WORD ORDER

The normal order of words in the Greek sentence generally follows the word order in English: subject, verb, object. However, for emphasis, for instance, the Greek sentence may place a part of speech in the first or last position in the sentence or clause.

EXERCISES

1. Memorize the vocabulary of Lesson 2, reciting the words out loud.

2. Practice writing the present active indicative of λύω.

3. Simplified Greek Reader – John 1:1-10. Read out loud putting stress on the accented syllable.

Second Declension O Stems; Meaning of the Cases

VOCABULARY

καί   — and, even, also   οὐ, οὐκ, οὐχ[1] — not
κύριος, ου, ὁ — Lord, sir   πᾶς, πᾶσα, πᾶν — all, every
λέγω   — I say, speak (cf.   ποιέω   — I make, do (poem)
        English words   σύ   — you
        ending in -logy)   τίς, τί[2]   — who? what? why?
ὁ, ἡ, τό   — the (masc., fem.,   (interrogative)
        neut. article)   τις, τι[2]   — someone, something,
ὅτι   — that, because   anyone, a certain
                                         one (indefinite)
                        ὡς   — as, that, how, about

EXPLANATIONS

In the vocabulary given thus far there have occurred several forms ending in -ος, e.g., ἄνθρωπος, θεός, κύριος. These nouns represent the second declension, being one of the three declensions in Greek. This type is presented first because it is the easiest of the three to master at this stage.

Each of the Greek declensions has gender, number and case. The <u>genders</u> are <u>masculine</u>, <u>feminine</u> and <u>neuter</u>; the <u>numbers</u> are <u>singular</u> and <u>plural</u>;[3] the <u>cases</u> in which the forms are declined[4] are <u>nominative</u>, <u>genitive</u>, <u>dative</u>, <u>accusative</u> and <u>vocative</u>.

The declension of κύριος and θεός, masculine nouns, as most of the second declension nouns ending in -ος are, is as follows:

	SINGULAR			PLURAL	
Nominative	κύριος	Lord		κύριοι	Lords
Genitive	κυρίου	of the Lord		κυρίων	of Lords
Dative	κυρίῳ	to or for the Lord		κυρίοις	to or for the Lords
Accusative	κύριον	Lord		κυρίους	Lords
Vocative	κύριε	Lord		κύριοι	Lords
Nominative	θεός	God		θεοί	Gods
Genitive	θεοῦ	of God		θεῶν	of Gods
Dative	θεῷ	to or for God		θεοῖς	to or for Gods
Accusative	θεόν	God		θεούς	God
Vocative	θεός	God		θεοί	Gods
	θεέ				

Greek nouns used with the definite article, ὁ, ἡ, τό (masculine, feminine and neuter) are called articular and are to be translated as "the....," e.g., "the man" or "the brother," etc.

---

[1]The κ and χ are added to οὐ when the following word begins with a vowel or with a vowel with rough breathing, respectively; e.g., οὐ λέγω; οὐκ εἶπον; οὐχ εὑρίσκω.

[2]Observe that the difference here is whether the accent is used or, as we shall see, how it is used with these forms. For their declension see page 44.

[3]In earlier Greek there was a dual number sometimes used to describe two persons or objects.

[4]To help describe the relationships of the words to other words in the sentence and to the thought.

Greek does not have an indefinite article like the English "a" or "an." When the Greek nouns do not have the definite article, they are normally to be translated with the English indefinite article; e.g., "a man" or "an apple." However, in the case of proper nouns, even when they are anarthrous (i.e., without the article), they are definite by nature and can be translated with the English article "the"; e.g., κύριος, the Lord; θεός, God or the God.

The <u>nominative</u> case is the naming case, and generally the subject of the sentence is put in this case. ὁ κύριος λέγει, the Lord speaks.

The <u>genitive</u> case is one of description, qualification, and separation. Thus, it carries, among other things, the idea of possession expressed in English by "of" or an affixed "s." ἀνθρώπου, of a man.

The <u>dative</u> case expresses the functions of personal interest (as indirect object), location and instrumentality. One of the most common uses is that of indirect object. ἀνθρώπῳ, to or for a man.

The <u>accusative</u> case expresses the idea of extension and is commonly used as the direct object of the verb. λύω τὸν κύριον, I loose the Lord.

The <u>vocative</u> case is one of direct address. κύριε, λέγω τῷ ἀνθρώπῳ, Lord, I am speaking to the man. Often the nominative form is used to express the vocative idea.

RECAPITULATION

CASE ENDING	FUNCTION
Nominative	Subject, naming case
Genitive	Description Quality
	Separation
Dative	Personal Interest
	Location
	Instrumentality
Accusative	Extension
Vocative	Direct address

There are a number of neuter second declension nouns in -ον.
They are declined as follows:

	SINGULAR		PLURAL	
Nominative	βιβλίον	a book	βιβλία	books
Genitive	βιβλίου	of a book	βιβλίων	of books
Dative	βιβλίῳ	to or for a book	βιβλίοις	to or for books
Accusative	βιβλίον	book	βιβλία	books
Vocative	βιβλίον	book	βιβλία	books

It is to be observed that as in the case of κύριος and θεός the ο
vowel predominates. It is to be further observed that the neuter second
declension nouns have in the nominative, accusative and vocative the
same form in the singular and the plural.

EXERCISES

1. Practice writing out the second declension forms in this lesson.
   Memorize them, sounding them out loud.

2. Study the second declension forms found on the accompanying First
   and Second Declension Chart. (next page)

3. Simplified Greek Reader: Translate with the aid of the Reader
   Notes, John 1:1-5.

4. Memorize the vocabulary in this and every lesson, sounding the
   words out loud. Mastering the meaning of these words will be of
   considerable help in obtaining a good working knowledge of New
   Testament Greek.

THE ARTICLE

EXPLANATIONS:

The article "the" in form consists of much the same endings as those in the second (or o) declension and the first (or η) declension with the letter τ preceding these endings, except in the case of the nominative singular and plural, masculine and feminine, which forms in the nominative singular are distinct, ὁ and ἡ. The neuter nominative and accusative singular form (τό) is different from the neuter second declension form. The declension is as follows:

Singular

	M.	F.	N.
N.	ὁ	ἡ	τό
G.	τοῦ	τῆς	τοῦ
D.	τῷ	τῇ	τῷ
A.	τόν	τήν	τό

Plural

	M.	F.	N.
N.	οἱ	αἱ	τά
G.	τῶν	τῶν	τῶν
D.	τοῖς	ταῖς	τοῖς
A.	τούς	τάς	τά

TYPES OF 2ND DECLENSION NOUNS AND ENDINGS

	Masculine	Feminine	Neuter	Masc.-Feminine	Neuter
N.	νόμος	ὁδός	δῶρον	-ος	-ον
G.	νόμου	ὁδοῦ	δώρου	-ου	-ου
D.	νόμῳ	ὁδῷ	δώρῳ	-ῳ	-ῳ
A.	νόμον	ὁδόν	δῶρον	-ον	-ον
V.	νόμε	ὁδέ	δῶρον	-ε	-ον
N.	νόμοι	ὁδοί	δῶρα	-οι	-α
G.	νόμων	ὁδῶν	δώρων	-ων	-ων
D.	νόμοις	ὁδοῖς	δώροις	-οις	-οις
A.	νόμους	ὁδούς	δῶρα	-ους	-α
V.	νόμοι	ὁδοί	δῶρα	-οι	-α

TYPES OF 1ST DECLENSION NOUNS

	Feminine			Masculine	
	-α (after ε, ι, ρ long in Gen. and Dat.)	short-α	long-η	-ας	-ης
N.	χώρα	ἀσθένεια	γλῶσσα	φωνή	νεανίας	προφήτης
G.	χώρας	ἀσθενείας	γλώσσης	φωνῆς	νεανίου	προφήτου
D.	χώρᾳ	ἀσθενείᾳ	γλώσσῃ	φωνῇ	νεανίᾳ	προφήτῃ
A.	χώραν	ἀσθένειαν	γλῶσσαν	φωνήν	νεανίαν	προφήτην
V.	χώρα	ἀσθένεια	γλῶσσα	φωνή	νεανία	προφήτα
N.	χῶραι	ἀσθένειαι	γλῶσσαι	φωναί	νεανίαι	προφῆται
G.	χωρῶν	ἀσθενειῶν	γλωσσῶν	φωνῶν	νεανιῶν	προφητῶν
D.	χώραις	ἀσθενείαις	γλώσσαις	φωναῖς	νεανίαις	προφήταις
A.	χώρας	ἀσθενείας	γλώσσας	φωνάς	νεανίας	προφήτας
V.	χῶραι	ἀσθένειαι	γλῶσσαι	φωναί	νεανίαι	προφῆται

1st DECLENSION ENDINGS

	Feminine			Masculine	
	-α (in all of sing.)	short-α	-η	-ας	-ης
N.	-α	-α	-η	-ας	-ης
G.	-ας	-ης	-ης	-ου	-ου
D.	-ᾳ	-ῃ	-ῃ	-ᾳ	-ῃ
A.	-αν	-αν	-ην	-αν	-ην
V.	-α	-α	-η	-α	-α
N.	-αι	-αι	-αι	-αι	-αι
G.	-ων	-ων	-ων	-ων	-ων
D.	-αις	-αις	-αις	-αις	-αις
A.	-ας	-ας	-ας	-ας	-ας
V.	-αι	-αι	-αι	-αι	-αι

Future Active Indicative of λύω

VOCABULARY

ἀδελφός, οῦ, ὁ — brother (Philadelphia)
ἀκούω — I hear
γῆ, γῆς, ἡ — earth
γινώσκω — I come to know
εἰς — toward, unto, into (with acc.)
ἐκ, ἐξ — out of, from (with gen., exodus, a going out)
θέλω — I will, wish

λαμβάνω — I take, receive (epilepsy, a seizing)
λόγος, ου, ὁ — word (logic)
μετά — with (with gen.) — after (with acc.)
οὐρανός, οῦ, ὁ — heaven
πιστεύω — I believe, trust
υἱός, οῦ, ὁ — son

EXPLANATIONS

In this lesson we are introduced to three new ω verbs given in the present tense, active voice, indicative mood, first person, singular form:

γινώσκω, λαμβάνω, πιστεύω.

By indicative is meant that this is the form of the verb used to indicate a factual statement; whether that statement is actually true or not is seen by examining the context. These three verbs are formed in the present active indicative just as in the case with λύω seen in Lesson 2. The future active indicative of these verbs is formed the same way, except that a σ is placed between the base or stem and the vowel and ending, as follows:

SINGULAR		PLURAL	
1. λύσω	I shall loose / I shall be loosing	1. λύσομεν	We shall loose / We shall be loosing
2. λύσεις	You will loose / You will be loosing	2. λύσετε	You will loose / You will be loosing
3. λύσει	He, she, it will loose / He will be loosing	3. λύσουσι(ν)	They will loose / They will be loosing

EXERCISES

1. Memorize vocabulary of Lesson 4.

2. Learn the future active indicative forms and meanings of λύω, and practice writing the other verbs in Lesson 4 in the future active indicative.

3. Simplified Greek Reader: John 1:6-10. Read out loud and translate with the aid of the Reader Notes.

Present Middle-Passive and Future Middle and
Passive Indicative of λύω

VOCABULARY

ἀλλά	— but, except
ἀποκρίνομαι	— I answer
γίνομαι	— I become, I am
ἐάν	— if
εἰ	— if
εἶδον	— I saw (idea). This is an aorist (past tense) form of a verb used very frequently.
ἐμαυτοῦ, σεαυτοῦ, ἑαυτοῦ	— of myself, of yourself, of himself, respectively (ἑαυτῶν, the plural, is used for all three persons.)
ἐν	— in, by, with, among (with dative)
ἡμέρα, ας, ἡ	— day (ephemeral, for a day)
μαθητής, οῦ, ὁ	— disciple
οὖν	— therefore, then, accordingly
οὕτως	— thus
ὑπό	— by (with genitive) under (with accusative, hypodermic)

EXPLANATIONS

The present tense middle-passive and the future middle and passive indicative
forms of the ω verb (like λύω) have endings which are different from
the active, while the variable vowel ο/ε before the ending is much the
same as in the active forms. It is to be remembered that the passive form
of the verb indicates that the subject of the sentence or clause is being acted
upon, while the middle form shows that the subject is acting to or for himself.
In the present tense, the middle and passive forms are identical, and distinction
in meaning is to be learned from the context while in the future the passive
forms differ from the middle. The passive forms and meanings are much more
frequently employed. The present tense, middle and passive, indicative is as
follows:

1. λύομαι   — I am loosed
     I am being loosed
     I loose myself
     I am loosing myself

1. λυόμεθα   — We are loosed
     We are being loosed
     We loose ourselves
     We are loosing ourselves

2. λύῃ   — You are loosed
     You are being loosed
     You loose yourself
     You are loosing yourself

2. λύεσθε   — You are loosed
     You are being loosed
     You loose yourselves
     You are loosing yourselves

3. λύεται   — He is loosed
     He is being loosed
     He looses himself
     He is loosing himself

3. λύονται   — They are loosed
     They are being loosed
     They loose themselves
     They are loosing themselves

The future tense, middle, indicative is the same in form as the present middle
or passive forms above except for the insertion of the extra tense sign σ
between the base or stem of the word and the variable or thematic vowel and
ending.

1.	λύσομαι – I shall loose myself I shall be loosing myself	1.	λυσόμεθα – We shall loose ourselves We shall be loosing ourselves
2.	λύσῃ – You will loose yourself You will be loosing yourself	2.	λύσεσθε – You will loose your- selves You will be loosing yourselves
3.	λύσεται – He will loose himself He will be loosing himself	3.	λύσονται – They will loose them- selves They will be loosing themselves

The future tense, passive, indicative is formed with the same endings
as the present passive, but the syllable θης is inserted before the
variable or thematic vowel and the endings, as follows:

SINGULAR		PLURAL	
1. λυθήσομαι	– I shall be loosed	1. λυθησόμεθα	– We shall be loosed
2. λυθήσῃ	– You will be loosed	2. λυθήσεσθε	– You shall be loosed
3. λυθήσεται	– He will be loosed	3. λυθήσονται	– They shall be loosed

The student will observe that stress is placed in the above translation
of the forms on the punctiliar (.) and linear or continuous (_____)
kind of action. In the present and future tenses either one may be
included in the meaning, depending on the context.

It is now time for the student to study the auxiliary "Verbal Prefixes
and Suffixes Chart" (next two pages), studying those columns which
present the present and future tenses, active, middle, and passive,
observing the base, the extra tense sign, the thematic vowel, and the
ending. What have been studied thus far have been the primary tense
endings which are used in the present, future, perfect, and future
perfect tenses.

In this lesson the student is introduced to the verbs γίνομαι and
ἀποκρίνουαι which are present middle and passive in form but do not
have a middle or passive meaning. Such a verb is called deponent, from
the Latin depono, "to place away or aside"; i.e., this type of verb in
a sense has placed aside the middle or passive meaning although it has
the middle or passive form, not the active form. There are a number of
deponent verbs.

EXERCISES

1. Memorize the vocabulary of Lesson 5.

2. Learn the present and future middle and passive forms and meanings
   of λύω and practice writing out these forms with the other verbs in
   Lesson 5.

3. Simplified Greek Reader: John 1:11-13. Translate using
   accompanying notes.

4. English to Greek exercises based on The Greek Reader, John 1:1-10.
   (a) The Word was God and the Word made the world.
   (b) The Word was the life of the world.
   (c) The light of the men was the life.
   (d) John bears witness concerning the light.

VERBAL PREFIXES AND SUFFIXES

SYSTEM	TENSE	AUGMENT (indic.)	REDUPLI- CATION	BASE	EXTRA TENSE SIGN	THEMATIC VOWEL	ENDING
Present	Pres. AMP			λυ		o/ε[1]	Prim.
	Impf. AMP	ἐ[2]		λυ		o/ε	Sec.
Future	Fut. AM			λυ	σ	o/ε	Prim.
1 Aor.	1 Aor. AM	ἐ		λυ	σα		Sec.
1 Pf. A.	1 Pf. A.		λε[3]	λυ	κ	α/ε	Prim.
	Plpf. A.	ἐ	λε	λυ	κ	ει	Sec.
Pf. MP	Pf. MP		λε	λυ			Prim.
	Plpf. MP	ἐ	λε	λυ			Sec.
	Fut. Pf. MP		λε	λυ	σ	o/ε	Prim.
1 Passive	Fut. P.			λυ	θησ	o/ε	Prim.
	Aor. P.	ἐ		λυ	θη		Sec.

1. a. In connection with the variable or thematic vowel o/ε (used with the present and future systems and with the future perfect and future passive tenses) o is used before μ and ν; ε is used elsewhere.

    b. The subjunctive lengthens the thematic vowel from o to ω and from ε to η.

    c. The optative combines its mood suffix ι or ιη with the variable vowel o/ε to form οι; or with (σ)α of the aorist to form αι; or with (θ)η or with the forms of εἰμί to form ει, so that the optative mood suffix signs are:

$$-οι$$
$$-αι$$
$$-ει$$

2. ἐ is a syllabic augment which is prefixed in the secondary tenses (imperfect, aorist and pluperfect) indicative to verbs beginning with a consonant. The second kind of augment is called temporal and lengthens the first syllable of verbs beginning with a vowel or diphthong. So:

UNAUGMENTED	becomes	AUGMENTED
α or ε		η
ι		ι
o		ω
υ		υ
αι or ᾳ		ῃ
οι		ῳ

3. There are two kinds of reduplication: syllabic and temporal.

    a. Syllabic reduplication means the reduplication of the initial
        consonant as a prefix in connection with verbs beginning
        with a single consonant (except ρ) and placing an ε after
        the reduplicated consonant; or in the case of verbs beginning
        with two consonants or a double consonant (ξ, ψ, or ζ) or with
        ρ reduplication is a simple ε prefixed. If the verb begins
        with a rough consonant the reduplication is a smooth or voice-
        less consonant of the same class.

    b. Temporal reduplication: in most verbs beginning with vowels
        or diphthongs the reduplication is like the augment.

PRIMARY ENDINGS

Active			Middle and Passive	
$-\mu\iota$	$-\omega$	$-\mu\epsilon\nu$	$-\mu\alpha\iota$	$-\mu\epsilon\vartheta\alpha$
$-\varsigma$		$-\tau\epsilon$	$-\sigma\alpha\iota^1$ $-\iota$	$-\sigma\vartheta\epsilon$
$-\sigma\iota$	$-\iota$	$-\omega\sigma\iota,$ $-o\upsilon\sigma\iota$	$-\tau\alpha\iota$	$-\nu\tau\alpha\iota$

SECONDARY ENDINGS

Active		Middle and Passive	
$-\nu$	$-\mu\epsilon\nu$	$-\mu\eta\nu$	$-\mu\epsilon\vartheta\alpha$
$-\varsigma$	$-\tau\epsilon$	$-\sigma o^2,$ $-o$	$-\sigma\vartheta\epsilon$
$-$	$-\nu,$ $-\sigma\alpha\nu$	$-\tau o$	$-\nu\tau o$

---

[1]In the present middle and passive indicative and the future middle
and passive indicative, second singular, of the λύω verb and other Greek
verbs the σ of the -σαι ending drops and the vowel α contracts with the
preceding ε to form η, and the ι becomes a subscript, so that the combined final formation becomes ῃ. However, this process does not occur
in this place in the present middle and passive formation of the regular
μι verbs, which keep the -σαι at this point. See pages 80, 83 and 85.

[2]In the imperfect middle and passive indicative, second singular,
of the λύω verb and other Greek verbs the σ of the -σο ending drops and
the vowel ο contracts with the preceding ε to form ου (e.g., ἐλύου), and
in the aorist middle indicative, second singular, the σ of the σο drops
and the ο contracts with the preceding α vowel to form ω (e.g., ἐλύσω).
However, this process does not occur in this place in the imperfect
middle and passive formation of the regular μι verbs, which keep the -σο
at this point. See pages 80, 83 and 85.

First Declension in α and η

VOCABULARY

ἄγγελος, ου, ὁ	– messenger, angel
ἅγιος, α, ον	– holy; plural, as a noun, it means saints
ἁμαρτία, ας, ἡ	– sin (hamartiology)
βασιλεία, ας, ἡ	– kingdom
δόξα, ης, ἡ	– glory (doxology)
ζωή, ῆς, ἡ	– life
καρδία, ας, ἡ	– heart (cardiac)
κόσμος, ου, ὁ	– world (cosmic)
νεκρός, ά, όν	– dead (necropolis)
νόμος, ου, ὁ	– law (Deuteronomy)
ὄχλος, ου, ὁ	– crowd, multitude (ochlocracy, mob rule)

EXPLANATIONS

First declension in α and η:

This declension is called the feminine declension and the forms are
declined as follows:

	1	2	3
		SINGULAR	
N. V.	ζωή	δόξα	ἁμαρτία
G.	ζωῆς	δόξης	ἁμαρτίας
D.	ζωῇ	δόξῃ	ἁμαρτίᾳ
A.	ζωήν	δόξαν	ἁμαρτίαν
		PLURAL	
N. V.	ζωαί	δόξαι	ἁμαρτίαι
G.	ζωῶν	δοξῶν	ἁμαρτιῶν
D.	ζωαῖς	δόξαις	ἁμαρτίαις
A.	ζωάς	δόξας	ἁμαρτίας

It is to be observed that:
1. The plural forms in each of the three categories are alike.
2. Forms (1) with η in the nominative have the η vowel throughout the
   endings of the singular; forms (2) whose stems end in ς, λ, λλ, or
   a double consonant (e.g., ξ) generally have α in the nominative
   (vocative) and accusative singular, with η in the genitive and dative
   of the singular[1]; and other forms (3) have α throughout the singular
   when the ending in the nominative is α and before the α is an ε, ι, or ρ.
3. The α in the nominative, genitive and accusative singular of the exclusively α forms (not the α-η forms) in most cases is long,[2] and the α in
   the accusative plural for all forms is long (compare ἁμαρτία).
4. The genitive plural is accented on the ultima, regardless of whether
   the noun was accented on the antepenult or penult, contrary to the
   noun rule of constant accent.

---

[1]Cf. H. E. Dana and J. R. Mantey, A Manual Grammar of the Greek New
Testament (New York: MacMillan, 1927), p. 36.

[2]There are, however, some feminine nouns (such as the abstract nouns
ἀλήθεια, truth, and εὔνοια, good will) that have short α in the nominative,
accusative and vocative singular. Cf. H. W. Smyth, Greek Grammar, rev.
(Cambridge: Harvard University Press, 1959), parag. 219.

5. And, first declension nouns, when accented on the ultima, have the circumflex on the genitive and dative singular and plural, but the acute accent elsewhere.

The adjective in o and α, η:

These forms incorporate the endings to be found in the first and second declensions as follows:

SINGULAR

	MASC.	FEM.	NEUTER	MASC.	FEM.	NEUTER
N.	ἀγαθός	ἀγαθή	ἀγαθόν	ἅγιος	ἁγία	ἅγιον
G.	ἀγαθοῦ	ἀγαθῆς	ἀγαθοῦ	ἁγίου	ἁγίας	ἁγίου
D.	ἀγαθῷ	ἀγαθῇ	ἀγαθῷ	ἁγίῳ	ἁγίᾳ	ἁγίῳ
A.	ἀγαθόν	ἀγαθήν	ἀγαθόν	ἅγιον	ἁγίαν	ἅγιον
V.	ἀγαθέ	ἀγαθή	ἀγαθόν	ἅγιε	ἁγία	ἅγιον

PLURAL

	MASC.	FEM.	NEUTER	MASC.	FEM.	NEUTER
N.	ἀγαθοί	ἀγαθαί	ἀγαθά	ἅγιοι	ἅγιαι	ἅγια
G.	ἀγαθῶν	ἀγαθῶν	ἀγαθῶν	ἁγίων[3]	ἁγίων[3]	ἁγίων[3]
D.	ἀγαθοῖς	ἀγαθαῖς	ἀγαθοῖς	ἁγίοις	ἁγίαις	ἁγίοις
A.	ἀγαθούς	ἀγαθάς	ἀγαθά	ἁγίους	ἁγίας	ἅγια
V.	ἀγαθοί	ἀγαθαί	ἀγαθά	ἅγιοι	ἅγιαι	ἅγια

EXERCISES

1. Memorize the vocabulary and paradigms in this lesson.

2. Translate in the Simplified Greek Reader, John 1:14-20. Read aloud and translate with the aid of the Greek Reader Notes.

3. Do the English to Greek exercises, based on the Greek Reader, John 1:11-13.

   a. He came into the world of men.
   b. Men did not receive the light.
   c. God makes men children of God.
   d. Men see the life of God.[4]

---

[3]Note the feminine genitive plural form is the same as the masculine and neuter genitive plural which have influenced it to be accented like the masculine and neuter forms of an adjective.

[4]Supplemental sentences for each chapter for practice in translating English to Greek are to be found on pages 105-109.

The Article, and First Declension Masculine and Second Declension Feminine Nouns

VOCABULARY

ἄν	– an untranslatable word, which causes a statement otherwise definite to be contingent
γράφω	– I write (phonograph)
ἔρχομαι	– I come, go (deponent)
ἐξέρχομαι	– I go out (deponent)
εἰσέρχομαι	– I go in or into, enter (deponent)
ἔργον, ου, τό	– work (energy)
ἐσθίω	– I eat (anthropophagous, man-eating)
καθώς	– as, even as
ὁδός, οῦ, ἡ	– way, road, journey (anode, cathode, electrical terminals)
πορεύομαι	– I go, proceed (deponent)
προφήτης, ου, ὁ	– prophet
τότε	– then, at that time (adverb)

EXPLANATIONS

The article "the" in form consists of much the same endings as those in the second (or ο) declension and the first (or η) declension with the letter τ preceding these endings, except in the case of the nominative singular and plural, masculine and feminine, which forms in the nominative singular are distinct, that is, ὁ and ἡ. The neuter nominative and accusative singular form (τό) is different from that of the neuter second declension form. The declension is as follows:

	SINGULAR			PLURAL		
	M.	F.	N.	M.	F.	N.
N.	ὁ	ἡ	τό	οἱ	αἱ	τά
G.	τοῦ	τῆς	τοῦ	τῶν	τῶν	τῶν
D.	τῷ	τῇ	τῷ	τοῖς	ταῖς	τοῖς
A.	τόν	τήν	τό	τούς	τάς	τά

The uses of the article and the adjective:
The article, like the English "the," is often needed to make a word definite,[1] such as, the boy, the man, rather than a boy or a man.

The adjective, being a describing word and dependent on a noun idea whether expressed or not, is governed by the following:

1. The adjective is to agree with the noun it modifies (or qualifies) in gender, number and case; e.g., ὁ ἀγαθὸς λόγος, ἡ ἀγία δόξα.

2. It may be used predicately without the use of the article as a predicate nominative adjective, since it cooperates with the verb in making an assertion about the subject; e.g., ὁ λόγος (is) ἀγαθός, ἡ δόξα (is) ἀγία.

3. It may be used attributively[2] directly with the noun (usually with the article before it), describing something characteristic about the noun; e.g., ὁ ἀγαθὸς ὄχλος, ἡ ἀγία δόξα, ὁ ὄχλος ὁ ἀγαθός, ἡ δόξα ἡ ἀγία.

---

[1]Sometimes in Greek, as in English, words are definite without the article. Compare proper nouns, such as Mary, John, etc.

[2]"A word or group of words standing between the article and its noun, or after the article, if its noun, with or without the article, precedes, is attributive." Smyth, op. cit., parag. 1154.

4. It may be used attributively as a noun, with or without the article, the gender of the noun concept used being understood by the gender of the adjective and its article employed together and by other noun concepts found in the immediate context. Examples of this use of the adjective with the article are:

οἱ ἅγιοι	(masc.)	the holy men
αἱ ἅγιαι	(fem.)	the holy women
τὰ ἅγια	(neut.)	the holy things

There are some important masculine first declension nouns in -ης, such as προφήτης, ου, ὁ, prophet, which is declined as follows:

	SINGULAR	PLURAL
N.	προφήτης	προφῆται
G.	προφήτου	προφητῶν
D.	προφήτῃ	προφήταις
A.	προφήτην	προφήτας
V.	προφῆτα	προφῆται

In addition, there are some feminine second declension nouns in -ος which are declined like λόγος but have the feminine article, as exampled by ἡ ὁδός (road, way), which is declined as follows:

	SINGULAR	PLURAL
N.	ἡ ὁδός	αἱ ὁδοί
G.	τῆς ὁδοῦ	τῶν ὁδῶν
D.	τῇ ὁδῷ	ταῖς ὁδοῖς
A.	τὴν ὁδόν	τὰς ὁδούς
V.	ἡ ὁδέ	αἱ ὁδοί

EXERCISES

1. Memorize the vocabulary and paradigms in this lesson.

2. Become thoroughly familiar with the uses of the article and the adjective.

3. Translate John 1:21-34 in the Simplified Greek Reader.

4. Translate the following sentences from English to Greek (based on the Simplified Greek Reader, John 1:14-34):

   a. John sees Jesus, and Jesus comes to him.
   b. The Word sees and knows men.
   c. The Spirit comes to Jesus and remains on him.
   d. Jesus, the Son of God, baptizes with the Holy Spirit.[3]

---

[3]See page 105 for Supplemental Sentences for Practice in Translating English to Greek.

Personal Pronouns

VOCABULARY

ἄλλος	- other, another (allegory, description of one thing under the image of another)
ἀμήν	- verily, truly, it is true (amen)
ἀπό	- with the gen., from (apostasy, stand off from)
ἀποστέλλω	- I send (with a commission, apostle)
αὐτός, αὐτή, αὐτό	- he, she, it, same, self
βάλλω	- I throw, put (ballistics)
ἐγώ	- I
ἐν	- with the dat., in, among, by
ἕως	- conj., until; with the gen., as far as
λαός, οῦ, ὁ	- people (laity)
νῦν	- now
σύ	- you
φωνή, ῆς, ἡ	- sound, voice (phonetics)

EXPLANATIONS

Personal Pronouns: <u>First, second and third person</u>. These are considered together because they have considerable in common, both as to their forms and usage.

The personal pronoun: The third personal pronoun αὐτός is the same in ending as the declension of the article[1] (except for the nominative singular masculine), and its declension is as follows:

SINGULAR

N.	αὐτός, he	αὐτή, she	αὐτό, it
G.	αὐτοῦ	αὐτῆς	αὐτοῦ
D.	αὐτῷ	αὐτῇ	αὐτῷ
A.	αὐτόν	αὐτήν	αὐτό

PLURAL

N.	αὐτοί, they	αὐταί	αὐτά
G.	αὐτῶν	αὐτῶν	αὐτῶν
D.	αὐτοῖς	αὐταῖς	αὐτοῖς
A.	αὐτούς	αὐτάς	αὐτά

The third personal pronoun αὐτός is used in the following ways:

1. Used independently in the oblique cases[2] in forms meaning his, him, her, their, them; sometimes it is used in the nominative case to mean, he, she, it;

2. Used with or without an accompanying noun but outside the governance of the article, or without the article, it means "self," as in the examples, αὐτὸς ὁ ἀδελφός or ὁ ἀδελφὸς αὐτός, the brother himself, and ἐγὼ Παῦλος αὐτός, I Paul myself.

---

[1]Drop the αὐ of αὐτός in each case to see the close similarity.

[2]Cases other than the nominative.

3. Used with an accompanying noun inside the governance of the article in an attributive sense to mean "same"; as ὁ αὐτὸς ἀδελφός or ὁ ἀδελφὸς ὁ αὐτός, the same brother.

The first and second personal pronouns, ἐγώ and σύ, respectively, have in the genitive singular and plural endings similar to the article, but otherwise the forms are different. They are as follows:

First personal pronoun

	Singular				Plural	
N.	ἐγώ		-I		ἡμεῖς	-we
G.	ἐμοῦ	μου	-of me		ἡμῶν	-of us
D.	ἐμοί	μοι	-to or for me		ἡμῖν	-to or for us
A.	ἐμέ	με	-me		ἡμᾶς	-us

Second personal pronoun

	Singular			Plural	
N.	σύ	-you		ὑμεῖς	-you
G.	σοῦ	-of you		ὑμῶν	-of you
D.	σοί	-to or for you		ὑμῖν	-to you
A.	σέ	-you		ὑμᾶς	-you

The forms ἐμοῦ, ἐμοί, ἐμέ, are emphatic in contrast to the enclitic[3] forms, μου, μοι, με . The forms σοῦ, σοί, σέ, are emphatic when accented; otherwise enclitic. For possession use the unemphatic forms and after prepositions the emphatic forms.[4] The student will at first have difficulty in distinguishing the plural forms of ἡμεῖς from ὑμεῖς. As a mnemonic aid observe that the Greek forms that begin with υ mean English "you"; the ones beginning with η are forms meaning "we" and "us."

EXERCISES

1. Memorize the vocabulary and paradigms in this lesson.

2. Master the uses of the pronouns given.

3. Be thoroughly familiar with the meanings of the prepositions in the cases they use.

4. Simplified Greek Reader: John 1:35-51.

5. English to Greek exercises based on the Greek Reader, John 1:35-41.
   a. John stands and two of (from) his disciples.
   b. The two disciples of John hear Jesus.
   c. The two disciples said, Rabbi (teacher), where do you stay (remain)?
   d. Andrew finds his brother, Simon.

---

[3] That is, forms without accent of their own, relying for emphasis on the preceding word. See Lesson One.

[4] Possession, ὁ λόγος σου, your word; ὁ λόγος μου, my word. After prepositions, ἀπ' ἐμοῦ, δι' ἐμοῦ, etc. However, note πρός με being used.

Explanation of the Demonstrative and Relative Pronouns

VOCABULARY

βλέπω	– I see
διά	– with gen., through; with accus., on account of
δοῦλος, ου, ὁ	– slave, servant
δύο	– two (dyad)
ἐγείρω	– I raise up
ἐκεῖνος, η, ο	– that (demonstrative pronoun)
κατά	– with gen., down from, against; with accus., according to, throughout, during
μέν	– postpositive particle, on the one hand, indeed (often used with δέ)
ὅς, ἥ, ὅ	– who, which (relative pronoun)
οὗτος, αὕτη, τοῦτο	– this, he, she, it (demonstrative pronoun)
πάλιν	– again (palimpsest, a MS. used again, the earlier writing having been erased; ψῆν, to erase)
παρά	– with gen., from; with dat., beside, in the presence of; with accus., alongside of (paragraph, orig. in MSS., a stroke along the margin)
περί	– with gen., concerning, about; with accus., around (perimeter, measure around)
πρός	– with accus., to, towards, with (proselyte, one who comes to another religion)
ὑπέρ	– with gen., in behalf of; with accus., above (hypercritical)

EXPLANATIONS

<u>The demonstrative pronoun:</u> οὗτος, this, and ἐκεῖνος, that, have endings which in the main are like those of the article. The forms of οὗτος are as follows:

	SINGULAR			PLURAL		
N.	οὗτος	αὕτη	τοῦτο	οὗτοι	αὗται	ταῦτα
G.	τούτου	ταύτης	τούτου	τούτων	τούτων	τούτων
D.	τούτῳ	ταύτῃ	τούτῳ	τούτοις	ταύταις	τούτοις
A.	τοῦτον	ταύτην	τοῦτο	τούτους	ταύτας	ταῦτα

It is to be observed that these endings are those of the first and second declensions in o and η and that all the forms of οὗτος have a prefixed τ except in the masculine and feminine nominative, singular and plural, that the forms of the feminine in η have an accompanying αυ in the preceding syllable except in the case of the genitive plural, and that the neuter plural nominative and accusative ending α has an accompanying αυ in the preceding syllable (example, ταῦτα).

The forms of the demonstrative pronoun ἐκεῖνος, η, ο follow the regular ending pattern of first and second declension nouns in o/η except that the neuter nominative and accusative singular ends in o (like the article τό), i.e., ἐκεῖνο. The declension of ἐκεῖνος is as follows:

	SINGULAR			PLURAL		
	MASCULINE	FEMININE	NEUTER	MASCULINE	FEMININE	NEUTER
N.	ἐκεῖνος	ἐκείνη	ἐκεῖνο	ἐκεῖνοι	ἐκεῖναι	ἐκεῖνα
G.	ἐκείνου	ἐκείνης	ἐκείνου	ἐκείνων	ἐκείνων	ἐκείνων
D.	ἐκείνῳ	ἐκείνῃ	ἐκείνῳ	ἐκείνοις	ἐκείναις	ἐκείνοις
A.	ἐκεῖνον	ἐκείνην	ἐκεῖνο	ἐκείνους	ἐκείνας	ἐκεῖνα

The relative pronoun: The endings of the relative pronoun are just like the article except that there is no τ before the endings, but rather a rough breathing mark (ʼ) is affixed, and the masculine nominative singular is ὅς instead of ὁ and the neuter is ὅ instead of τό. It is to be observed that all the relative pronoun forms are accented. (Compare the forms of the article ὁ, ἡ, οἱ, αἱ.)

The forms of the relative pronoun are as follows:

	SINGULAR			PLURAL		
N.	ὅς	ἥ	ὅ	οἵ	αἵ	ἅ
G.	οὗ	ἧς	οὗ	ὧν	ὧν	ὧν
D.	ᾧ	ᾗ	ᾧ	οἷς	αἷς	οἷς
A.	ὅν	ἥν	ὅ	οὕς	ἅς	ἅ

Uses of the personal, demonstrative and relative pronouns: **First and second personal pronouns:** It is to be observed, of course, that the first and second personal pronoun concepts are resident in the subject meanings of the appropriate verbal forms, such as λύω, I loose, λύεις, you loose. However, often the first and second personal pronoun forms are used in addition to the idea resident in the verb forms, and so express emphasis, such as in the sentence, ἐγὼ καὶ λύω, I also loose. The first and second personal pronouns are also used in other relationships, such as the object of the verb, as in λύω σέ, I loose you, the object of prepositions, etc.

The demonstrative pronoun, which is a pronoun that particularly points out a person or thing, may be used: 1) alone to refer to some noun or pronoun referred to elsewhere in the context, whether expressed or unexpressed, such as οὗτος, this man (referred to elsewhere), or ἐκείνη, that woman; and 2) in the predicate position with an accompanying noun, such as οὗτος ὁ ἀδελφός, ὁ ἀδελφὸς οὗτος, this brother,[1] and ἐκεῖναι αἱ ἐκκλησίαι, αἱ ἐκκλησίαι ἐκεῖναι, those churches.

The relative pronoun is a word which relates to another word in the context, usually expressed (although sometimes not), called the antecedent. As a general rule the relative pronoun must be in agreement with the antecedent in gender and number, but not necessarily in case. Observe the following examples: ὁ ἀδελφὸς ὅν βλέπω ἔρχεται, the brother, whom I see, comes; ὁ ἀδελφὸς ᾧ λέγεις ἔρχεται, the brother to whom you speak comes; ὁ ἀδελφὸς περὶ οὗ λέγεις ἔρχεται, the brother concerning whom you speak comes.

Generally, however, when the antecedent is in the genitive or the dative case and the relative pronoun is the object of its verb and would be expected to be in the accusative case, the relative pronoun is attracted into the case of its antecedent, as is exampled in the following sentence where the antecedent noun is in the genitive and the relative pronoun follows suit: λέγει περὶ τοῦ ἀνθρώπου οὗ βλέπεις, he speaks concerning

---

[1] Observe that Greek puts in an article where English does not.

the man whom you see.[2]

The relative pronoun may be used with the antecedent being unexpressed in Greek, such as in the sentence, κύριε, ὃν βλέπεις ἔρχεται, Lord, <u>he whom</u> you see is coming. The relative pronoun together with its gender includes the antecedent idea of "he."

<u>Prepositions and their uses</u>: In the vocabulary of this lesson there are a number of prepositions, such as ἀπό, κατά, etc. Prepositions are "helping" words which stand before (pre-position) the words they are to help and assist in indicating the relationship of these words to the subject, verb, etc. The prepositions "take" different cases with different meanings, falling in line with the function of the different cases. For examples observe ἀπό with the genitive, meaning "from" (the genitive including the separation idea), and ἐν with the dative, meaning "in", "by" (the dative including the ideas of location and instrument).

Some prepositions "govern" more than one case, and, therefore, indicate different meanings with different cases, such as κατά with the genitive, meaning, "down from, against"; and with the accusative, meaning, "according to, throughout" (the accusative having the extension idea).

In succeeding lessons additional prepositions will be added to the student's dictionary storehouse. Study the prepositions chart in the New Testament Greek Syntax Chart found later in this book (see pages 207-212).

EXERCISES

1. Memorize the vocabulary and paradigms in this lesson.

2. Master the use of the pronouns given.

3. Become thoroughly familiar with the meanings of the prepositions in the cases they use.

4. Translate in the Simplified Greek Reader John 2:1-12.

5. Translate the following sentences from English to Greek, based on John 1:42-51:

   a. Simon, who was the son of John, finds Philip.

   b. Philip finds Nathanael and brings (bears) him to Jesus, whom he saw.

   c. Jesus says, I know you whom I saw under the fig tree.

   d. You will see these things.

---

[2]The long forms of ὅς, that is, ὅστις, ἥτις, ὅ τι (or, ὅ,τι), whoever, whatever, are not attracted into the case of the antecedent. Cf. Luke 2:10, and Rom. 9:4.

Perfect Active, Middle-Passive of λύω

VOCABULARY

ἀγαθός, ή, όν	– good
ἀλήθεια, ας, ἡ	– truth
ἀποθνῄσκω	– I die
ἐκκλησία, ας, ἡ	– a community, congregation, church (ecclesiastical)
θάνατος, ου, ὁ	– death (thanatopsis, a view of, or meditation on, death)
κρίνω	– I judge, decide (critic)
μένω	– I remain
οἶκος, ου. ὁ	– house (economy, household management)
ὅσος, η, ον	– as great as, as many as
πῶς	– how? (interrogative particle)
ψυχή, ῆς, ἡ	– soul, life, self (psycho-)

EXPLANATIONS

To review, the primary tenses in Greek are the present, future, perfect and future perfect.[1] There have already been presented to the student the present and the future indicative, active, middle and passive. This lesson now presents the perfect indicative, active, middle and passive. Up to this point the verbal forms studied have had variable vowels and personal endings as suffixes, but no prefix. The perfect tense of Greek has a prefix added to the base or stem, consisting ordinarily of a syllable made up of a reduplication of the consonant beginning the stem of the word followed by ε (for the sake of pronunciation), such as λε-λυ--. Then, as a suffix to the stem there is added, in the active, a κ, followed, in most cases, by an α vowel and other necessary personal endings. The first person singular form, then, looks like this: λέ-λυ-κα. In the perfect middle and passive the prefix formation is the same, but the suffix does not include the κ but consists of only the primary middle and passive personal endings added directly to the stem, as exampled in the form λέ-λυ-μαι.

In past lessons stress has been placed on the kind of action expressed by Greek verbs with linear (————) and point (●) action, both of these kinds of action being involved in the meaning of the present and future. In the perfect there is a combination of point and linear action, to indicate a state of completion which continues (●————, γέγραπται, it stands written), or action which has just now come to a state of completion (————● , τετέλεσται, it is finished, it has just now been finished, John 19:30). Often the Greek perfect can be translated by using forms of the English "have," but the student needs to remember the completed action with duration which is resident in the meaning of these forms. See the Greek Syntax Chart for further details. (See pages 194ff.)

---

[1]There is little use of the future perfect (action completed in the future) in the New Testament.

The perfect forms of λύω and their translation are as follows:

Perfect active indicative

λέλυκα	I have loosed (━━━●)	λελύκαμεν	We have loosed
λέλυκας	You have loosed	λελύκατε	You have loosed
λέλυκε(ν)	He has loosed	λελύκασι(ν)	They have loosed
		λελύκαν	

Perfect middle and passive indicative

λέλυμαι[2]	I have loosed myself(━━━●)	λελύμεθα	We have loosed ourselves
	I have been loosed (●━━━)		We have been loosed
λέλυσαι	You have loosed yourself	λέλυσθε	You have loosed yourself
	You have been loosed		You have been loosed
λέλυται	He has loosed himself	λέλυνται	They have loosed themselves
	He has been loosed		They have been loosed

In the case of verbs whose stems begin with a vowel, as ἁμαρτάνω, or a
consonant cluster, as σταυρόω, the prefix of the perfect usually consists
of either a lengthening of the initial vowel, as ἡμάρτηκα, or, in the
case of an initial consonant cluster, prefixing an ε, as ἐσταύρωκα. For
further details see the Verb Chart for the perfect prefixes and suffixes, p. 177.

EXERCISES

1. Memorize the vocabulary.

2. Master the forms and translations of the perfect indicative,
   active, middle, and passive.

3. Be able to discuss the distinction between linear and
   punctiliar kinds of action.

4. Simplified Greek Reader: John 2:13-22.

5. English to Greek exercises based on the Greek Reader, John 2:1-12.
   a. A wedding occurred (came about) in Cana of Galilee.
   b. It was the third day.
   c. Jesus and his disciples who were in Galilee came to (unto)
      the wedding.
   d. The mother of Jesus says to him, "The men whom you see do
      not have wine."

---

[2]See the chart on Greek Tenses, page 177, for rules for the formation of the perfect. In the middle and passive, perfect and pluperfect,
where the stem ends in a mute consonant (π, β, φ; τ, δ, θ; κ, γ, χ),
there is likely to be an assimilation or accommodation of the mute to
the initial consonant of the middle-passive ending, as exampled by
δεδίω (χ) γμαι.

Imperfect Active, Middle-Passive of λύω

VOCABULARY

ἀγάπη, ης, ἡ — love
ἀπέρχομαι — I depart
δεῖ — (impersonal verb) It is necessary
ἐξουσία, ας, ἡ — authority
ἴδιος, α, ον — one's own (idiosyncrasy)
μέλλω — I am about to
ὅλος, η, ον — whole
ὅτε — when (conjunction)
σῴζω — I save (soteriology, the study of the doctrines of salvation)
ὥρα, ας, ἡ — hour (horoscope, prediction based on the hour of a person's birth)

EXPLANATIONS

Secondary tenses:

We have observed that the secondary tenses are the imperfect, aorist and pluperfect (or, past-perfect). Whereas the present and future verb forms have no prefix (or, augment) added to the stem, in the imperfect and aorist there is a prefixed ε which is called a syllabic augment, e.g., ἐ-λυ; in the case of a verb beginning with a vowel, there is a lengthening of this vowel, called a temporal augment, e.g., ἦγον (from ἄγω, I lead).

As to suffixes in the secondary tenses, it is to be noted that following the stem there is added the variable vowel ο/ε, in the imperfect, followed by the secondary personal endings (see the Greek Verbal Prefixes and Suffixes Chart on pages 15 and 168).

As to **tense and kind of action**, the imperfect presents past time and only continuous (————) kind of action.

The forms of λύω in the imperfect indicative, active, middle and passive, are as follows:

ACTIVE

ἔλυον	I was loosing	ἐλύομεν	We were loosing
ἔλυες	You were loosing	ἐλύετε	You were loosing
ἔλυε(ν)	He was loosing	ἔλυον[1]	They were loosing

MIDDLE AND PASSIVE

ἐλυόμην	I was loosing myself	ἐλυόμεθα	We were loosing ourselves
	I was being loosed		We were being loosed
ἐλύου[2]	You were loosing yourself	ἐλύεσθε	You were loosing yourselves
	You were being loosed		You were being loosed
ἐλύετο	He was loosing himself	ἐλύοντο	They were loosing themselves
	He was being loosed		They were being loosed

---

[1]Observe that the first singular and third plural are identical in form.

[2]ἐλύου presents a contraction between the variable vowel and the ending. Originally forms like this would have been ἐ-λύεσο; the σ was weak, dropped out, and the resultant ε-ο contracted to ου.

EXERCISES

1. Memorize the vocabulary.

2. Master the forms and translations of the imperfect indicative active, middle, and passive.

3. Simplified Greek Reader: John 2:23-3:8.

4. English to Greek exercises based on the Greek Reader, John 2:1-12.
   a. Six stone water pots were there.
   b. They were filling the water pots and were bringing (bearing) the wine.
   c. The head of the feast says, "You keep the good wine until now."
   d. After this, Jesus was going down to Capernaum and was staying (remaining) there.

Aorist Active, Middle, and Passive of λύω

VOCABULARY

ἀλλήλων	– of one another (parallel, alongside one another)
ἄρτος, ου, ὁ	– bread, loaf
ἄρχομαι	– (middle use) I begin (ἄρχω, active– I rule)
δικαιοσύνη, ης, ἡ	– righteousness
εἰρήνη, ης, ἡ	– peace (Irene)
ἐκβάλλω	– I cast out, put out
ἐνώπιον	– with the genitive, before
ἔτι	– still, yet, even
θάλασσα, ης, ἡ	– sea, lake (thalassocracy)
καιρός, οῦ, ὁ	– fitting season, opportunity, time
οἰκία, ας, ἡ	– house
ὀφθαλμός, οῦ, ὁ	– eye (ophthalmology)
προσεύχομαι	– I pray (deponent)
πρῶτος, η, ον	– first (protozoa)
τέκνον, ου, τό	– child
φοβέομαι	– I fear (deponent) (phobia)

EXPLANATIONS

Secondary tenses continued:

The Aorist: As in the case of the imperfect indicative secondary tense, the aorist (also a secondary tense) indicative has the prefixed augment, either syllabic or temporal (see page 15). The aorist indicative stem is suffixed with a tense sign σ and a predominate α vowel in the active and middle, followed by the secondary personal endings. Examples are: ἔλυσα, aorist active indicative, first person singular; and ἐλυσάμην, aorist middle indicative, first person singular.

It is to be observed that the aorist passive indicative is separate in form from the aorist middle indicative, and formed by the addition to the stem of the passive tense sign θη[1] before the secondary active personal endings. For example: ἐλύθην, aorist passive indicative, first person singular.

The tense of the aorist indicative is past and the kind of action is punctiliar (•), which is to be contrasted with the imperfect indicative which indicates past time continuous action (——).

The forms of the aorist indicative and their translations are as follows:

ACTIVE

ἔλυσα[2]	I loosed (•)	ἐλύσαμεν	We loosed
ἔλυσας	You loosed	ἐλύσατε	You loosed
ἔλυσε(ν)	He loosed	ἔλυσαν	They loosed

---

[1]Observe that the future passive indicative has this same passive tense sign together with the future tense sign σ.

[2]Notice the predominance of the α vowel following the σ so that the full indication of the aorist active and middle indicative is ε---σα.

<u>Middle</u>

ἐλυσάμην	I loosed myself	ἐλυσάμεθα	We loosed ourselves
ἐλύσω[1]	You loosed yourself	ἐλύσασθε	You loosed yourselves
ἐλύσατο	He loosed himself	ἐλύσαντο	They loosed themselves

<u>Passive</u>

ἐλύθην[2]	I was loosed	ἐλύθημεν	We were loosed
ἐλύθης	You were loosed	ἐλύθητε	You were loosed
ἐλύθη	He was loosed	ἐλύθησαν	They were loosed

EXERCISES

1. Memorize the vocabulary of this lesson.

2. Learn the paradigms and translations of the secondary tenses.

3. Simplified Greek Reader, John 3:8-15.

4. English to Greek exercises based on the Greek Reader, John 2:13-25.
   a. The feast of the Jews was near and Jesus was going up to Jerusalem. Men were loosed from their sins.
   b. Jesus finds men in the temple.
   c. They were selling cattle, sheep, and doves.
   d. Jesus said, "Take up these things from here."
   e. Many in Jerusalem believed in him.

---

[1]ἐλύσω is a contracted form from a form like ἐλύσασο with the second σ, as weak, dropping, and α-ο contracting to ω .

[2]Observe that the aorist passive indicative personal endings are like those in the imperfect active indicative, the θη being used to carry the passive idea.

Pluperfect Active, Middle-Passive of λύω, and the Verb εἰμί

VOCABULARY

αἴρω	– I take up, take away
ἀναβαίνω	– I go up
ἄρχω	– I rule
διδάσκω	– I teach (didactic)
δύναμαι	– I am powerful, able
ἕκαστος, η, ον	– each
ἐκεῖ	– there
ἕτερος, α, ον	– other, another, different (heterodox, holding another doctrine)
ἕτοιμος, η, ον	– ready, prepared
κάθημαι	– I sit (deponent)
καλός, ή, όν	– beautiful, good
ὅπου	– where, whither
πίπτω	– I fall
προσέρχομαι	– I come to (deponent)
τόπος, ου, ὁ	– place (topography)

EXPLANATIONS

The Pluperfect: The third Greek secondary tense is the plu- (or, past) perfect which is used less regularly than other tenses (except the future perfect which is used infrequently). The formation of this pluperfect tense employs as a prefix the reduplication principle found in the perfect tense, with a prefixed ε augment added, as ε-λε-λυ-. As a suffix, the pluperfect adds to the stem κ plus ει, plus the secondary personal endings, in the active; in the middle and passive the secondary personal endings, without κ, alone are added as a suffix directly to the stem of the verb, as exampled by ἐλελύμην.

The tense of the pluperfect is past time and the kind of action is a combination of the point, or definite action (●), and the continuous, or linear (——————), in combinations of ——————● and ●——————, all conceived of as having been in a completed state in past time. Compare the perfect, γέγραπται, It **stands** written, with the pluperfect, ἐγέγραπτο, It **stood** written.

The forms of the pluperfect indicative and their translation are as follows:

ACTIVE

ἐλελύκειν[1]	I had loosed (and the condition continued)	ἐλελύκειμεν	We had loosed
ἐλελύκεις	You had loosed	ἐλελύκειτε	You had loosed
ἐλελύκει	He had loosed	ἐλελύκεισαν	They had loosed

---

[1]See again the chart on Greek Tenses, with analysis of the Formation of the Perfect Tense (page 177). In the middle and passive perfect and pluperfect, where the stem ends in a mute consonant, i.e., πβφ, τδθ, and κγχ (see page 2), there is likely to be an assimilation or accommodation of the mute to the initial consonant of the middle-passive ending, exampled in ἐγεγρά(φ)μμην.

MIDDLE AND PASSIVE

ἐλελύμην	I had loosed myself I had been loosed (•——— , ———•)	ἐλελύμεθα	We had loosed ourselves We had been loosed
ἐλέλυσο	You had loosed yourself You had been loosed	ἐλέλυσθε	You had loosed yourselves You had been loosed
ἐλέλυτο	He had loosed himself He had been loosed	ἐλέλυντο	They had loosed themselves They had been loosed

The verb "to be," εἰμί: This important, often used verb, although belonging to the -μι type verb, needs to be introduced here. εἰμί, by its very nature, in being a verb of existence, has only three tenses in the indicative: present, imperfect and future, there being only active forms in the present and imperfect, and middle deponent forms in the future.

The indicative forms of εἰμί and their translations are as follows:

PRESENT

εἰμί [2]	I am	ἐσμέν	We are
εἶ	You are	ἐστέ	You are
ἐστί(ν)	He is	εἰσί(ν)	They are

IMPERFECT

ἤμην	I was	ἦμεν	We were
ἦς	You were	ἦτε	You were
ἦν	He was	ἦσαν	They were

FUTURE

ἔσομαι	I shall (or, will) be	ἐσόμεθα	We shall (or, will) be
ἔσῃ [3]	You will be	ἔσεσθε	You will be
ἔσται	He will be	ἔσονται	They will be

The negatives οὐ and μή used with verbal forms: The negative οὐ is used basically with the indicative forms of the verb, with μή being used in the other moods.[4] Before questions both οὐ and μή may be used, the former indicating that a positive response is to be expected (e.g., "You were there, weren't you?"), and the latter indicating a negative answer is expected (e.g., "You weren't there, were you?").

EXERCISES

1. Memorize the vocabulary of the lesson.
2. Learn the paradigms and translations of the secondary tense, pluperfect, of λύω, and the present, imperfect and future indicative of εἰμί.
3. Translate in the Simplified Greek Reader, John 3:16-21.

---

[2]For this type of accent on the present indicative of εἰμί see the discussion (p. 35) on enclitics and proclitics. All the forms of the present of εἰμί except εἶ are enclitic. The imperfect and future forms of εἰμί are not enclitic.

[3]The form ἔσῃ is a contraction of an earlier form like ἔσεσαι in which the second σ, being weak, dropped and the resultant ε-αι contracted to ῃ. Note that in the future forms of εἰμί there is a similarity to the future middle elements (tense sign σ, variable vowel and primary endings) of λύω.

[4]Subjunctive, imperative, optative, participle and infinitive.

4. English to Greek exercises based on the Greek Reader, John 2:13–25.
   a. You are making the temple a house of business (a business mart).
   b. Jesus answered and said to them, "You will destroy (loose) this temple. I will raise it up in three days."
   c. The disciples continued to believe the Scripture and the Word of God.
   d. Jesus continually knew men and did not (continually) entrust himself to them.

Proclitics, Enclitics; Second Aorist Verbs

VOCABULARY

αἷμα, ατος, τό	– blood (anemia, without blood)
ἀνοίγω	– I open
βαπτίζω	– I baptize
δίκαιος, α, ον	– right, just, righteous
δώδεκα	– twelve (dodecagon)
ἐμός, ἐμή, ἐμόν	– my, mine (possessive pronoun)
εὐαγγέλιον, ου, τό	– the good news, gospel
ἱερόν, οῦ, τό	– temple (area, compound) (hierarchy)
κεφαλή, ῆς, ἡ	– head (encephalitis)
ὄνομα, ατος, τό	– name
πέμπω	– I send
πίστις, εως, ἡ	– faith, belief, trust
πονηρός, ά, όν	– evil

EXPLANATIONS

Proclitics and Enclitics: As we learned in a preceding lesson (Introduction, Lesson 1), a proclitic is a word (like the article in its forms ὁ and ἡ) which goes so closely with (or leans heavily on) the following word that it does not have an accent of its own, as in the case of ὁ ἀδελφός (the brother) and ἡ φωνή (the voice).

On the other hand, we learned that an enclitic is a word, of one syllable, or sometimes two, which goes so closely with the preceding word that it usually has no accent of its own. It does, however, frequently affect the accenting of the previous word or sometimes keeps its own accent; so the following special rules are to be observed:

1. When the word preceding the enclitic has an acute accent on the antepenult or a circumflex on the penult, then that word takes an additional acute on its ultima as though it were one word with the enclitic, as ἄνθρωπός σου (your man), ἄνθρωπός ἐστιν (a man is), or δῶρόν μου (my gift), δῶρόν ἐστιν (a gift is).[1]

2. When, however, the ultima of the enclitic's preceding word is accented with an acute, there is no additional accent or change to a grave accent as ἀδελφός σου (your brother).

3. An enclitic or proclitic immediately preceding an enclitic will take its own acute accent, as εἴς με, ἄνθρωπός μού ἐστιν.

4. A two-syllable enclitic will retain its own accent when:
    a. the preceding word has an acute accent on the penult, as ὥρα ἐστίν.
    b. the enclitic begins the clause or sentence, or calls for special emphasis as ἔστιν δὲ ἀδελφός. (ἔστιν is accented on the penult when it begins the sentence.)

---

[1]Thus the rules are fulfilled that there is to be an accent on one of the three last syllables of a word and that a circumflex is not to stand on the antepenult.

<u>The Second Aorist Verbs</u>: The student has learned the aorist active
indicative of λύω, that is, the forms ἔλυσα, etc. This can be called the
first aorist. Some verbs do not have first aorist forms with the -σα,
etc., suffix syllables. Rather, we may say that in the place of these
first aorist suffix endings the <u>second aorist</u> verb often has a change
from the stem or base form used in the present system of that verb and
uses the imperfect type endings. Observe the examples: ὁράω, I see;
ὄψομαι, I will see; εἶδον (second aorist), I saw; or, γίνομαι, I
become; γενήσομαι, I will become; ἐγενόμην,[2] I became.

It is to be observed that the meaning of the second aorist indicative
(past tense, punctiliar action) is the same as that of the first aorist;
it is only the formation of the word which is different.

The conjugation of the second aorist verbs, εἶδον and ἐγενόμην,
is as follows:

εἶδον	I saw,	ἐγενόμην	I became,
εἶδες	etc.	ἐγένου	etc.
εἶδε(ν)		ἐγένετο[3]	
εἴδομεν		ἐγενόμεθα	
εἴδετε		ἐγένεσθε	
εἶδον		ἐγένοντο	

EXERCISES

1. Memorize the vocabulary of the lesson.

2. Following the principles set forth regarding the accenting of enclitics,
   correctly accent the following forms and phrases:

   a. ἄνθρωπος μου
   b. δῶρον σου
   c. μαθητης σου
   d. πνεῦμα ἐστιν
   e. ζήτουσιν σε
   f. κράβατον σου
   g. ἄνθρωποι μου εἰσιν
   h. δόξα ἐστιν
   i. κύριος ἐστιν
   j. ἄλλοι εἰσιν

3. Simplified Greek Reader, John 3:22-30.

4. English to Greek exercises based on the Greek Reader, John 3:1-15.
   a. Nicodemus was a man of (from) the Pharisees.
   b. This one comes (came) to Him and spoke to Him.
   c. Jesus answered and said to him, "It is necessary for a man to
      be born again."
   d. You heard the sound (voice) of the Spirit, but you do not know
      where he goes.
   e. Man does not go up to heaven, but the Son of Man must be lifted up.
      Men believed in Him.

[2]Second aorist deponent.

[3]This is frequently used to mean, "It came to pass."

Third Declension

VOCABULARY

αἰών, ῶνος, ὁ	- age (aeon)
ἀνήρ, ἀνδρός, ὁ	- man, husband (polyandry, having many husbands)
ἀποκτείνω	- I kill
γυνή, γυναικός, ἡ	- woman, wife (misogynist, a person who hates women)
ἑπτά	- seven (heptagon)
εὑρίσκω	- I find
καταβαίνω	- I go down
μᾶλλον	- more
πατήρ, πατρός, ὁ	- father (paternal)
πίνω	- I drink
πνεῦμα, ατος, τό	- spirit
χάρις, ιτος, ἡ	- grace (charismatic)
χείρ, χειρός, ἡ	- hand (chirography)

EXPLANATIONS

Third Declension: The student has already mastered the second or o declension masculine and neuter nouns and also the feminine first α/η declension forms.

The Greek third declension is somewhat more complicated, but can readily be mastered if the pattern of endings be compared with the endings of other nouns of this declension and also with the endings of the first and second declensions. This lesson will concern itself with Type 1 of the endings which are summarized in the Third Declension Chart:[1]

	MASCULINE-FEMININE	NEUTER
	SINGULAR	
N.V.	------	------
G.	-ος (cf. 1st declen. fem. gen. sing. in ας/ης)	-ος
D.	-ι (cf. 1st and 2nd declen. dat. sing. ending in iota subscript)	-ι
A.	-α (short), ν	- (same as the nominative)
	PLURAL	
N.V.	-ες	-α (short)
G.	-ων (cf. 1st and 2nd declen. genitive plural in -ων)	-ων
D.	-σι(ν) (cf. 1st and 2nd declen. (-φι, ξι) dat. plural ending in ις [οις, αις] whereas the 3rd declen. ends in -σι)	-σι(ν)
A.	-ας (short)	-α (same as the nominative; short)

---

[1]See pp. 172-174 for the Third Declension Chart. Type 1 of the third declension involves stems ending in the following consonantal combinations: mutes (or stops; see page 2); -ντ- stems; stems in -τ- and -ας; stems in ρ; and stems in ν. See page 172.

Observe that the nominative singular of this declension must be learned by observation in vocabulary and lexical lists.

Nouns of _Type 1_ of this declension found in the vocabulary of Lesson 15 include:

SINGULAR

N.	ἡ σάρξ	ἡ χάρις	ὁ πατήρ (πατερ)	τὸ ὄνομα
G.	σαρκός[2]	χάριτος	πατρός[3]	ὀνόματος
D.	σαρκί[2]	χάριτι	πατρί[3]	ὀνόματι
A.	σάρκα	χάριν	πατέρα	ὄνομα
V.	σάρξ	χάρις	πάτερ	ὄνομα

PLURAL

N.	σάρκες	χάριτες	πατέρες	ὀνόματα
G.	σαρκῶν[2]	χαρίτων	πατέρων	ὀνομάτων
D.	σαρξί(ν)[2]	χάρισι(ν)	πατράσι(ν)	ὀνόμασι(ν)
A.	σάρκας	χάριτας	πατέρας	ὀνόματα
V.	σάρκες	χάριτες	πατέρες	ὀνόματα

EXERCISES

1. Memorize the vocabulary of this lesson.

2. Translate John 3:31–36 in the Simplified Greek Reader.

3. Do the English to Greek exercises based on the Greek Reader, John 3:16–36:

    a. God loved the world; men believe in his Son and have eternal life.
    b. Some (men) practice (do) the truth and work the works of God.
    c. Jesus and his disciples came into the land of Judea and they were baptizing.
    d. Men were coming to John and he was baptizing.
    e. They said to John, "Jesus was with you across the Jordan."
    f. John said, "I am not the Christ."
    g. God sends the Son who speaks the words of God.
    h. Men disobey the Son and the wrath of God remains on them.

---

[2]Monosyllabic third declension nouns are accented on the ultima of the genitive and dative, singular and plural.

[3]Syncopated (see W. W. Goodwin, Greek Grammar, revised by C.B. Gulick [Boston: Ginn and Company, 1930], parag. 65): the dropping of a short vowel between two consonants.

Third Declension Continued

VOCABULARY

ἀγαπητός, ή, όν	– beloved
αἰώνιος, ον	– eternal (aeonian)
γένος, ους, τό	– nation, race, kind, sort
ἔθνος, ους, τό	– nation, in the plural, Gentiles (ethnology)
ἐντολή, ῆς, ἡ	– commandment
θέλημα, ατος, τό	– will (monothelite, one holding that Christ had but one, a divine will)
καρπός, οῦ, ὁ	– fruit
μήτηρ, μητρός, ἡ	– mother (maternal)
ὄρος, ὄρους, τό	– mountain (orology, the study of mountains)
οὔτε	– neither, nor
πλοῖον, ου, τό	– boat
πρεσβύτερος, ου, ὁ	– elder (presbyter)
πῦρ, πυρός, τό	– fire (pyre)
σάββατον, ου, τό	– Sabbath
στόμα, ατος, τό	– mouth (stomach)
σῶμα, ατος, τό	– body (somatic)
ὕδωρ, ὕδατος, τό	– water (hydroplane)

EXPLANATIONS

Third Declension, Type 2: In Lesson 15 the student learned the ending characteristics of Type 1 of the Third Declension. Type 2, which is presented in this lesson, has some endings which are similar to those of Type 1, such as the dative singular and the genitive and dative plural. The Type 2 nouns are neuter in gender and have stems ending in σ-. Such nouns show the following endings:

SINGULAR

N.V.	-ος
G.	-ους (Since the stem or base of these nouns is -εσ-, where the case ending -ος is added, the first -σ- drops, and εος contracts to ους)
D.	-ει
A.	-ος

PLURAL

N.V.	-η
G.	-ων
D.	-εσι(ν)
A.	-η

Third declension nouns, Type 2, are declined as follows:
(τὸ ἔθνος, stem, ἐθνεσ-; τὸ γένος, stem, γενεσ-)

SINGULAR

N.V.	ἔθνος	γένος
G.	ἔθνους (from ἔθνεϕος)	γένους (from γένεϕος)
D.	ἔθνει	γένει
A.	ἔθνος	γένος

PLURAL

N.V.	ἔθνη[1]	γένη[1]
G.	ἐθνῶν (ἐθνέων)	γενῶν (γενέων)
D.	ἔθνεσι(ν)	γένεσι(ν)
A.	ἔθνη	γένη

EXERCISES

1. Memorize the vocabulary of this lesson.

2. Learn the characteristic features of Type 2 of the Third Declension.

3. Translate in the Simplified Greek Reader John 4:1-6.

4. Do the English to Greek exercises based on the Greek Reader, John 4:1-6, and on the material in Lessons 1-16.[2]

   a. The Pharisees heard that Jesus made and baptized disciples.
   b. Jesus himself did not baptize but his disciples baptized men.
   c. Jesus went out of Judea and came to a city of Samaria, Sychar.

---

[1]It is to be observed that a neuter plural subject in Greek may take a singular verb.

[2]More English to Greek exercises for Lesson 16 are available on page 106.

The Greek Moods Explained

VOCABULARY

ἄγω	– I lead
ἀπολύω	– I release, dismiss
δαιμόνιον, ου, τό	– demon
ἔξω	– without; with gen.–outside
ἱμάτιον, ου, τό	– garment
κηρύσσω	– I proclaim, preach
νύξ, νυκτός, ἡ	– night
οὐδέ	– and not, not even, neither, nor
πιστός, ή, όν	– faithful, believing
πούς, ποδός, ὁ	– foot (podium)
πρόσωπον, ου, τό	– face (prosopography, description of personal appearance)
ῥῆμα, ατος, τό	– word (rhetoric)
σημεῖον, ου, τό	– sign (semaphore, bearing a sign)
συνάγω	– I gather together (synagogue)
τρεῖς, τρία	– three (triad)
ὑπάγω	– I go, depart
φέρω	– I carry, bear, lead (Christopher, bearing Christ)
φῶς, φωτός, τό	– light (phosphorus, photography)
χαίρω	– I rejoice
χάρις, ιτος, ἡ	– grace
ὧδε	– hither, here

EXPLANATIONS

The Moods: Mood in grammar refers to the way the verbal statement is made, whether stated as a fact or in some other way. Thus far the student has been exposed only to the indicative mood, the mood in which the verbal statement is made as a fact (whether indeed the statement is factual is to be determined by the context). Example: ὁ ἄνθρωπος λύει τὸν ἀπόστολον , the man looses (in fact) the apostle.

In Greek, there are several other moods:

1) The subjunctive, in which the verbal statement is made as a probable or possible action or situation. Example: If he should (or shall) go, I shall hear him.

2) The imperative, in which the verbal statement is made as a command. Example: You, loose the child.

3) The participle, which is a verbal adjective hybrid, and as an adjective can and does modify nouns, pronouns, adjectives, and subjects in verbs, and, as a verb, carries action or being.

4) The infinitive, which is a verbal noun hybrid, and thus as a noun may be used as a subject or object or verbal complement, and as a verb carries action or being.

5) Infrequently in the New Testament there is found the optative form of the verb, in which the verbal statement is made as a possible or potential or desirable action or situation.

Example: Let it not be! (Romans 6:2). May God Himself sanctify you wholly (1 Thessalonians 5:23).

We have observed in Lesson 13 but do so again here that the negative for the indicative is οὐ (οὐκ before vowels; οὐχ before rough breathing), and for the other moods regularly μή. In questions of all sorts introduced by "not," οὐ is used expecting a positive reply (Is he not going? He is going, isn't he?), and μή introduces questions which expect a negative response (He isn't going, is he?).

EXERCISES

1. Memorize the vocabulary of this lesson.

2. Learn the principles concerning the nature of Greek moods.

3. Simplified Greek Reader, John 4:7-15.

4. English to Greek exercises based on the Greek Reader, John 4:7-15, and the material in Lessons 1-16.

    a. A woman of Samaria comes (came) to the well of Jacob and she sees (saw) Jesus.

    b. Jesus said to her, "You do not know the gift of God, the water of life."

    c. The woman said to Him, "Where, therefore, do you have the water of life?"

    d. When a man drinks of the water of life from me, he shall not thirst at all forever.

    e. The woman said to Jesus, "Lord, I wish this water of life."

Third Declension Continued; Interrogative and Indefinite Pronouns

VOCABULARY

ἀρχή, ῆς, ἡ	– beginning (archaic)
ἀσπάζομαι	– I greet, salute
γραμματεύς, έως, ὁ	– scribe (grammatical), teacher of the law
διδάσκαλος, ου, ὁ	– teacher (didactic)
δύναμις, εως, ἡ	– power (dynamite)
εὑρίσκω·	– I find (Eureka – I have found it)
θρόνος, ου, ὁ	– throne
λοιπός, ή, όν	– remaining; as a noun, the rest; as an adverb, for the rest, henceforth
μή	– not, lest
οὐδείς, οὐδεμία, οὐδέν; μηδείς, μηδεμία, μηδέν	– no one, nothing, none
πόλις, πόλεως, ἡ	– city (Neapolis, new city, Acts 16:11)
ὑπάρχω	– I am, exist (neut. subst. – one's belongings)
χαρά, ᾶς, ἡ	– joy, delight

EXPLANATIONS

Third Declension, Type 3: In previous lessons the student has learned the ending characteristics of Types 1 and 2 of the Third Declension. The endings of Type 3, introduced in this lesson, are similar to the two preceding types in the genitive singular (ending in oς), the dative singular (ending in -ι), and in the genitive and dative plural (ending in -ων and -σι respectively). The nouns of Type 3 are basically masculine and feminine in gender and have stems in the semi-vowels ι and υ. The characteristics of this type are:

	SINGULAR	PLURAL
N.V.	----------	-εις (ες)
G.	-ως, ος	-ων
D.	-ει	-σι (ν)
A.	-ν (α)	-εις (ας)

Of this Type 3 of the third declension, representative nouns are declined as follows:

SINGULAR

N.	ἡ πόλις	ὁ βασιλεύς (βασιλευ-)
G.	πόλεως[1]	βασιλέως
D.	πόλει	βασιλεῖ (βασιλέϊ)
A.	πόλιν	βασιλέα
V.	πόλι	βασιλεῦ

PLURAL

N.V.	πόλεις (πόλεες)	βασιλεῖς (βασιλέες)
G.	πόλεων[1]	βασιλέων
D.	πόλεσι(ν)	βασιλεῦσι(ν)
A.	πόλεις	βασιλεῖς[2]

---

[1]Observe the irregular accent on the antepenult although the ultima is long; this is because the earlier form of the word as πόλη-ος by transfer of quantity became πόλεως, with the accent remaining the same as on the earlier form. The accent of the genitive plural then followed the pattern of the genitive singular. See H. W. Smyth, Greek Grammar (Cambridge: Harvard University Press, 1959), paragraphs 268-272.

[2]An alternate earlier form of the accusative plural was βασιλέας.

The student is now ready to study carefully, for comparative purposes, the New Testament Greek Third Declension Chart by W. H. Mare (pp. 172–174).

The _interrogative_ and _indefinite_ pronouns in Greek have the same declined forms, the basic difference being that the interrogative forms (meaning, Who? Which? and What?) have the regular accent throughout on the first syllable of the word, while the indefinite forms (meaning, someone, something, a certain one, a certain thing) are enclitic (and follow the rules of enclitics given above). The acute accent, when it occurs on the ultima of the interrogative use of this pronoun, does not change to a grave when it is followed by other words without intervening punctuation. It is to be observed that the one set of forms serves for the masculine-feminine genders throughout. The neuter has its own set of forms. These forms are declined as follows:

	INTERROGATIVE PRONOUN SINGULAR			INDEFINITE PRONOUN SINGULAR	
	M.F.	N.		M.F.	N.
N.	τίς (who?)	τί (what?)	N.	τις (someone)	τι (something)
G.	τίνος	τίνος	G.	τινός	τινός
D.	τίνι	τίνι	D.	τινί	τινί
A.	τίνα	τί	A.	τινά	τι

	PLURAL			PLURAL	
N.	τίνες	τίνα	N.	τινές	τινά
G.	τίνων	τίνων	G.	τινῶν	τινῶν
D.	τίσι(ν)	τίσι(ν)	D.	τισί(ν)	τισί(ν)
A.	τίνας	τίνα	A.	τινάς	τινά

EXERCISES

1. Memorize the vocabulary of this lesson.

2. Learn the characteristic features of Type 3 of the Third Declension.

3. Learn the forms of the interrogative and indefinite pronouns.

4. Translate in the Simplified Greek Reader, John 4:16–23.

5. Do the English to Greek exercises based on the Greek Reader, John 4:16–23:
   a. The woman has five husbands.
   b. She said, "You are the prophet who is coming."
   c. The Samaritans worshiped in this mountain, but the Jews worshiped in Jerusalem.
   d. The true worshipers of God will worship him in spirit and in truth.

The Present Active Participle

VOCABULARY

ἀρχιερεύς, έως, ὁ	– chief priest, high priest
βασιλεύς, έως, ὁ	– king (Basil)
δέχομαι	– I receive (deponent)
δοξάζω	– I glorify (doxology)
εἷς, μία, ἕν	– one
ἤδη	– now, already
κράζω	– I cry out
μέσος, η, ον	– middle, in the midst (Mesopotamia, in the middle of the rivers)
οὐχί	– strengthened form of "not"
συναγωγή, ῆς, ἡ	– synagogue
φημί	– I say

EXPLANATIONS

The Participle – The Greek participle can be classified as a hybrid concept, being a combination of both **verb** (it has tense, kind of action, voice, and can have an object and adverbial modifiers) and **adjective** (it qualifies the action of the main verb, can take the article and modify a noun, and has gender and case as well as number). For all practical purposes, at this stage of our study, the present participle should be translated with an -ing, like the English, see**ing**, hear**ing**, or know**ing**.

The present participle indicates action that occurs at the same time as that of the main verb, so that the participle, translated initially with -ing, can then be more freely translated as, while seeing or while he sees; example, βλέπων τὸν ἄνθρωπον ἔρχεται , Seeing the man, he comes; or, While he is seeing the man, he comes. The **forms** of the present active participle, in the three genders and both numbers, are as follows (the masculine and neuter follow the third declension, the feminine the first declension):

SINGULAR

	M.	**F.**	**N.**
N.	λύων (he loosing)	λύουσα (she loosing) [1]	λῦον (it loosing)
G.	λύοντος	λυούσης	λύοντος
D.	λύοντι	λυούσῃ	λύοντι
A.	λύοντα	λύουσαν	λῦον

PLURAL

	M.	**F.**	**N.**
N.	λύοντες	λύουσαι	λύοντα
G.	λυόντων	λυουσῶν	λυόντων
D.	λύουσι(ν)	λυούσαις	λύουσι (ν)
A.	λύοντας	λυούσας	λύοντα

The present participial forms of the verb εἰμί, I am, are like the endings of the participle of λύω above, as follows:

---

[1] Compare the declension of δόξα, page 17.

	Masculine	SINGULAR Feminine	Neuter
N.	ὤν	οὖσα	ὄν
G.	ὄντος	οὔσης	ὄντος
D.	ὄντι	οὔσῃ	ὄντι
A.	ὄντα	οὖσαν	ὄν

		PLURAL	
N.	ὄντες	οὖσαι	ὄντα
G.	ὄντων	οὐσῶν	ὄντων
D.	οὖσι(ν)	οὔσαις	οὖσι(ν)
A.	ὄντας	οὔσας	ὄντα

It has been stated above that the participle, like the adjective, may take an article. This means, therefore, that the participle, like the adjective, can be in the underline{attributive} or underline{predicate} positions. Thus, when in the attributive position with the article, the participle is to be translated as, the one who sees, while when it is without the article it is to be translated as, seeing, or while he is seeing. Example:

ὁ βλέπων, The one who sees
   βλέπων, Seeing, or while he is seeing

The participle, when used without the article, is called the underline{circumstantial} participle, because it qualifies the circumstances of the action connected to the main verb. The underline{attributive} participle, with the article, like the adjective, tells something about the noun (idea) with which it is associated and thereby describes the noun in some way. Example:

ὁ βλέπων ἄνθρωπος,   The seeing man, the man who sees

βλέπων ὁ ἄνθρωπος ἔρχεται, Seeing, or while he is seeing, the man comes
                           (here βλέπων qualifies the activity involved
                           in ἔρχεται; i.e., it tells what is happening
                           in the circumstances when the man comes).

The forms and meaning of the participle in this lesson must be mastered. As the student masters the participle, he will be greatly helped in understanding Greek sentences and syntax.

EXERCISES

1. Memorize the vocabulary in this lesson.

2. Master the forms of the present active participle and the principles of syntax which govern the use of the participle presented in this lesson.

3. Simplified Greek Reader, John 4:24-30.

4. English to Greek exercises based on the Greek Reader, John 4:22-30. (The underlining indicates that a participle is called for.)
   a. She knows that Messiah is coming and, underline{believing} in him, she went away into the city.
   b. The underline{men who hear} the woman came out of the city and were coming to underline{him who speaks} the Word of God.
   c. underline{While she hears} Jesus, the woman knows that she has sin in her.
   d. The salvation underline{which is} from God is according to the Word of the Lord.

The Participle Explained; Principal Parts of the Verb

VOCABULARY

ἄχρι, ἄχρις	- with the genitive, as far as, up to; as a conjunction, until
γραφή, ῆς, ἡ	- writing, Scripture (Hagiographa, the holy writings, the poetic books of the O.T.)
διό	- wherefore
ἐπαγγελία, ας, ἡ	- promise
εὐαγγελίζω	- I bring good news, preach good news
ἤ	- or
λίθος, ου, ὁ	- stone (monolith)
μέγας, μεγάλη, μέγα	- large, great (megaphone)
μόνος, η, ον	- alone, only (monologue)
παραβολή, ῆς, ἡ	- parable
πολύς, πολλή, πολύ	- much; plural, many (polytheism)
χρόνος, ου, ὁ	- time (chronology)

EXPLANATIONS

Principal parts of some important verbs: The principal parts of a verb are
those tense forms which, when given, provide sufficient structure for the
student to conjugate or recognize the conjugated forms of all the tenses.
The regular verb, such as λύω, will have six principal parts as follows
(which will normally be given in the Greek to English lexicon):

1. Present active indicative first person singular - λύω.
   From this base, or stem, λυ-, can be constructed all of the forms
   of the present and imperfect.

2. Future active indicative first person singular - λύσω.
   From this form, λυ- plus σ, the sign of the future, can be constructed
   all of the future active and middle forms.

3. Aorist active indicative first person singular - ἔλυσα.
   From this form, with or without the augment ε (or its equivalent),
   can be constructed all of the forms of the aorist active and middle.

4. Perfect active indicative first person singular - λέλυκα.
   From this form can be constructed all of the perfect, pluperfect and
   future perfect active forms.

5. Perfect middle-passive indicative first person singular - λέλυμαι.
   From this form can be constructed all of the perfect, pluperfect
   and future perfect middle and passive forms.

6. Aorist passive indicative first person singular - ἐλύθην.
   From this form, with or without the augment ε (or its equivalent),
   can be constructed all of the aorist, future and future perfect
   passive forms.

Learn the principal parts of the following verbs:

1. γίνομαι, γενήσομαι, ἐγενόμην, γέγονα,[1] γεγένημαι, ἐγενήθην -
   I become, happen, come to pass.

---

[1]This is the second perfect with α added to the stem or base, but
without κ.

2. ἔρχομαι,[1] ἐλεύσομαι, ἦλθον, ἐλήλυθα, _____, _____[2] - I come, go.

3. ἐσθίω, φάγομαι, ἔφαγον,[3] _____ - I eat.

4. λαμβάνω, λήμψομαι, ἔλαβον,[3] εἴληφα,[4] εἴλημμαι, ἐλήμφθην -
I take, receive.

5. λύω, λύσω, ἔλυσα, λέλυκα, λέλυμαι, ἐλύθην - I loose.

6. πιστεύω, πιστεύσω, ἐπίστευσα, πεπίστευκα, πεπίστευμαι, ἐπιστεύθην -
I believe.

7. πορεύομαι, πορεύσομαι, ἐπορευσάμην, πεπόρευμαι, ἐπορεύθην -
I go (deponent, usually with passive forms).

Further explanations: In a previous lesson the student was introduced to the
meaning and conjugation of the present participle of λύω. In addition, stress
was placed on the participle used in the attributive position (with the
article) and in the predicate position (the circumstantial participle).

Further, it is to be noted that the time of the present participle, being
related to that of the main verb, is coincidental with the time of the main
verb which governs the overall time situation of the sentence. Example:
βλέπων αὐτόν, ὁ ἄνθρωπος λέγει τῷ κυρίῳ, Seeing him (or, While seeing him),
the man speaks to the Lord; βλέπων αὐτόν, ὁ ἄνθρωπος εἶπε τῷ κυρίῳ, Seeing
him (or, While seeing him), the man spoke to the Lord. The "seeing"
circumstance in each case is going on at the time of the main verb, whether
"he speaks" (when he is seeing him) or "he spoke" (while he was seeing him).

Now the student is ready to consider the aorist participle which carries
punctiliar kind of action. Its time is antecedent to the time of the main
verb, or sometimes coincidental with the time of the main verb, whether that
verb is past, present or future. Example: ἰδὼν αὐτόν, ὁ ἄνθρωπος λέγει
τῷ κυρίῳ, Having seen him (or, After he had seen him or, When he had seen him),
the man speaks to the Lord; ἰδὼν αὐτόν, ὁ ἄνθρωπος εἶπε τῷ κυρίῳ, Having
seen him (or, After he had seen him or, When he had seen him or, When he
saw him), the man spoke to the Lord.

---

[1]In the case of deponent verbs (i.e., middle or passive in form but active
in meaning) of course, the present middle and passive indicative, first person
singular, is the form under which these verbs are listed in the Greek to
English lexicon under normal circumstances.

[2]Some verbs are not conjugated in all of the tenses.

[3]This is a second aorist, a form not using the suffix syllable σα, but
(we could say) in its place, having a change in the spelling of the stem or
base (examples, φαγ- instead of the present stem ἐσθι-; λαβ- instead of the
present stem λαμβαν-) and using endings like the imperfect of the λύω verb.

[4]This is the second perfect with α added to the stem or base, but without κ.

Compare the attributive use of the aorist participle, as ὁ ἄνθρωπος
ὁ ἰδὼν αὐτὸν λέγει τῷ κυρίῳ, The man, the one who has seen him, speaks
to the Lord.

EXERCISES

1. Memorize the vocabulary in this lesson.

2. Learn the principal parts of the verbs given in this lesson.

3. Simplified Greek Reader, John 4:31-37.

4. English to Greek exercises based on the Greek Reader, John 4:24-37.
   a. The woman, the one who sees Christ, goes away into the city.
   b. God is (a) spirit, and the men, the ones who worship him, are his sons.
   c. Jesus sees the men, the ones who speak to the woman.
   d. The one who sows and the one who reaps receive wages.

The Aorist Active Participle

VOCABULARY

γλῶσσα, ης, ἡ	– tongue, language (glossolalia)
δεξιός, ά, όν	– right (opposite left)
ἐλπίς, ίδος, ἡ	– hope
ἔσχατος, η, ον	– last (eschatology)
εὐθύς, εὐθέως	– straightway, immediately
θεωρέω	– I look at, behold (theorem, theory)
μακάριος, α, ον	– blessed, happy
μηδέ	– but not, nor, not even
παιδίον, ου, τό	– infant, child
πείθω	– I persuade
σοφία, ας, ἡ	– wisdom (philosophy)
τέ	– and (an enclitic particle, weaker in force than καί)

EXPLANATIONS

The forms of the aorist active participle in the three genders and both numbers, singular and plural, are as follows (the masculine and neuter follow again the third declension endings, and the feminine the first declension):

SINGULAR

	Masculine	Feminine	Neuter
N.	λύσας	λύσασα	λῦσαν
G.	λύσαντος	λυσάσης	λύσαντος
D.	λύσαντι	λυσάσῃ	λύσαντι
A.	λύσαντα	λύσασαν	λῦσαν

PLURAL

	Masculine	Feminine	Neuter
N.	λύσαντες	λύσασαι	λύσαντα
G.	λυσάντων	λυσασῶν[1]	λυσάντων
D.	λύσασι(ν)	λυσάσαις	λύσασι(ν)
A.	λύσαντας	λυσάσας	λύσαντα

It is to be observed that the aorist participle, not being indicative, does not have the indicative time augment, ε-.

In Lesson 14 we studied the indicative forms of the second aorist verb. We are now ready to study the declension of the second aorist active participle of that type verb, using the second aorist active participial forms of εἶδον as an example. These forms are as follows:

SINGULAR

	Masculine	Feminine	Neuter
N.	ἰδών[2]	ἰδοῦσα	ἰδόν
G.	ἰδόντος	ἰδούσης	ἰδόντος
D.	ἰδόντι	ἰδούσῃ	ἰδόντι
A.	ἰδόντα	ἰδοῦσαν	ἰδόν

---

[1]Remember that the feminine first declension genitive plural is accented on the ultima.

[2]Observe that, not being the indicative, the participle here does not have the ε- augment, and that being a second aorist active participle, it is irregularly accented.

PLURAL

Masculine	Feminine	Neuter
N. ἰδόντες	ἰδοῦσαι	ἰδόντα
G. ἰδόντων	ἰδουσῶν	ἰδόντων
D. ἰδοῦσι(ν)	ἰδούσαις	ἰδοῦσι(ν)
A. ἰδόντας	ἰδούσας	ἰδόντα

EXERCISES

1. Learn the vocabulary of Lesson 21.

2. Learn the meaning and conjugation of the second aorist participle of λύω.

3. Learn the second aorist active participial forms of ἰδών (εἶδον).

4. Translate in the Greek Reader John 4:38-45.

5. Translate the following sentences from English to Greek (based on the material in this lesson and on John 4:31-37 of the Simplified Greek Reader):

   a. Jesus said to her, "Having seen me, do you believe the Word of God?"

   b. The man who has come to the Father will have eternal life.

   c. Having loosed her waterpot (the waterpot of her) from her hand, the woman went to the men of the city.

   d. She said to them, "The Christ, the one who spoke to me, is the truth."

   e. The men, having heard (after they heard) the word, went out of the city.

The Present Middle-Passive and Aorist Middle Participles

VOCABULARY

ἁμαρτωλός, όν	- adjective, sinful; as a noun, sinner
ἄρα	- then, therefore
ἔρημος, ον	- adjective, solitary, deserted; as a noun, ἡ ἔρημος, wilderness, desert
καθίζω	- I seat, sit (cathedral, i.e., the church which contains the bishop's seat)
κρίσις,[1] εως, ἡ	- judgment (crisis)
οὐκέτι	- adverb, no longer
πλείων, πλεῖον, or πλέον	- adjective, larger, more
πρό	- preposition with the genitive, before (prologue)
σπείρω	- I sow
τρίτος, η, ον	- third
τυφλός, ή, όν	- blind (typhlosis, medical blindness)
φυλακή, ῆς, ἡ	- guard, prison, watch

EXPLANATIONS

More principal parts of verbs:

1. ἀποθνῄσκω, ἀποθανοῦμαι,[2] ἀπέθανον - I die.

2. ἄρχω, ἄρξω, ἦρξα - I rule (it takes a genitive object); the middle form means, I begin.

3. βάλλω, βαλῶ,[2] ἔβαλον, βέβληκα, βέβλημαι, ἐβλήθην - I throw, cast.

4. βλέπω, βλέψω, ἔβλεψα - I see (for the future and aorist tenses of "see" often forms of ὁράω [future ὄψομαι, aorist εἶδον and εἶδα, and perfect ἑώρακα] are used).

5. διδάσκω, διδάξω, ἐδίδαξα, (δεδίδαχα), (δεδίδαγμαι), ἐδιδάχθην - I teach.

6. πίπτω, πεσοῦμαι,[2] ἔπεσον (second aorist), or ἔπεσα (first aorist), πέπτωκα - I fall.

7. σῴζω, σώσω, ἔσωσα, σέσωκα, σέσω(σ)μαι, ἐσώθην - I save.

Thus far the student has been introduced to the present and aorist active participial forms. Now he is ready to consider the middle and passive forms of the participle, whose endings contain a middle and/or passive element and final case endings which again are like those in the first declension (for the feminine forms) and the second declension (for the masculine and neuter forms).

Again, since the participle stresses in its verbal aspect the kind of action that is characteristic of regular verbal forms in the indicative, middle and passive participles are to be found in the present (stressing continuous, or sometimes simple or punctiliar kind of action), aorist (point

---

[1]-σις is a certain type of noun ending indicating action. κρίσις is related to κρίνω, I judge.

[2]These are special forms of the future which do not employ an σ suffix.

action) and perfect.[3] This lesson will set forth the present middle-passive and aorist middle forms of the participle.

The present middle and passive[4] forms of the participle of λύω are as follows:

SINGULAR

Masculine		Feminine		Neuter	
N. λυόμενος	(he loosing for	λυομένη	(she loosing for	λυόμενον	(it loos-
G. λυομένου	himself; he being	λυομένης	herself; she	λυομένου	ing for it-
D. λυομένῳ	loosed)	λυομένῃ	being loosed)	λυομένῳ	self; it
A. λυόμενον		λυομένην		λυόμενον	being loosed)

PLURAL

N. λυόμενοι	λυόμεναι	λυόμενα
G. λυομένων	λυομένων	λυομένων
D. λυομένοις	λυομέναις	λυομένοις
A. λυομένους	λυομένας	λυόμενα

It is to be observed that the masculine and neuter forms given above follow the second declension, while the feminine follows the η type first declension. It is to be noted further that the aorist participles do **not** have the tense augment of the indicative.

The aorist middle participle has distinct endings from the passive participle which are as follows:

SINGULAR

Masculine		Feminine		Neuter	
N. λυσάμενος	(he having loosed	λυσαμένη	(she having	λυσάμενον	(it having
G. λυσαμένου	himself, or for	λυσαμένης	loosed herself,	λυσαμένου	loosed it-
D. λυσαμένῳ	himself)	λυσαμένῃ	or for herself)	λυσαμένῳ	self, or
A. λυσάμενον		λυσαμένην		λυσάμενον	for itself)

PLURAL

N. λυσάμενοι	λυσάμεναι	λυσάμενα
G. λυσαμένων	λυσαμένων	λυσαμένων
D. λυσαμένοις	λυσαμέναις	λυσαμένοις
A. λυσαμένους	λυσαμένας	λυσάμενα

It is to be noted that following the aorist element -σα, the masculine and neuter endings are like the second declension, and the feminine endings are like the first declension in -η.

EXERCISES

1. Memorize the vocabulary in this lesson.
2. Learn the principal parts of the seven verbs listed in this lesson.
3. Memorize the present middle and passive and aorist middle forms of the participle of λύω.
4. Translate in the Greek Reader John 4:46-50.
5. Translate the following sentences from English to Greek (based on the Greek Reader, John 4:46-49):
   a. The nobleman came to Jesus who healed his child.

---

[3]The future participle is very little used in the New Testament, so that we will not include it in our study here.

[4]Like the present middle and passive indicative, the middle and passive forms of the participle are the same, the context determining whether the particular form is to be taken as middle or passive, the passive idea, however, predominating in usage.

b. After Jesus saw the man (or, <u>Jesus having seen</u> the man), the Jews spoke to the disciples.
c. <u>Having seen</u> Jesus, the man spoke to Jesus concerning his son.
d. The man says, 'My son is dying. Will you heal him?"

The Aorist Passive Participle; the Genitive
Absolute; Second Aorist Middle Participle

VOCABULARY

ἀπαγγέλλω   – I announce
ἔμπροσθεν   – with the genitive, in front of, before
ἔτος, ους, τό   – (third declension neuter noun) year (the
                                     Etesian winds blow annually)
κακός, ή, όν   – adjective, evil, bad (cacophony, bad sound)
μικρός, ά, όν   – adjective, small (microscope)
παραλαμβάνω   – I receive, take along
ποῦ   – interrogative adverb, where, whither
προσφέρω   – I bring to, offer
σωτηρία, ας, ἡ   – salvation (soteriology)
τοιοῦτος, -αύτη, -οῦτον,   – qualitative adjective, of such a quality,
    or, -οῦτο   such, similar, like
φόβος, ου, ὁ   – fear, terror (phobia)
χρεία, ας, ἡ   – a need

EXPLANATIONS

The aorist passive participial forms of λύω are as follows:

SINGULAR

Masculine	Feminine	Neuter
N. λυθείς	λυθεῖσα	λυθέν
G. λυθέντος	λυθείσης	λυθέντος
D. λυθέντι	λυθείσῃ	λυθέντι
A. λυθέντα	λυθεῖσαν	λυθέν

PLURAL

N. λυθέντες	λυθεῖσαι	λυθέντα
G. λυθέντων	λυθεισῶν	λυθέντων
D. λυθεῖσι(ν)	λυθείσαις	λυθεῖσι(ν)
A. λυθέντας	λυθείσας	λυθέντα

The aorist passive participial forms use the passive syllable θη (or, θε[ι]
here) together with the third declension endings for the masculine and
neuter and the first declension endings in η and α for the feminine.

The Genitive Absolute: The student has observed that the Greek participle
can be used predicatively (i.e., outside the "control" of the article) and
thus describe more vividly the qualifying verbal activity of a noun or
pronoun; thus this participle in the predicate position is called the circumstantial participle. In this connection, Greek often uses the circumstantial
participle in a special grammatically independent construction in which a
circumstantial participle and an accompanying noun or pronoun are both put
in the genitive case with no direct grammatical connection with any part of
the main or independent clause. Thus, the construction in the genitive is
absolute, or grammatically independent from the main clause, and so it is
called the genitive absolute. For example: τοῦ ἀνθρώπου βλέποντος αὐτόν,
οἱ μαθηταὶ εἶπον τὸν λόγον, The man seeing him (or, While the man was seeing
him), the disciples spoke the word; τοῦ ἀνθρώπου ἰδόντος αὐτόν, οἱ
μαθηταὶ εἶπον τὸν λόγον, The man having seen him (or, After the man had
seen him), the disciples spoke the word; αὐτοῦ βλέποντος τὸν κύριον, οἱ
μαθηταὶ εἶπον τὸν λόγον, He seeing (or, While he was seeing) the Lord, the
disciples spoke the word. The genitive absolute is used frequently in Greek.

Again, observe that the tense of the participle is related to that of the main verb, the present participle being coincidental (or, at the same time as) with that of the main verb; and the aorist participle being antecedent to (or sometimes coincidental with) the time of the main verb.

The second aorist participle of γίνομαι, which is used deponently (as is the present form), is declined as follows:

SINGULAR

Masculine	Feminine	Neuter
N. γενόμενος (he having	γενομένη (she having	γενόμενον (it hav-
G. γενομένου become)	γενομένης become)	γενομένου ing be-
D. γενομένῳ	γενομένῃ	γενομένῳ come)
A. γενόμενον	γενομένην	γενόμενον

PLURAL

N. γενόμενοι	γενόμεναι	γενόμενα
G. γενομένων	γενομένων	γενομένων
D. γενομένοις	γενομέναις	γενομένοις
A. γενομένους	γενομένας	γενόμενα

Observe that the second aorist middle base or stem is γενομεν- and is used with the second declension endings in the masculine and neuter and with the first declension endings in η for the feminine. Also observe, as with other participial forms, the second aorist middle participle does not use the augment ε- which belongs with the indicative.

EXERCISES

1. Learn the vocabulary of Lesson 23.

2. Study carefully the attributive and the predicate uses of the participle. What is the relation of the time of the present participle to the main verb? And of the time of the aorist participle to the main verb?

3. What is a genitive absolute and how does it relate to the main clause of the sentence?

4. Translate in the Greek Reader John 4:51-5:5.

5. Translate the following sentences from English to Greek (based on the Greek Reader, John 4:50-54, and on other parts of the Reader):
   a. The nobleman, the one who believed the word of Jesus (or, the one having believed the word of Jesus), went away into Capernaum.
   b. When he came down into the city (or, he having come down into the city), his servants (the servants of him) came to him.
   c. Jesus did this sign, after he had made the water wine (or, having made the water wine).
   d. When the nobleman believed, Jesus went away from Galilee and came to Jerusalem.
   e. While Jesus comes into Cana of Galilee (or, Jesus coming into Cana of Galilee), a nobleman comes out of Capernaum.

LESSON TWENTY-FOUR

The Perfect Active Participle

VOCABULARY

ἁμαρτάνω	- I sin (cf., hamartiology)
ἅπας, ἅπασα, ἅπαν	- all, whole (alternate form of πᾶς)
γενεά, ᾶς, ἡ	- generation (genealogy)
διώκω	- I pursue, persecute
ἐγγίζω	- I come near
θαυμάζω	- I marvel, wonder at
θηρίον, ου, τό	- a wild beast (theriomorphic, having animal form)
μέρος, ους, τό	- a part (pentamerous, of five parts)
ὅμοιος, α, ον	- like (Homoiousian, one holding that the Father and the Son in the Godhead are of like substance)
σεαυτοῦ, ῆς	- of yourself (reflexive pronoun)
σπέρμα, ατος, τό	- seed (sperm)

EXPLANATIONS

More Principal Parts of Verbs:

1. ἄγω, ἄξω, ἤγαγον (second aorist), ἦχα (perfect), ἦγμαι, ἤχθην - I lead.

2. βαπτίζω, βαπτίσω, ἐβάπτισα, βεβάπτικα, βεβάπτισμαι, ἐβαπτίσθην - I baptize.

3. εὑρίσκω, εὑρήσω, εὗρον (second aorist), εὕρηκα, (εὕρημαι), εὑρέθην - I find.

4. κηρύσσω, κηρύξω, ἐκήρυξα, (κεκήρυχα), (κεκήρυγμαι), ἐκηρύχθην - I proclaim, I preach.

5. πέμπω, πέμψω, ἔπεμψα, (πέπομφα), (πέπεμμαι), ἐπέμφθην - I send.

6. πίνω, πίομαι, ἔπιον, πέπωκα, (πέπομαι), ἐπόθην - I drink.

7. προσεύχομαι, προσεύξομαι, προσηυξάμην - I pray.

In the last few lessons the student has studied both the present and aorist participles in their active, middle and passive forms. At this point, to complete the scheme of this important part of Greek grammatical structure, it is in order to introduce the perfect participial forms. It must be remembered that the perfect tense includes, at the beginning of the word, the principle of reduplication of the first consonant with a connecting -ε-, or its equivalent,[1] in the active, middle and passive forms. Following the base, or stem, of the word, in the active forms, there is added the suffix κα (third singular, κε) plus the primary endings; in the middle and passive forms, there is no κα, but rather the middle and passive primary endings are added directly to the base, or stem. For example: λέλυκα, perfect active indicative, first person singular, meaning, I have loosed (●——), I just loosed (——●); λέλυμαι, perfect middle or passive indicative, first person singular, meaning, I have loosed for myself or, I have been loosed, I stand loosed.

---

[1]Verbs which begin with a vowel lengthen the beginning vowel in lieu of reduplication.

The perfect active participle is as follows:

SINGULAR

λελυκώς (he having loosed)	λελυκυῖα	λελυκός
λελυκότος	λελυκυίας	λελυκότος
λελυκότι	λελυκυίᾳ	λελυκότι
λελυκότα	λελυκυῖαν	λελυκός

PLURAL

λελυκότες	λελυκυῖαι	λελυκότα
λελυκότων	λελυκυιῶν	λελυκότων
λελυκόσι(ν)	λελυκυίαις	λελυκόσι(ν)
λελυκότας	λελυκυίας	λελυκότα

The student is to observe that the perfect active participle is irregularly accented on the penult (except for the masculine nominative singular, the neuter nominative and accusative singular, and the feminine genitive plural, where the accent is on the ultima).

EXERCISES

1. Learn the vocabulary of Lesson 24.

2. Memorize the principal parts of the seven verbs listed in this lesson.

3. Learn the forms of the perfect active participle. Review again the use of the genitive absolute.

4. Translate in the Greek Reader, John 5:6-13.

5. Translate the following sentences from English to Greek (cf. the Greek Reader, John 5:1-11, and other parts of the Reader):
   a. When Jesus came into Jerusalem, his disciples came into the house.
   b. Jesus saw the pool which had five porches.
   c. Jesus said to the one who was sick: "Will you be healed?"
   d. While Jesus comes to the water (or, Jesus coming to the water), the man who was thirty and eight years old and was lying down, is not cast into the pool.
   e. The man who was healed said to the Jews: "He made me well."

The Perfect Middle-Passive Participle

VOCABULARY

ἀνάστασις, εως, ἡ	- resurrection (Anastasia, a girl's name)
δεύτερος, α, ον	- second (Deuteronomy)
ἐάν	- if (with the subjunctive)
ἐπιγινώσκω	- I come to know, recognize, know fully
θεραπεύω	- I heal (therapeutic)
θλῖψις, εως, ἡ	- tribulation, affliction
ναός, οῦ, ὁ	- temple
οἶδα	- I know (second perfect with a present meaning)
ὅταν	- whenever (ὅτε + ἄν [ἐάν], with the subjunctive)
πᾶς, πᾶσα, πᾶν	- all, every
σήμερον	- today
τιμή, ῆς, ἡ	- honor, price (Timothy, God honoring)

EXPLANATIONS

The perfect middle and passive forms and translation of this form of the participle are as follows (the forms are identical for the middle and passive):

SINGULAR

N.	λελυμένος (he, having	λελυμένη (she, having	λελυμένον (it, having
G.	λελυμένου been loosed)	λελυμένης been loosed)	λελυμένου been loosed)
D.	λελυμένῳ (●——; ——●)	λελυμένῃ (●——; ——●)	λελυμένῳ (●——; ——●)
A.	λελυμένον	λελυμένην	λελυμένον

PLURAL

N.	λελυμένοι	λελυμέναι	λελυμένα
G.	λελυμένων	λελυμένων	λελυμένων
D.	λελυμένοις	λελυμέναις	λελυμένοις
A.	λελυμένους	λελυμένας	λελυμένα

It is to be observed that the perfect middle and passive participle is accented on the penult, which is an exception to the rule that the verb has a recessive accent (see page 3).

Examples of usage of the perfect participial forms are as follows:

1. ὁ λελυκὼς τὸν ἄνθρωπον λέγει τῷ κυρίῳ,
   The one having loosed the man (●——; ——●) (or, the one who has loosed the man) speaks to the Lord. (This is the attributive use of the participle.)

2. λελυκὼς τὸν ἄνθρωπον, λέγει τῷ κυρίῳ,
   Having loosed (or, When he has loosed) the man, he speaks to the Lord. (This is the predicate use of the participle.)

3. ὁ λελυμένος ὑπὸ τοῦ ἀνθρώπου λέγει τῷ κυρίῳ,
   The one having been loosed (and standing loosed, ●——; ——●) by the man speaks to the Lord. (This is the attributive use of the participle.)

4. λελυμένος ὑπὸ τοῦ ἀνθρώπου, λέγει τῷ κυρίῳ,
   Having been loosed (or, When he was loosed, ●——; ——●) by the man, he speaks to the Lord.

Genitive absolute construction:

5. λελυκότος τοῦ ἀδελφοῦ τὸν ἄνθρωπον, ὁ 'Ιησοῦς ἔρχεται εἰς τὴν πόλιν,
The brother having loosed the man, Jesus comes into the city (or,
After the brother has loosed the man, Jesus comes into the city).

6. λελυμένου τοῦ ἀδελφοῦ, ὁ 'Ιησοῦς ἔρχεται εἰς τὴν πόλιν,
The brother having been loosed (having stood loosed), Jesus
comes into the city (or, After the brother has been loosed, Jesus
comes into the city).

EXERCISES

1. Learn the vocabulary of Lesson 25.

2. Learn the perfect middle and passive participial forms.

3. Translate in the Simplified Greek Reader John 5:14-19.

4. Translate the following sentences from English to Greek, using for
helps material in this lesson and in the Greek Reader, John 5:10-13,
and other parts of the Reader:[1]

   a. The man who had been loosed (or, who stood loosed) came to
   the Jews.

   b. The Jews having persecuted Jesus (or, when the Jews had
   persecuted Jesus), the man who was healed went into his
   house.

   c. The man told (to) the Jews that the one who healed (or, had
   healed) him was Jesus.

   d. A crowd being in the place (or, while the crowd was in the place),
   Jesus went out of the city.

---

[1]Supplemental sentences for this lesson for practice in translating
English to Greek are to be found on page 107.

The Subjunctive

VOCABULARY

ἅπτομαι	– I touch
διέρχομαι	– I pass through
δύναμις, εως, ἡ	– power (dynamite)
ἐργάζομαι	– I work (energy)
θύρα, ας, ἡ	– door
καινός, ή, όν	– new
λογίζομαι	– I account, reckon (logic)
ὀλίγος, η, ον	– little, few (oligarchy)
ὅπως	– with the subjunctive (as is also ἵνα), that, in order that
οὐαί	– woe! alas!
παραγίνομαι	– I come, arrive
περισσεύω	– I abound
πρόβατον, ου, τό	– a sheep
χωρίς	– with the genitive, without, apart from

EXPLANATIONS

More Principal Parts of Verbs:

1. ἀσπάζομαι, _____, ἠσπασάμην (first aorist) – I greet, salute.

2. γινώσκω, γνώσομαι, ἔγνων, ἔγνωκα, ἔγνωσμαι, ἐγνώσθην – I know.

3. δέχομαι, δέξομαι, ἐδεξάμην, _____, δέδεγμαι, ἐδέχθην – I receive (deponent).

4. δοξάζω, δοξάσω, ἐδόξασα, (δεδόξακα), δεδόξασμαι, ἐδοξάσθην – I glorify.

5. εὐαγγελίζω, (εὐαγγελίσω), εὐηγγέλισα, (εὐηγγέλικα), εὐηγγέλισμαι, εὐηγγελίσθην – I preach the good news.

6. κράζω, κράξω, ἔκραξα, κέκραγα, _____ – I cry out.

7. πείθω, πείσω, ἔπεισα, πέποιθα, πέπεισμαι, ἐπείσθην – I persuade.

Thus far in considering the verb, this study has concentrated on the indicative mood (which is the mood of statement of fact) and the participle (the hybrid: verb-adjective). Beyond these verbal forms there are moods which indicate ways of saying things other than using the statement of fact or a verbal-adjective adjunct, such as the participle.

Subjunctive:

The subjunctive is a mood in which the statement made indicates the probability or possibility of the event which is posited occurring. To accomplish this, the conditional and purpose clauses, etc., are used with distinctive subjunctive verb forms in which basically the ο/ε variable vowels are lengthened to ω/η. The forms of the present subjunctive are as follows:

	Active		Middle-Passive	
1.	λύω	λύωμεν	λύωμαι	λυώμεθα
2.	λύῃς	λύητε	λύῃ	λύησθε
3.	λύῃ	λύωσι(ν)	λύηται	λύωνται

The forms of the aorist subjunctive are as follows:[1]

	Active	Middle	Passive
1.	λύσω	λύσωμαι	λυθῶ[2]
2.	λύσῃς	λύσῃ	λυθῇς
3.	λύσῃ	λύσηται	λυθῇ
1.	λύσωμεν	λυσώμεθα	λυθῶμεν
2.	λύσητε	λύσησθε	λυθῆτε
3.	λύσωσι(ν)	λύσωνται	λυθῶσι(ν)

It is to be observed that the subjunctive has present and aorist forms[3] but has no imperfect or future ones. The present subjunctive forms stress durative (or, linear) kind of action, and the aorist subjunctive forms stress the punctiliar (or, point, or, definite) kind of action, and the time concepts are basically carried by the indicative verb in the particular sentence involved.

EXERCISES

1. Learn the vocabulary of Lesson 26.

2. Memorize the principal parts of the seven verbs given in the lesson.

3. Memorize the present and aorist forms of the subjunctive.

4. Translate in the Greek Reader, John 5:20-24.

5. Translate the following sentences from English to Greek (based on the material in this lesson and on the Greek Reader, John 5:14-24):
   a. Jesus did this new miracle and Jews persecuted him.
   b. He did this for his sheep.
   c. The Father sent the Son who has the judgment.
   d. The one who believes in Jesus believes in the word and does not see death.

---

[1]The perfect forms of the subjunctive are not frequently used and will not be included here.

[2]This seemingly irregular accent is due to a contraction of the passive element -θε-, with the subjunctive vowels ω/η, as λυθέ-ω (λυθῶ), λυθέ-ῃς (λυθῇς), etc. [3]There are the regular first aorist forms, and second aorist forms for second aorist verbs.

Uses of the Subjunctive

VOCABULARY

ἄξιος, α, ον	– worthy (axiom; in philosophy and psychology, axiological, pertaining to the science of value)
δικαιόω	– I justify, pronounce righteous
ἐπιθυμία, ας, ἡ	– eager desire, passion
ἐτοιμάζω	– I prepare
ἱκανός, ἡ, όν	– sufficient, able, considerable
κλαίω	– I weep
μνημεῖον, ου, τό	– tomb, monument
ὅστις, ἥτις, ὅ,τι (or, ὅ τι)	– whoever, whichever, whatever
πάντοτε	– always
πάσχω	– I suffer
πράσσω	– I do, perform (praxis, practice, as opposed to theory)
τέλος, ους, τό	– end (teleology)

Examples of the use of the subjunctive in the ἵνα clause for purpose are:

ὁ 'Ιησοῦς ἔρχεται ἵνα λύῃ ἡμᾶς ἀπὸ τῶν ἁμαρτιῶν ἡμῶν, Jesus comes in order that he may be loosing (present subjunctive) us from our sins;

ὁ 'Ιησοῦς ἔρχεται ἵνα λύσῃ ἡμᾶς ἀπὸ τῶν ἁμαρτιῶν ἡμῶν, Jesus comes (in order) that he may loose (aorist subjunctive, point action) us from our sins;

ὁ 'Ιησοῦς ἦλθεν ἵνα λύῃ ἡμᾶς ἀπὸ τῶν ἁμαρτιῶν ἡμῶν, Jesus came (in order) that he might be loosing (present subjunctive used in relation to an aorist indicative verb) us from our sins;

ὁ 'Ιησοῦς ἦλθεν ἵνα λύσῃ ἡμᾶς ἀπὸ τῶν ἁμαρτιῶν ἡμῶν, Jesus came (in order) that he might loose (aorist subjunctive used in relation to an aorist indicative verb) us from our sins.

Conditional Use of the Subjunctive: The subjunctive can be used in a conditional "if" clause, with the introductory word ἐάν (or sometimes ἄν, or even εἰ) to indicate that the condition is probable or is very likely to come to pass - at least the condition is stated in these terms. The subjunctive forms used in such cases are to be translated (at this stage of the student's learning) with an introductory "should" or "shall"[1] to indicate the probability or possibility of the conditional part of the sentence.

Examples of this type of condition[2] are as follows: ἐὰν ὁ 'Ιησοῦς λύῃ ἀνθρώπους ἀπὸ τῶν ἁμαρτιῶν αὐτῶν σωθήσονται, If Jesus shall (or, should) be loosing (or, looses at any time) men from their sins, they shall be saved; ἐὰν ὁ 'Ιησοῦς λύσῃ ἀνθρώπους ἀπὸ τῶν ἁμαρτιῶν αὐτῶν σωθήσονται, If Jesus shall (or, should) loose (aorist subjunctive, point action) men from their sins, they shall be saved.

---

[1] It is to be noted that the "shall" used here does not mean that the event is necessarily going to happen.

[2] A. T. Robertson in his grammar calls this the third class condition.

In contrast, the indicative factual condition with the introductory word, εἰ, states the condition as a fact whether it is actually true or not. Examples of this are:

εἰ ὁ Ἰησοῦς λύει ἀνθρώπους ἀπὸ τῶν ἁμαρτιῶν αὐτῶν σωθήσονται,

If Jesus looses (as he is in fact doing) men from their sins, they shall be saved,

εἰ ὁ Ἰησοῦς ἔλυσεν ἀνθρώπους ἀπὸ τῶν ἁμαρτιῶν αὐτῶν σωθήσονται,

If Jesus has loosed (as in fact he has) men from their sins, they shall be saved.

As can be seen in comparing the ἐάν plus the subjunctive with the εἰ plus the indicative conditions, it is a matter of viewpoint, perspective, and intent which is involved in the differences in these two kinds of conditions.

The hortatory subjunctive or subjunctive of exhortation:

The subjunctive can be used in an independent clause in the first person plural to express exhortation to mutual activity. Examples:

ἔχωμεν εἰρήνην πρὸς τὸν θεόν , <u>Let us have</u> (or continue to have; present subjunctive) peace with God;
ἔσχῶμεν εἰρήνην πρὸς τὸν θεόν , <u>Let us have</u> (point action; aorist subjunctive) peace with God.

The Deliberative Subjunctive:

The subjunctive is also used in a deliberative way with the first person in the sense of "What are we to do?" Rendered more freely, "What shall we do?"

λέγωμεν αὐτοῖς; "Are we to speak (or, be speaking; present subjunctive) to them?" Or, "Shall we speak to them?";

εἴπωμεν αὐτοῖς; "Are we to speak (point action; aorist subjunctive) to them?"

The subjunctive uses the negative μή where the indicative uses οὐ.

EXERCISES

1. Learn the vocabulary of Lesson 27.

2. Thoroughly master the uses of the subjunctive in ἵνα clauses, conditions, exhortation, and deliberation.

3. Translate in the Greek Reader, John 5:25-29.

4. Translate the following sentences from English to Greek (based on the material in this lesson and on the Greek Reader, John 5:25-29):

    a. The one <u>who</u> hears the Lord comes to Him <u>in order that</u> he <u>may know</u> His word.

    b. Jesus spoke (said) the Word of God <u>in order that</u> men <u>might be saved</u> (aorist tense).

c. Let us hear (or, be hearing) the word of the Lord in order that
    we may be saved.

d. The ones who have heard the voice of the Son of God shall live.

e. If we should believe in the Lord, we shall know his Word.

f. If God sends (as in fact he does) his Son into the world, men
    shall believe on Him.

g. Are we to believe (or shall we believe) in the Son of God (in
    order) that we may be saved?

The Infinitive; Using the Lexicon

VOCABULARY

ἀγρός, οῦ, ὁ	- field (agrarian)
ἄρχων, οντος, ὁ	- ruler (monarch)
ἐμαυτοῦ	- of myself
διάβολος, ου, ὁ	- slanderous; as noun, accuser, the devil
εὐθέως (εὐθύς)	- immediately
μαρτυρία, ας, ἡ	- testimony, evidence
ὀπίσω	- behind, after; with the gen., behind, after (opisthograph, a manuscript written on both front and back, Rev. 5:1)
οὖς, ὠτός, τό	- ear (otology)
πέντε	- five
περιτομή, ῆς, ἡ	- circumcision
πτωχός, ή, όν	- poor; poor man
ὑποστρέφω	- I return
ὥσπερ	- just as, even as

More Principal Parts of Verbs:

1. ἁμαρτάνω, ἁμαρτήσω, ἡμάρτησα or 2 aorist ἥμαρτον, ἡμάρτηκα, (ἡμάρτημαι), (ἡμαρτήθην) - I sin.

2. ἀπαγγέλλω, ἀπαγγελῶ, 1 aorist ἀπήγγειλα, 2 aorist passive ἀπηγγέλην - I report, announce, tell, proclaim.

3. διώκω, διώξω, ἐδίωξα, δεδίωκα, δεδίωγμαι, ἐδιώχθην - I pursue, persecute.

4. ἐγγίζω, ἐγγιῶ or ἐγγίσω, ἤγγισα, ἤγγικα - I come near.

5. θαυμάζω, θαυμάσομαι, ἐθαύμασα, τεθαύμακα, aorist passive ἐθαυμάσθην - I wonder, marvel, wonder at.

6. θεραπεύω, θεραπεύσω, ἐθεράπευσα, (τεθεράπευκα), τεθεράπευμαι, ἐθεραπεύθην - I heal.

7. προσφέρω, προσοίσω, προσήνεγκα or προσήνεγκον,[1] προσενήνοχα, (προσενήνεγμαι), προσηνέχθην - I bring to (with the accusative of the thing brought and the dative of the person to whom it is brought).

8. σπείρω, (σπερῶ), ἔσπειρα, _____ , ἔσπαρμαι, ἐσπάρην[2] - I sow.

EXPLANATION

The student has studied the indicative mood of the statement of fact and also the subjunctive mood of probability and possibility. In addition considerable emphasis has been placed on the participle, the verbal-adjective hybrid.

Now it is time to investigate the infinitive and imperative moods.

---

[1]This verb has a first and second aorist with κ instead of ς.

[2]This is a second aorist passive form with the η vowel, but no θ(η).

The infinitive:

Whereas the participle is a verbal-adjective, the infinitive is a verbal-noun hybrid. Thus the infinitive contains the <u>kind of action</u> elements of the verb in emphasizing durative (or, linear) and punctiliar action and the substantive characteristics of the noun, being able to be used as a subject, object, object of a preposition, etc. In English the infinitive forms are expressed as, to loose, to be loosing, etc. In the New Testament infinitives are to be found mainly in the present and aorist and sometimes in the perfect.[3] The infinitive forms, active, middle and passive, are as follows:

<u>Infinitive</u>

	Active		Middle-Passive	
Present	λύειν[4]	– to loose, to be loosing	λύεσθαι[4]	– to be loosed, to loose oneself
Aorist	λῦσαι	– to loose (●)	λύσασθαι	– to loose oneself (●)
			λυθῆναι	– to be loosed (●)
Perfect	λελυκέναι	– to have loosed (●——; ——●)	λελύσθαι	– to have been loosed, to have loosed oneself (●——; ——●)

Examples of uses of the infinitive are as follows:

<u>As subject</u>: 1) τὸ λύειν τὸν ἵππον ἐστὶν ἀγαθόν,
To loose the horse is good.

2) τὸ λυθῆναι ἀπὸ τῶν ἁμαρτιῶν ἐστιν ἀγαθόν,
To be loosed (●) from your sins is good.

<u>As object</u>: 1) ἀγαπᾶτε λύειν τὸν ἵππον,
You love to loose the horse.

2) θέλετε λυθῆναι ἀπὸ τῶν ἁμαρτιῶν ὑμῶν,
You wish to be loosed from your sins.

<u>As object of a preposition</u>:

1) ἐν τῷ λύειν τὸν ἄνθρωπον τὸν ἵππον,
ὁ κύριος εἶπε τοῖς μαθηταῖς,
While the man loosed (or, was loosing,——) the horse, the Lord spoke to the disciples. (Literally, In the <u>to loose</u> with reference to the man [an accusative of general reference] the horse [the direct object of the infinitive], the Lord spoke to the disciples.)

2) μετὰ τὸ λυθῆναι ὑμᾶς ἀπὸ τῶν ἁμαρτιῶν ὑμῶν ἡ εἰρήνη
τοῦ κυρίου προσελεύσεται πρὸς ὑμᾶς,
After you[5] are loosed (●) from your sins, the peace of the Lord will come to you.

---

[3]There is a future infinitive, but it is rarely used in the New Testament.

[4]Second aorist active and middle stems are expected to take the -ειν and -εσθαι type endings of the present tense, e.g., ἐλθεῖν and γενέσθαι.

[5]ὑμᾶς (after λυθῆναι) is the accusative of general reference (to be loosed with reference to you) and is to be thought of as the subject of the infinitive.

<u>As purpose</u>: 1) ἦλθε βλέπειν τὸν κύριον, He came to see[6] (or,
in order to see) the Lord.

2) ἦλθον βλέπεσθαι ὑπὸ τοῦ κυρίου, They came to be seen
(or, in order to be seen) by the Lord.

EXERCISES

1. Learn the vocabulary of Lesson 28.

2. Memorize the principal parts of the eight verbs given in this lesson.

3. Learn the infinitive forms presented in this lesson.

4. Master the uses of the infinitive.

5. Translate from the Simplified Greek Reader John 5:30-35, using the
vocabulary lists and lexicon.

As verse 30 is examined, the following principles are to be observed
in using the Greek Lexicon by Arndt, Gingrich and Danker:[7]

a. Look up the words needed as they are alphabetically listed in the
lexicon.

b. With verbs like the deponent δύναμαι (page 207), observe that there
are listed various important forms of the verb; and then the meanings
are given numerically. Look at the meanings broadly at first, and then
if you have greater need of information, examine the details of meanings
and the references. An * at the end of an entry means all the passages
in our New Testament and early Christian literature are cited; two ** means
all the New Testament passages are given.

c. With an adverb like οὐ (page 590), observe that the discussion of the way
the form is used in the literature and presented in the grammars is listed
first, and then the meanings are outlined and discussed.

d. In the case of a noun like κρίσις (page 452), observe that the noun, its
genitive form and article are given first, so that the student will know the
gender and type of declension of the noun. Then a brief survey of the
literature in which the noun κρίσις is found is given. (Look up the ab-
breviations to authors, literature, etc., given in a section at the front of
the lexicon.) Then, again, the meanings are outlined and explained.

6. Translate the following sentences from English to Greek, using the material
in this lesson and that found in the Reader, John 5:30-35:

a. I came to the Lord in order to be loosed (•) from my sins.
b. I am not able to come (———) to the Lord in order that he might save (•) me.
c. <u>To see</u> the Lord is to have peace.
d. I said these things in order that you might be saved.

---

[6]This is another way to express purpose besides ἵνα and the subjunctive.

[7]W. F. Arndt, F. W. Gingrich, and Frederick Danker, <u>A Greek to English Lexicon
of the New Testament</u>, Second Edition, Revised and Augmented (Chicago: University of
Chicago Press, 1979).

The Imperative

VOCABULARY

ἄρτι — now, just now
βούλομαι — I wish, determine
ἐκπορεύομαι — I go out
ἐπιστρέφω — I turn to, return
καλῶς — well
μάρτυς, -υρος, ὁ — witness (martyr)
ὀργή, ῆς, ἡ — anger
ὀφείλω — I owe, ought
πειράζω — I test, tempt
προσευχή, ῆς, ἡ — prayer
τέσσαρες, ων — four (Diatessaron of Tatian, A.D. 170 harmony of Gospels; literally, through the four)
ὑποτάσσω — I subject, put in subjection (hypotaxis, subordination of clauses)

The Imperative:

The imperative is the mood of command whether positive or negative (this latter is called prohibition). The basic tenses of the imperative are present and aorist. Obviously the imperative forms are in the second and third persons, the first person being taken care of by the hortatory (or, exhortation) subjunctive. The forms are as follows:

Present

Active		Middle Passive	
λῦε	- you loose (——)	λύου	- you be loosed
λυέτω	- let him loose	λυέσθω	- let him be loosed
λύετε	- you (plural) loose	λύεσθε	- you (plural) be loosed
λυέτωσαν	- let them loose	λυέσθωσαν	- let them be loosed

Aorist

Active		Middle		Passive	
λῦσον	- you loose (•)	λῦσαι	- you loose yourself (•)	λύθητι	- you be loosed (•)
λυσάτω		λυσάσθω		λυθήτω	
λύσατε		λύσασθε		λύθητε	
λυσάτωσαν		λυσάσθωσαν		λυθήτωσαν	

The negative for the infinitive and imperative is μή.

Examples:

1) εἶπεν λῦε τὸ πλοῖον, He said, "Loose (——) the boat."

2) εἶπεν λύσατε τὸν ἄνθρωπον, He said, "Loose (•) the man."

3) εἶπεν μὴ λύετε τὸ πλοῖον, He said, "Do not be loosing the boat."

4) εἶπεν μὴ λύσητε[1] τὸν ἄνθρωπον, He said, "Do not loose (•) the man."

---

[1]The aorist punctiliar prohibition is expressed by using the aorist subjunctive with μή.

EXERCISES

1. Learn the vocabulary of Lesson 29.

2. Learn the imperative forms presented in this lesson.

3. Master the uses of the imperative.

4. Translate from the Greek Gospel of John, Chapter 5:36-40 (using the vocabulary lists and lexicons).

5. Translate the following sentences from English to Greek (based on the material in this lesson and in John 5:36-40):

   a. The Lord said to me, "Come to me."

   b. The man said, "Do not send (———) me away. I want (wish) to see the Lord."

   c. I have the witness from God because he is my Father.

   d. The Scriptures which bear witness (are bearing witness) concerning me have in them eternal life.

LESSON THIRTY

The Contract Verbs

VOCABULARY

αἰτέω	- I ask
ἀκολουθέω	- I follow (takes the dative) (cf. acolyte, the assistant who carries the wine and water and the lights at Mass; he follows the priest)
ἀσθενέω	- I am weak, am sick
βλασφημέω	- I revile, blaspheme
δέω	- I bind (diadem, literally something bound around or across)
διακονέω	- I wait upon, serve (deacon)
δοκέω	- I think, seem (docetism, the early heresy that Christ's body was phantasmal or of celestial substance which merely seemed human)
εὐλογέω	- I bless (eulogize)
εὐχαριστέω	- I give thanks (Eucharist)
ζητέω	- I seek
καλέω	- I call, name, invite
κατοικέω	- I inhabit, dwell
κρατέω	- I grasp (plutocratic)
μαρτυρέω	- I bear witness, testify
μετανοέω	- I repent
μισέω	- I hate (misogynist, a woman-hater)
οἰκοδομέω	- I build, edify
παρακαλέω	- I exhort, encourage
περιπατέω	- I walk
τηρέω	- I keep
φωνέω	- I call (phonetic)

Principal Parts of Verbs:

1. ἀγαπάω, ἀγαπήσω, ἠγάπησα, ἠγάπηκα, ἠγάπημαι, ἠγαπήθην - I love.

2. αἰτέω, αἰτήσω, ᾔτησα, ᾔτηκα, (ᾔτημαι), ᾐτήθην - I ask (in the sense of request), I ask for.

3. δικαιόω, δικαιώσω, ἐδικαίωσα, _____, δεδικαίωμαι, ἐδικαιώθην - I justify.

4. ἐργάζομαι, (ἐργάσομαι), ἠργασάμην, εἴργασμαι, _____, - I work, accomplish.

5. ἑτοιμάζω, ἑτοιμάσω, ἡτοίμασα, ἡτοίμακα, ἡτοίμασμαι, ἡτοιμάσθην - I prepare.

6. κλαίω, κλαύσω and κλαύσομαι, ἔκλαυσα, ____, (κεκλαύσομαι), (ἐκλαύσθην) - I weep, cry.

7. λογίζομαι, (Attic fut. λογιοῦμαι), ἐλογισάμην, (λελόγισμαι), ἐλογίσθην - I reckon, calculate, evaluate.

8. πάσχω, (πείσομαι), ἔπαθον, πέπονθα - I suffer, experience.

Verb types other than the λύω types. Thus far in the study of Greek the
student has learned the structure and conjugation of the omega, ω, verb,
as λύω. There are three other types of verbal structure which now need
to be studied. These other verbal types do not differ in all tenses from
the omega type, but the variations in structure occur mainly in the
present, imperfect, and future tenses. These verbal types are called
contract, liquid, and μι verbs.

The Contract Verbs

These verbs, as can be observed in the examples in the vocabulary of
Lesson 30, vary from λύω in having the vowels α, ε, or ο as the end
of the verb base before the regular variable vowel ο/ε and endings are
added as suffixes. Acting differently than consonants or such as the
semi-vowel or consonant υ in λύω, this α, ε, or ο at the end of the
verb base combines with the variable vowel ο/ε to form what is
linguistically called a contraction of two vowels. An analysis of the
vowel contractions which occur in these contract verbs in the present and
imperfect is to be seen in the accompanying chart entitled: Rules for
Contract Verbs. It is to be noted that the α in the end of the base of
those contract verbs like ἀγαπά-ω "overcomes" a following ε, and combines
into some form of α; also the ο vowel at the end of the base of those
contract verbs like δικαιό-ω "overcomes" ε, η, or ο and produces a contraction in which the ο vowel predominates, as οι, ου or ω.

Even though there are contractions of vowels before the endings of these
verbs, it is to be observed that often the student can without any
difficulty recognize the form because the regular consonant-vowel
syllable endings used with λύω are added to the end of the forms, as
-μεν, -τε, etc.

RULES FOR CONTRACT VERBS:

There are certain verbs which have an α, ε , or ο before the suffix endings
in I, II amp which contract with the variable vowel before the consonant
suffix endings. If the α, ε, or ο is accented, the contraction receives
the circumflex accent (this occurs most of the time and will help the
student recognize a contract verb). Find out from what vowel or diphthong
the contraction comes.

Note that α and ᾳ contractions come from combinations which have an α as
the first vowel of the combination.

Note that ει contractions come from ε or ει combinations.

Note that η and ῃ contractions come from combinations of ε + η and ε + ῃ.

Note that οι, ου, ω contractions come from combinations which contain
an ο, ου, or ω vowel.

If the contracted vowel on the end of the word is:	Then it comes from:
α	α+ε τιμᾶτε
α	α+ει τιμᾶν (I a 31)
α	α+η τιμᾶτε
ᾳ	α+ει τιμᾷ
ᾳ	α+η τιμᾷς
ει	ε+ε ἐφίλει
ει	ε+ει φιλεῖ
η	ε+η φιλῆτε
ῃ	ε+η φιλῇ
οι	ο+ει δηλοῖ
οι	ο+η δηλοῖ
ου	ο+ε δηλοῦτε
ου	ο+ει δηλοῦν (I a 31)
ου	ο+ο ἐδήλουν
ου	ο+ου δηλοῦσα
ου	ε+ο φιλοῦμεν
ου	ε+ου φιλοῦσα
ω	α+ο τιμῶμεν
ω	α+ου τιμῶσα
ω	α+ω τιμῶν
ω	ε+ω φιλῶ
ω	ο+η δηλῶτε
ω	ο+ω δηλῶ

It is to be noted that outside of the present and imperfect tenses the vowel which ends the verb base or stem lengthens (and there is no contraction) and the regular endings are added, as, for example, ζητήσω, I will seek. The present and imperfect forms of the contract verb types (in εω) are as follows:

Present

	Active	Middle–Passive
Indicative		
1.	ζητῶ (εω)	ζητοῦμαι (εο)
2.	ζητεῖς (εει)	ζητῇ (εη)
3.	ζητεῖ (εει)	ζητεῖται (εε)
1.	ζητοῦμεν (εο)	ζητούμεθα (εο)
2.	ζητεῖτε (εε)	ζητεῖσθε (εε)
3.	ζητοῦσι (ν) (εου)	ζητοῦνται (εο)
Subjunctive		
1.	ζητῶ (εω)	ζητῶμαι (εω)
2.	ζητῇς (εη)	ζητῇ (εη)
3.	ζητῇ (εη)	ζητῆται (εη)
1.	ζητῶμεν (εω)	ζητώμεθα (εω)
2.	ζητῆτε (εη)	ζητῆσθε (εη)
3.	ζητῶσι (ν) (εω)	ζητῶνται (εω)
Infinitive		
	ζητεῖν (εει)	ζητεῖσθαι (εε)

Present

Active Participle		Middle-Passive Participle
Masc. ζητῶν (εω)		ζητούμενος (εο)
Fem. ζητοῦσα (εου)		ζητουμένη (εο)
Neut. ζητοῦν (εο)		ζητούμενον (εο)

Imperative		Imperative
2. ζήτει (εε)		ζητοῦ (εου)
3. ζητείτω (εε)		ζητείσθω (εε)
2. ζητεῖτε (εε)		ζητεῖσθε (εε)
3. ζητείτωσαν (εε)		ζητείσθωσαν (εε)
-ούντων		-είσθων (εε)

Imperfect

Active Indicative		Middle-Passive Indicative
1. ἐζήτουν (εο)		ἐζητούμην (εο)
2. ἐζήτεις (εε)		ἐζητοῦ (εου)
3. ἐζήτει (εε)		ἐζητεῖτο (εε)
1. ἐζητοῦμεν (εο)		ἐζητούμεθα (εο)
2. ἐζητεῖτε (εε)		ἐζητεῖσθε (εε)
3. ἐζήτουν (εο)		ἐζητοῦντο (εο)

EXERCISES

1. Learn the vocabulary of Lesson 30.

2. Memorize the principal parts of the eight verbs given.

3. Learn the contract εω verb forms given and also the principles
   set forth. Study the chart of Rules for Contract Verbs.

4. Translate from the Greek Reader, John 5:41-47 (using the vocabulary lists and lexicons).

5. Translate the following sentences from English to Greek (based on
   the material in this lesson and John 5:30-47).

   a. If I should bear witness concerning the Lord, he will bear
      witness in heaven concerning me.

   b. I tell you this that (in order that) you might remain (————)
      in him.

   c. I have borne witness (•) to these works which (ἅ) you are doing.

   d. Hear the Scriptures because the Lord speaks to you through them.

The Contract Verbs Continued; The Liquid Verbs

VOCABULARY

ἀγαπάω	– I love
ἐπερωτάω	– I ask, question
ἐρωτάω	– I ask, request, entreat
ἐρῶ	– I shall say
ζάω	– I live
ὁράω	– I see
πλανάω	– I lead astray (planet, to the ancients an apparently wandering celestial body)
σταυρόω	– I crucify
φανερόω	– I make manifest

EXPLANATION

It is to be noted that outside of the present and imperfect tenses the
vowel which ends the verb base or stem of these contract verbs lengthens
(and there is no contraction) and the regular endings are added, as for
example, δικαιώσω, I will justify, and ἀγαπήσω, I will love. The present
and imperfect forms of the contract verb types (in αω and οω) are as
follows:

Present

	Active	Middle-Passive
Indicative		
1.	ἀγαπῶ (αω)	ἀγαπῶμαι (αο)
2.	ἀγαπᾷς (αει)	ἀγαπᾷ (αη)
3.	ἀγαπᾷ (αει)	ἀγαπᾶται (αε)
1.	ἀγαπῶμεν (αο)	ἀγαπώμεθα (αο)
2.	ἀγαπᾶτε (αε)	ἀγαπᾶσθε (αε)
3.	ἀγαπῶσι(ν) (αου)	ἀγαπῶνται (αο)
Subjunctive		
1.	ἀγαπῶ (αω)	ἀγαπῶμαι (αω)
2.	ἀγαπᾷς (αη)	ἀγαπᾷ (αη)
3.	ἀγαπᾷ (αη)	ἀγαπᾶται (αη)
1.	ἀγαπῶμεν (αω)	ἀγαπώμεθα (αω)
2.	ἀγαπᾶτε (αη)	ἀγαπᾶσθε (αη)
3.	ἀγαπῶσι(ν) (αω)	ἀγαπῶνται (αω)
Imperative		
2.	ἀγάπα (αε)	ἀγαπῶ (αου)
3.	ἀγαπάτω (αε)	ἀγαπάσθω (αε)
2.	ἀγαπᾶτε (αε)	ἀγαπᾶσθε (αε)
3.	ἀγαπάτωσαν (αε)	
	-ώντων (αο)	ἀγαπάσθωσαν (αε)
		-άσθων (αε)
Infinitive		
	ἀγαπᾶν (αει)	ἀγαπᾶσθαι (αε)
Participle		
	ἀγαπῶν (αω)	ἀγαπώμενος (αο)
	ἀγαπῶσα (αου)	ἀγαπωμένη (αο)
	ἀγαπῶν (αο)	ἀγαπώμενον (αο)

Imperfect

	Active	Middle-Passive
Indicative		
1.	ἠγάπων (αο)	ἠγαπώμην (αο)
2.	ἠγάπας (αε)	ἠγαπῶ (αου)
3.	ἠγάπα (αε)	ἠγαπᾶτο (αε)
1.	ἠγαπῶμεν (αο)	ἠγαπώμεθα (αο)
2.	ἠγαπᾶτε (αε)	ἠγαπᾶσθε (αε)
3.	ἠγάπων (αο)	ἠγαπῶντο (αο)

Present

	Active	Middle-Passive
Indicative		
1.	δικαιῶ (οω)	δικαιοῦμαι (οο)
2.	δικαιοῖς (οει)	δικαιοῖ (οη)
3.	δικαιοῖ (οει)	δικαιοῦται (οε)
1.	δικαιοῦμεν (οο)	δικαιούμεθα (οο)
2.	δικαιοῦτε (οε)	δικαιοῦσθε (οε)
3.	δικαιοῦσι(ν) (οου)	δικαιοῦνται (οο)
Subjunctive		
1.	δικαιῶ (οω)	δικαιῶμαι (οω)
2.	δικαιοῖς (οη)	δικαιοῖ (οη)
3.	δικαιοῖ (οη)	δικαιῶται (οη)
1.	δικαιῶμεν (οω)	δικαιώμεθα (οω)
2.	δικαιῶτε (οη)	δικαιῶσθε (οη)
3.	δικαιῶσι (οω)	δικαιῶνται (οω)
Imperative		
2.	δικαίου (οε)	δικαιοῦ (οου)
3.	δικαιούτω (οε)	δικαιούσθω (οε)
2.	δικαιοῦτε (οε)	δικαιοῦσθε (οε)
3.	δικαιούτωσαν (οε)	δικαιούσθωσαν (οε)
	-ούντων (οο)	-ούσθων (οε)
Infinitive	δικαιοῦν (οει)	δικαιοῦσθαι (οε)
Participle		
	δικαιῶν (οω)	δικαιούμενος (οο)
	δικαιοῦσα (οου)	δικαιουμένη (οο)
	δικαιοῦν (οο)	δικαιούμενον (οο)

Imperfect

	Active	Middle-Passive
Indicative		
1.	ἐδικαίουν (οο)	ἐδικαιούμην (οο)
2.	ἐδικαίους (οε)	ἐδικαιοῦ (οου)
3.	ἐδικαίου (οε)	ἐδικαιοῦτο (οε)
1.	ἐδικαιοῦμεν (οο)	ἐδικαιούμεθα (οο)
2.	ἐδικαιοῦτε (οε)	ἐδικαιοῦσθε (οε)
3.	ἐδικαίουν (οο)	ἐδικαιοῦντο (οο)

Although there are contractions of vowels in these contract verb forms, there is no difference between contract verbs and the regular ω (omega) verbs such as λύω in the concepts of time and kind of action.

Liquid Verbs:

Those verbs whose stems or bases end in λ, μ, ν or ρ are called liquid verbs (as these four letters are called liquid consonants). In the present and imperfect these verbs are conjugated just like λύω, but in their <u>future</u> forms they do not add an σ, but act as though their bases ended in ε which then contracts with the variable vowel ο/ε.[1] Thus the future of these verbs have forms which look like present contract forms of the contract verb ζητέω, ζητῶ. Examples of μένω, I remain, are as follows:

	Present Active	Future Active
1.	μένω	μενῶ
2.	μένεις	μενεῖς
3.	μένει	μενεῖ
1.	μένομεν	μενοῦμεν
2.	μένετε	μενεῖτε
3.	μένουσι(ν)	μενοῦσι(ν)

In the aorist the liquid verbs are generally different also in not adding an σ to the base, such as ἔλυσα, but rather, generally showing an internal difference from the present in the base or stem, and then adding the first aorist vowel and endings.

Examples:

μένω, I remain, μενῶ, I will remain, ἔμεινα (aorist), I remained.

ἀποστέλλω, I send, ἀποστελῶ, I will send, ἀπέστειλα, I sent.

1.	ἔμεινα[2]	ἀπέστειλα
2.	ἔμεινας	ἀπέστειλας
3.	ἔμεινε(ν)	ἀπέστειλε(ν)
1.	ἐμείναμεν	ἀπεστείλαμεν
2.	ἐμείνατε	ἀπεστείλατε
3.	ἔμειναν	ἀπέστειλαν

Although these liquid verb forms are to some extent different in the future and aorist, the tense and kind of action concepts are the same as in the λύω verb.

---

[1]"Verb stems ending in λ, μ, ν, ρ add -εσ⁰/ε-; then σ drops and ε contracts with the following vowel." H. W. Smyth, <u>Greek Grammar</u>, parag. 535.

[2]In the First (Sigmatic) Aorist System "verb-stems ending in λ, μ, ν, ρ lose σ and lengthen their vowel in compensation (37): α to η (after ι or ρ to ᾱ), ε to ει, ῐ to ῑ, ῠ to ῡ." Smyth, <u>Greek Grammar</u>, parag. 544.

EXERCISES

1. Learn the vocabulary of Lesson 31.

2. Learn the contract (αω and οω) and liquid verb forms and principles.

3. Translate from the Greek Gospel of John Chapter 6:1-6 (using the vocabulary lists and lexicons).

   Beginning with this lesson the student will no longer be using the John Greek Reader, but will be translating directly from the Greek Gospel of John beginning at John 6:1.

4. Translate the following sentences from English to Greek (based on the material in this lesson and John 5:30-6:6).

   a. How are you able to see the Lord? You are not seeking to know his Word.

   b. He who hates his sin will love the Lord and will follow him.

   c. Jesus was doing miracles (or signs) and many people were believing in him.

   d. When Philip speaks to the crowd, Jesus will remain in the mountain.

The μι Verbs

VOCABULARY

ἀναγινώσκω	- I read
ἀποδίδωμι	- I give back, pay; middle, I sell
ἀρνέομαι	- I deny
βιβλίον, ου, τό	- a book (Bible)
γεννάω	- I beget (cf. hydrogen, as being considered the generator of water)
δεικνύω or δείκνυμι	- I show (in logic, apodeictic, of clear demonstration)
διαθήκη, ης, ἡ	- a covenant
διακονία, ας, ἡ	- waiting at table, service, ministry
δίδωμι	- I give
δυνατός, ή, όν	- powerful, possible (cf. dynamite)
ἐγγύς	- near
ἔξεστι(ν)	- It is lawful
ἐπιτίθημι	- I lay upon
ἐχθρός, ά, όν	- hating; noun, enemy
ἥλιος, ου, ὁ	- sun (helium)
ἱερεύς, έως, ὁ	- priest (hierarchy)

Principal Parts of Verbs:

1. ἀκολουθέω, ἀκολουθήσω, ἠκολούθησα, ἠκολούθηκα - I come after, I follow (with the dative).

2. βούλομαι, (βουλήσομαι), _____, (βεβούλημαι), ἐβουλήθην - I wish, I am willing.

3. ἐπιστρέφω, ἐπιστρέψω, ἐπέστρεφα, ἐπέστροφα, _____, ἐπεστράφην (second aorist passive) - I turn (back), return.

4. ὀφείλω, ὤφειλον (imperfect), (ὀφειλήσω), (ὠφείλησα), ὤφελον (second aorist), (ὠφείληκα) - I owe, I am indebted.

5. πειράζω, πειράσω, ἐπείρασα, _____, πεπείρασμαι, ἐπειράσθην - I try, I make trial of.

6. περισσεύω, περισσεύσω, ἐπερίσσευσα - Be more than enough, be left over.

7. πράσσω, πράξω, ἔπραξα, πέπραχα, _____, ἐπράχθην - I do, I accomplish.

8. ὑποτάσσω, _____, ὑπέταξα, _____, ὑποτέταγμαι, ὑπετάγην (second aorist passive) - I subject, I subordinate.

EXPLANATION

In Lessons 30 and 31 the student studied those forms of the contract and liquid verbs where they use vowel contractions before primary and secondary endings, or where, in the case of the liquid verbs, there will be an -α vowel aorist without a preceding σ (like ἔλυσα, as in the case of ἔμεινα and ἀπέστειλα.

The μι verbs:

The μι type verb forms add some distinctive suffixes to the verb base and also show a reduplication of the initial consonant of the base followed by a connecting -ι, in the present and imperfect tenses, as, for example, δί-δω-μι, I give. In one of the beginning lessons the student was introduced to a very common μι verb, εἰμί, I am. There are three basic examples of New Testament μι verbs that are given for analysis, as follows: δί-δω-μι, I give; τί-θη-μι, I place, put; ἵ-στη-μι (originally this form was σίστημι, but the initial σ dropped and was replaced by rough breathing). It is to be observed that the base or stem of δίδωμι is δω(δο); that of τίθημι is θη(θε); and that of ἵστημι is στη(στα).[1]

There are certain characteristics which apply to all three types, and then there are some distinctives which pertain to each type. The student is to master the summary of these characteristics to be found on the accompanying page of Rules for Verbs.

The paradigms for the present, imperfect and aorist of the δίδωμι verb are as follows:

δίδωμι

Present Active	Imperfect Active	Present M.P.	Imperfect M.P.
1. δίδωμι[2]	ἐδίδουν	δίδομαι	ἐδιδόμην
2. δίδως	ἐδίδους	δίδοσαι	ἐδίδοσο
3. δίδωσι(ν)	ἐδίδου	δίδοται	ἐδίδοτο
1. δίδομεν	ἐδίδομεν	διδόμεθα	ἐδιδόμεθα
2. δίδοτε	ἐδίδοτε	δίδοσθε	ἐδίδοσθε
3. διδόασι(ν)	ἐδίδοσαν	δίδονται	ἐδίδοντο

---

[1]Smyth (Greek Grammar, parag. 416) identifies these verbs as belonging to the root class of μι verbs. "The conjugation of μι verbs differs from that of -ω-verbs only in the present, imperfect and second aorist active and middle; and (rarely) in the second perfect. The μι forms are made by adding the endings directly to the tense-stem without any thematic vowel, except in the subjunctive of all verbs, and in the optative of verbs ending in -νυμι." Smyth, Greek Grammar, parag. 412.

[2]Do not confuse this δω base with the subjunctive.

Pres. Act. Subj.	Pres. M.P. Subj.	Pres. Act. Impv.	Pres. M. P. Impv.
1. διδῶ[3]	διδῶμαι		
2. διδῷς	διδῷ	δίδου	δίδοσο
3. διδῷ	διδῶται	διδότω	διδόσθω
1. διδῶμεν	διδώμεθα		
2. διδῶτε	διδῶσθε	δίδοτε	δίδοσθε
3. διδῶσι(ν)	διδῶνται	διδότωσαν	διδόσθωσαν
		-ντων	-σθων

Present Active Infinitive

διδόναι

Present Middle-Passive Infinitive

διδόσθαι

Present Active Participle	Present Middle-Passive Participle
M. διδούς	διδόμενος
F. διδοῦσα	διδομένη
N. διδόν	διδόμενον

Aorist Active Indicative	Aorist Middle Indicative	Aorist Passive Indicative
1. ἔδωκα	ἐδόμην	ἐδόθην
2. ἔδωκας	ἔδου	ἐδόθης
3. ἔδωκε(ν)	ἔδοτο	ἐδόθη
1. ἐδώκαμεν	ἐδόμεθα	ἐδόθημεν
2. ἐδώκατε	ἔδοσθε	ἐδόθητε
3. ἔδωκαν	ἔδοντο	ἐδόθησαν

Aorist Active Subjunctive	Aorist Middle Subjunctive	Aorist Passive Subjunctive
1. δῶ	δῶμαι	δοθῶ
2. δῷς	δῷ	δοθῇς
3. δῷ	δῶται	δοθῇ
1. δῶμεν	δώμεθα	δοθῶμεν
2. δῶτε	δῶσθε	δοθῆτε
3. δῶσι(ν)	δῶνται	δοθῶσι(ν)

Aorist Active Imperative	Aorist Middle Imperative	Aorist Passive Imperative
2. δός	δοῦ	δόθητι
3. δότω	δόσθω	δοθήτω
2. δότε	δόσθε	δόθητε
3. δότωσαν	δόσθωσαν	δοθήτωσαν
-ντων	-σθων	-θέντων

Aorist Active Infinitive	Aorist Middle Infinitive	Aorist Passive Infinitive
δοῦναι	δόσθαι	δοθῆναι

Aorist Active Participle	Aorist Middle Participle	Aorist Passive Participle
δούς, δοῦσα, δόν	δόμενος, δομένη, δόμενον	δοθείς, δοθεῖσα, δοθέν

---

[3]Observe the contraction of the base (or stem) vowel with the subjunctive long vowels.

EXERCISES

1. Learn the vocabulary of Lesson 32.

2. Memorize the principal parts of the eight verbs given.

3. Learn the μι verb forms given and the distinctive characteristics which are given in The Rules for μι Verbs listed below.

    μι Verbs

    a. General Rules: these verbs

        1. are regular (similar to λύω) in III, V, VI[4]
        2. reduplicate the first letter of the stem in I, II
        3. do not reduplicate the first letter of the stem in IV
        4. The active infinitives in I, IV, end in ναι.

    b. δίδωμι:

        1. Has the ο/ω type vowels as part of the verb stem.
        2. Has ω in Ia singular, but ο in Ia plural.
        3. Has ου in IIa singular, but ο in IIa plural.
        4. Has ω throughout I amp (and IV am) subjunctive.
        5. Has κ (instead of ς) in IVa ind. only.

4. Translate from John, Chapter 6:7-15 (using the vocabulary lists and lexicons).

5. Translate the following sentences from English to Greek, based on the material in this lesson and on John 6:7-15.

    a. He gives the priest the book in order that he may read the gospel.

    b. They were staying in the house and they said, "Come to the Lord."

    c. The Lord said to the disciples, "Make the men (to) arise. I lay upon them my word of truth."

    d. When the Lord spoke, the disciples gathered together the fragments which the multitude did not eat.

---

[4]See the number system on pages 6 and 7.

The μι Verbs Continued

VOCABULARY

τίθημι	- I place, put, set
ὑπομονή, ῆς, ἡ	- patient endurance, perseverance
φυλάσσω	- I guard, keep, protect
ὥστε	- that, so that, with the result that (often followed by the accusative and the infinitive); therefore, thus, accordingly

EXPLANATION

The paradigms for the present, imperfect and aorist of the τίθημι verb are as follows:

Pres.Act.Ind.	Impf.Act.Ind.	Pres.M.P.Ind.	Impf.M.P.Ind.	Pres.Act.Subj.
1. τίθημι	ἐτίθην	τίθεμαι	ἐτιθέμην	τιθῶ[1]
2. τίθης	ἐτίθεις	τίθεσαι	ἐτίθεσο	τιθῇς
3. τίθησι(ν)	ἐτίθει	τίθεται	ἐτίθετο	τιθῇ
1. τίθεμεν	ἐτίθεμεν	τιθέμεθα	ἐτιθέμεθα	τιθῶμεν
2. τίθετε	ἐτίθετε	τίθεσθε	ἐτίθεσθε	τιθῆτε
3. τιθέασι(ν)	ἐτίθεσαν	τίθενται	ἐτίθεντο	τιθῶσι(ν)

Pres.M.P.Subj.	Pres.Act.Impv.	Pres.M.P.Impv.	Pres.Act.Inf.
1. τιθῶμαι			τιθέναι
2. τιθῇ	τίθει	τίθεσο	
3. τιθῆται	τιθέτω	τιθέσθω	
1. τιθώμεθα			
2. τιθῆσθε	τίθετε	τίθεσθε	
3. τιθῶνται	τιθέτωσαν	τιθέσθωσαν	
	-ντων	-σθων	

Pres.Act.Part.	Pres.M.P.Part.	Pres.M.P.Inf.
τιθείς	τιθέμενος	τίθεσθαι
τιθεῖσα	τιθεμένη	
τιθέν	τιθέμενον	

Aor.Act.Ind.	Aor.Mid.Ind.	Aor.Act.Subj.	Aor.Mid.Subj.
1. ἔθηκα	ἐθέμην	θῶ	θῶμαι
2. ἔθηκας	ἔθου	θῇς	θῇ
3. ἔθηκε(ν)	ἔθετο	θῇ	θῆται
1. ἐθήκαμεν	ἐθέμεθα	θῶμεν	θώμεθα
2. ἐθήκατε	ἔθεσθε	θῆτε	θῆσθε
3. ἔθηκαν	ἔθεντο	θῶσι(ν)	θῶνται

---

[1]Observe the contraction of the base, or stem, vowel with the subjunctive long vowel.

Aor. Act. Impv.	Aor. Mid. Impv.	Aor. Act. Inf.	Aor. Mid. Inf.
θές	θοῦ	θεῖναι	θέσθαι
θέτω	θέσθω		

Aor. Act. Impv.	Aor. Mid. Impv.	Aor. Pass. Ind.	Aor. Pass. Subj.
θέτε	θέσθε	ἐτέθην	τεθῶ
θέτωσαν	θέσθωσαν	ἐτέθης	τεθῇς
	-σθων	ἐτέθη	τεθῇ

Aor. Act. Part.	Aor. Mid. Part.		
θείς	θέμενος	ἐτέθημεν	τεθῶμεν
θεῖσα	θεμένη	ἐτέθητε	τεθῆτε
θέν	θέμενον	ἐτέθησαν	τεθῶσι(ν)

		Aor. Pass. Impv.	Aor. Pass. Inf.
		τέθητι	τεθῆναι
		τεθήτω	

		Aor. Pass. Impv.	Aor. Pass. Part.
		τέθητε	τεθείς
		τεθήτωσαν	τεθεῖσα
		-έντων	τεθέν

EXERCISES

1. Learn the vocabulary of Lesson 33.

2. Learn the μι verb forms given and the distinctive characteristics which are given in the Rules for μι Verbs below.

   The μι verb τίθημι:

   a. Has the ε/η type vowels as a part of the verb stem.
   b. Has η as the stem vowel in I (present) a singular, but ε in I a plural.
   c. Has η and ει as the stem vowels in II (imperfect) a 1 and II a 2 and 3 respectively, but ε in the II a plural.
   d. Has κ (instead of σ) in IV (aorist) a in the indicative only.

3. Translate from John 6:16-23 using the vocabulary lists and lexicons.

4. Translate the following sentences from English to Greek (based on the material in this lesson and John 6:7-23).

   a. When he had given thanks (or having given thanks), Jesus gave the bread to the ones sitting down (or reclining).

   b. The Lord said, "Gather together the bread. I wish to go to the boat."

   c. To have the cup of the Lord is a good thing.

   d. Guard your hearts. Put prayer in your life.

The μι Verbs Continued; Aorist of γινώσκω
Forms of εἰμί; Second Aorist of ἔρχομαι

VOCABULARY

ἀνίστημι	- I cause to rise, I arise
ἀπόλλυμι	- I destroy; middle, I perish (Apollyon, the angel of the bottomless pit, Rev. 9:11)
ἀφίημι	- I let go, permit, forgive (aphesis, the gradual loss of a short unaccented initial vowel, exampled by "squire" for "esquire")
ἵστημι	- I cause to stand, I stand
καυχάομαι	- I boast
λαλέω	- I speak (cf. glossolalia, the gift of speaking in tongues)
μέλος, ους, τό	- member
μήτε	- and not, neither....nor
οἶνος, ου, ὁ	- wine
παρίστημι	- I am present, offer, stand by
πλῆθος, ους, τό	- multitude, crowd
ποῖος, α, ον	- what kind of? what?
ποτήριον, ου, τό	- cup
προσκυνέω	- I worship, bow low
συνέρχομαι	- I come together

EXPLANATION

The paradigms for the present, imperfect and aorist of the ἵστημι verb are as follows:

Pres.Act.Ind.	Impf.Act.Ind.	Pres.M.P.Ind.	Impf.M.P.Ind.
1. ἵστημι	ἵστην[1]	ἵσταμαι	ἱστάμην[1]
2. ἵστης	ἵστης	ἵστασαι	ἵστασο
3. ἵστησι(ν)	ἵστη	ἵσταται	ἵστατο
1. ἵσταμεν	ἵσταμεν	ἱστάμεθα	ἱστάμεθα
2. ἵστατε	ἵστατε	ἵστασθε	ἵστασθε
3. ἱστᾶσι(ν)	ἵστασαν	ἵστανται	ἵσταντο

Pres.Act.Subj.	Pres.M.P.Subj.	Pres.Act.Impv.	Pres.M.P.Impv.
1. ἱστῶ	ἱστῶμαι		
2. ἱστῇς	ἱστῇ	ἵστη	ἵστασο
3. ἱστῇ	ἱστῆται	ἱστάτω	ἱστάσθω
1. ἱστῶμεν	ἱστώμεθα		
2. ἱστῆτε	ἱστῆσθε	ἵστατε	ἵστασθε
3. ἱστῶσι(ν)	ἱστῶνται	ἱστάτωσαν -ντων	ἱστάσθωσαν -σθων

Pres.Act.Inf.	Pres.Act.Part.	Pres.M.P.Inf.	Pres.M.P.Part.
ἱστάναι	ἱστάς ἱστᾶσα ἱστάν	ἵστασθαι	ἱστάμενος ἱσταμένη ἱστάμενον

[1]The ι here does not show a visible lengthening, but the student is to consider the imperfect initial ι as long here.

Aor.Act.Ind.	Aor.Act.Subj.	Aor.Act.Impv.	Aor.Act.Inf.	Aor.Act.Part.
1. ἔστην[2] (I	στῶ		στῆναι	στάς
2. ἔστης stood)	στῇς	στῆθι		στᾶσα
3. ἔστη	στῇ	στήτω		στάν
1. ἔστημεν	στῶμεν			
2. ἔστητε	στῆτε	στῆτε		
3. ἔστησαν	στῶσι(ν)	στήτωσαν		
		στάντων		

Aor.Pass.Ind.	Aor.Pass.Subj.	Aor.Pass.Impv.	Aor.Pass.Inf.	Aor.Pass.Part.
1. ἐστάθην	σταθῶ		σταθῆναι	σταθείς
2. ἐστάθης	σταθῇς	στάθητι		σταθεῖσα
3. ἐστάθη	σταθῇ	σταθήτω		σταθέν
1. ἐστάθημεν	σταθῶμεν			
2. ἐστάθητε	σταθῆτε	στάθητε		
3. ἐστάθησαν	σταθῶσι(ν)	σταθήτωσαν		
		-έντων		

Additional Paradigms
Aorist of γινώσκω

Aor. Ind.	Act. Subj.	Act. Impv.	Act. Inf.	Act. Part.
1. ἔγνων[3]	γνῶ		γνῶναι	γνούς
2. ἔγνως	γνῷς	γνῶθι		γνοῦσα
3. ἔγνω	γνῷ	γνώτω		γνόν
1. ἔγνωμεν	γνῶμεν			
2. ἔγνωτε	γνῶτε	γνῶτε		
3. ἔγνωσαν	γνῶσι(ν)	γνώτωσαν		

εἰμί (I am)

	Pres. Subj.	Pres. Impv.	Pres. Inf.	Pres. Part.
1.	ὦ		εἶναι	ὤν
2.	ᾖς	ἴσθι		οὖσα
3.	ᾖ	ἔστω		ὄν
1.	ὦμεν			
2.	ἦτε	ἔστε		
3.	ὦσι(ν)	ἔστωσαν		

Second Aorist of ἔρχομαι, I come, and λείπω, I leave

ἦλθον - I came   ἔλιπον - I left

Act. Impv.	Act. Inf.	Act. Part.	Act. Impv.	Act. Inf.	Act. Part.
2. ἐλθέ	ἐλθεῖν	ἐλθών	λίπε	λιπεῖν	λιπών
3. ἐλθέτω		ἐλθοῦσα	λιπέτω		λιποῦσα
		ἐλθόν			λιπόν
2. ἔλθετε			λίπετε	Mid. Inf.	Mid. Part.
3. ἐλθέτωσαν			λιπέτωσαν	λιπέσθαι	λιπόμενος, η, ον

---

[2]These are second aorist forms. First aorist active indicative forms are
ἔστησα, ἔστησας, etc., I set, or placed, etc.

[3]The aorist base or stem of γινώσκω is γνο (γνω).

EXERCISES

1. Learn the vocabulary of Lesson 34.

2. Learn the μι verb forms given and the distinctive characteristics which are given in <u>The Rules for μι Verbs</u> listed below and also εἰμί and 2 Aor. of ἔρχομαι and γινώσκω.

   <u>μι Verbs</u>

   ἵστημι:

   a. Has the α/η type vowels as a part of the verb stem.
   b. Has ἱ as redupl. in I and II.
   c. Has α vowel in I and II (in most forms).
   d. Has η in I, II a sing., but α in I, II a plural.
   e. Has IV, and 2IV forms as well.

3. Translate from John, chapter 6:24-30 (using the vocabulary lists and lexicons).

4. Translate the following sentences from English to Greek (based on the material in this lesson and on John 6:24-30).

   a. The crowd (or multitude) was about to come and seize Jesus that (in order that) they might make him a king.

   b. Having embarked (gotten into) in a boat, the disciples were progressing (coming) across the sea.

   c. Standing on the water, Jesus sees the disciples in the boat and says to them, "Stop fearing (don't fear). I am he."

   d. They came together in the boat and worshipped him.

Use of the Relative and Syntax of the Cases

VOCABULARY

ἀγοράζω	- I buy (cf. agora, marketplace)
ἀκάθαρτος, ον	- unclean
ἄνεμος, ου, ὁ	- wind (anemometer)
ἀρνίον, ου, τό	- lamb
γέ	- indeed, even, really, at least
διάκονος, ου, ὁ	- servant, deacon
διδαχή, ῆς, ἡ	- teaching (cf. didactic)
ἐλεέω	- I have mercy (cf. eleemosynary)
ἐλπίζω	- I hope
ἐπικαλέω	- I call, name; middle, I invoke, appeal to
ἐπιτιμάω	- I rebuke, warn
καθαρίζω	- I cleanse (catharsis)
ναί	- truly, yes
ὁμοίως	- likewise
παραγγέλλω	- I command, charge
παρέρχομαι	- I pass by, pass away, arrive
παρρησία, ας, ἡ	- boldness, confidence
πλήν	- however, only; with gen. - except
σκανδαλίζω	- I cause to stumble, offend (scandalize)
σκότος, ους, τό	- darkness (scotoscope, a field glass for seeing at night)
συνείδησις, εως, ἡ	- conscience
φαίνω	- I shine, appear (phenomenon, phantom)
φεύγω	- I flee
φυλή, ῆς, ἡ	- tribe (in zoology, a phylum is one of the large basic divisions of the animal kingdom)

Principal Parts of Verbs:

1. βλασφημέω, _____, 1 aor. ἐβλασφήμησα, _____, 1 aor. pass., ἐβλασφημήθην - I revile, defame, blaspheme.

2. δέω, _____, ἔδησα, δέδεκα, δέδεμαι, ἐδέθην - I bind, tie.

3. δοκέω, δόξω, 1 aor. ἔδοξα - (transitive) -- I think, believe, suppose; (intransitive), seem.

4. ἐρωτάω, ἐρωτήσω, ἠρώτησα, (ἠρώτηκα), (ἠρώτημαι), ἠρωτήθην - I ask (originally of asking a question, but in the New Testament also asking in the sense of requesting).

5. εὐλογέω, εὐλογήσω, εὐλόγησα, εὐλόγηκα, εὐλόγημαι, εὐλογήθην - I bless, praise.

6. καλέω, καλέσω, ἐκάλεσα, κέκληκα, κέκλημαι, ἐκλήθην - I call, call by name, address.

7. κρατέω, κρατήσω, ἐκράτησα, ____, κεκράτημαι, ____, - I take hold of, grasp, seize, hold.

EXPLANATION

In Lesson 9 (pages 23, 24) the student was introduced to the forms and uses of the relative pronoun, ὅς, ἥ, ὅ. It will be remembered that the forms of the relative pronoun, except for the nominative masculine and feminine singular and plural, are identical with those of the article, ὁ, ἡ, τό, except that the relative pronoun has a rough breathing <u>throughout</u> and in the oblique cases (those cases outside of the nominative) and the neuter nominative the forms do not begin with a τ.

As to use, the student learned that the relative pronoun introduces a dependent clause in the sentence, and that it must agree with the <u>antecedent</u> (i.e., the word to which the relative pronoun refers) in gender and number, but not necessarily in case. The relative pronoun, when the direct object of its dependent verb, is sometimes attracted into the case of the <u>antecedent</u> when <u>the latter</u> is in the genitive or dative case.

It <u>is</u> now time for the student to practice further the use of the relative pronoun. The following are examples:

1. John 6:9 - ἔστιν παιδάριον ὧδε ὃς ἔχει πέντε ἄρτους
   κριθίνους.....
   "There is a small boy here <u>who</u> has five barley loaves." ὅς is subject nominative in its own clause but agrees with its antecedent in number, and as masculine agrees functionally (natural gender) with παιδάριον (which is neuter grammatically).

2. John 6:13 - ἐγέμισαν δώδεκα κοφίνους κλασμάτων...ἃ ἐπερίσσευσαν.....

   "They filled twelve baskets of the fragments . . . which were in excess." Here the relative is the neuter plural subject of its dependent clause and agrees with its antecedent (κλασμάτων) in gender and number.

3. John 6:21 - ἐγένετο τὸ πλοῖον ἐπὶ τῆς γῆς εἰς ἣν ὑπῆγον.

   "The boat came to the land <u>into which</u> they were going." Here the relative ἥν is the accusative object of εἰς and agrees with its antecedent γῆς in gender (fem.) and number (sing.).

4. John 6:27 - ἐργάζεσθε...τὴν βρῶσιν τὴν μένουσαν εἰς ζωὴν αἰώνιον, ἣν ὁ
   υἱὸς τοῦ ἀνθρώπου ὑμῖν δώσει.
   "Continue to work for the food which remains unto life eternal <u>which</u> the Son of Man will give to you." The relative ἥν is the accusative object of δώσει and agrees with its antecedent in gender (fem.) and number (sing.).

5. John 6:11 - διέδωκεν...ὁμοίως καὶ ἐκ τῶν ὀφαρίων ὅσον ἤθελον.

   "He distributed likewise also of the fish as much as (that which) they (each one) wished (imperfect)." The correlative relative ὅσον is neuter accusative object of ἤθελον and includes in the one word a reference to the antecedent quantity, "as much as," and the relative concept, "that which."

SYNTAX OF THE CASES:

In review of some of the syntactical uses of the cases, the student will observe the following:

1. Nominative

   Subject - John 7:1, Jesus was walking in Galilee.

   Predicate nominative - Matt. 16:18, you are Peter.

2. Vocative (direct address)

   The same form as the nominative - Mark 14:36, Abba, Father. (ὁ πατήρ)

   The vocative form - John 17:1, πάτερ, Father.

3. Accusative (the case of extension)

   Direct object of the verb - John 7:4, manifest yourself to the world.

   Extension of space - John 6:19, they rowed twenty-five or thirty stadia.

   Extension of time - John 1:39, they remained with him that day.

   Object of the preposition - John 6:15 (with εἰς), he withdrew again into the mountain.

   Accusative of general reference ("subject" idea of the infinitive) - Luke 2:27, In the bringing the child with reference to his parents = When the parents brought the child.

With this lesson the student is to use the Greek parsing number system which he will find on pages 6 and 7 of this book.

EXERCISES

1. Learn the vocabulary of Lesson 35.

2. Memorize the principal parts of the verbs in this lesson.

3. Review the forms and syntax of the relative pronoun.

4. Review the uses of the nominative, vocative, and accusative cases set forth in this lesson.

5. Translate John 6:31-40.

6. Translate the following sentences from English to Greek (based upon the material in this lesson and John 6:19-31).
   a. The man whom he sees says, "Don't fear (or, stop fearing)."
   b. When the Lord blessed the bread, the people ate at the place in which they were remaining.
   c. The Lord Jesus gave to them as much as (that which) they wished to eat.
   d. Do you believe on Jesus Christ whom the Father sent?
   e. What are we to do that we may see God?

Syntax of the Cases Continued; Parsing Exercises

VOCABULARY

ἀληθινός, ή, όν	– true
γαμέω	– I marry (monogamous)
γνῶσις, εως, ἡ	– knowledge
ἐνδύω	– I put on, clothe
ἐπεί	– when, since
ἡγέομαι	– I am chief, think, regard
θυσία, ας, ἡ	– sacrifice
ἰσχυρός, ά, όν	– strong
κρίμα, ατος, τό	– judgment (cf., crisis)
μάχαιρα, ης,[1] ἡ	– sword

EXPLANATIONS

Syntax of the Cases, continued:

In Lesson 35 the student reviewed some of the uses of the nominative, vocative and accusative cases. In this lesson a brief review and further explanation of the genitive and dative cases will be considered with illustrations given from the New Testament.

Genitive Case

It has been observed in an earlier lesson that the Greek genitive case has in it both a genitive, or <u>descriptive</u> or <u>qualitative</u>, function and also an ablative, or <u>source</u>, function.[2]

A. Genitive function (containing the ideas of description, qualification, or specification):

1. Possession (and genitive of relationship).

2. Genitive absolute
   John 6:18, a great wind blowing (i.e., because a great wind was blowing).

3. Object of the preposition
   John 4:5, near the place.
   John 6:19, near the boat.

4. Genitive of the object of the verb
   Luke 17:32, Remember <u>the wife</u> of Lot.

5. Genitive of time within which
   Matt. 24:20, within winter.

---

[1]The declension of this noun in the genitive and dative singular is an exception to the general rule set forth in Lesson 6 that first declension forms have α throughout the singular when the ending in the nominative is α and the letter before the α is ε, ι or ρ. However, the Ptolemaic papyri decline it as a rule μαχαίρας, μαχαίρᾳ; likewise so does the Septuagint. See Arndt and Gingrich, <u>A Greek to English Lexicon of the New Testament</u> (Chicago: University of Chicago Press, 1957), μάχαιρα.

[2]Some have explained this phenomenon on the basis of two separate cases, the genitive case and the ablative case. It is true that the Indo-European parent language had an eight-case system, including the genitive and the ablative cases.

B. Ablative function (containing the ideas of source, origin, or separation):

   1. The genitive-ablative function with the preposition (as, with ἐκ, ἀπό, etc.)
       John 1:44, And Philip was from Bethsaida.

   2. The genitive-ablative function with adjectives
       John 6:45, and all will be taught by God (i.e. from that source).

Dative Case

The dative case includes three functions: The dative-locative function or the dative of place; the dative-instrumental association function; and the dative-personal interest function.

A. The dative-locative function:

   1. Dative-locative of time when
       John 20:1, on the first day of the Sabbath.

   2. Dative-locative with prepositions (as ἐν, ἐπί, παρά, etc.)
       John 19:25, they stood by the cross.

B. Dative-instrumental association function:

   1. Dative-instrumental association function with prepositions (as, σύν) Luke 1:56, And Mary remained with her.

   2. Dative-instrumental function of means
       Matt. 3:12, He will burn it with unquenchable fire.

C. Dative-personal interest function:

   1. Dative-personal interest of indirect object
       John 6:27, ...eternal life which the Son of man will give to you.

   2. Dative-personal interest with certain verbs
       Luke 15:29, I am serving you.

EXERCISES

1. Learn the vocabulary of Lesson 36.

2. Review the syntactical principles of the genitive and dative cases as set forth in this lesson.

3. Translate John 6:41-51 (use your Greek lexicon in your preparation).

4. Translate the following sentences from English to Greek (based on the material in this lesson and on John 6:19-45).
    a. Jesus gave to you the true bread from heaven in order that you might be saved.
    b. After the crowd came to Jesus, the disciples who were near the place were wishing to hear the Word of God.
    c. When Jesus preached on that day, the crowd requested (or, asked) that the disciples give them loaves of bread.
    d. Jesus said to his disciples, "I am the bread of life which comes down from heaven."

e. Jesus told the people, you must be (it is necessary for <u>you</u> to be) taught <u>by</u> the Son of God.

f. <u>In (or, on) the last day</u> I will raise up the ones who believe in me and they shall stand <u>by me in</u> heaven.

g. We will be <u>with the Lord</u> in heaven because we have been saved <u>by</u> his power and authority.

5. Parse the following verb forms:

1. λαμβάνεις	31. παρελαμβάνετε
2. διδάσκω	32. ἀπέθνῃσκον
3. ἔχομεν	33. διδασκόμεθα
4. γράφετε	34. ἀνέβαινον
5. λύουσι	35. ἦμεν
6. ἔχεις	36. ἔβλεπεν
7. λαμβάνομεν	37. ἦς
8. λύω	38. ἐστίν
9. λέγει	39. ἐλύεσθε
10. λέγουσι	40. ἐλύετε
11. γράφει	41. ἐλυόμην
12. βλέπεις	42. ἐδιδασκόμεθα
13. ἐγείρει	43. ἐξεπορεύετο
14. λέγομεν	44. ἐλέγετο
15. μένουσι	45. ἐβλέπετο
16. εἴχομεν	46. ἐδέχου
17. εἶ	47. συνήρχοντο
18. εἰσί	48. ἀπέθνῃσκε(ν)
19. λύονται	49. ἠκούοντο
20. ἀγόμεθα	50. ἦγον
21. εἰσέρχονται	51. ἀκούουσι(ν)
22. ἐξέρχεσθε	52. ἠρχόμην
23. βαπτίζονται	53. λύσῃ
24. σῴζεται	54. λυσόμεθα
25. ἀποκρινόμεθα	55. ἀπέλυσε(ν)
26. σῴζῃ	56. ἐπιστεύσαμεν
27. λύομαι	57. σώσει
28. ἔλυον	58. λύσεις
29. ἠκούομεν	59. ἀναβλέψουσι(ν)
30. ἀκούομεν	60. ἐθαύμασαν

The Verb οἶδα; The ἵνα Object Clause; Conditional
Sentences; and The New Testament Optative Paradigm

VOCABULARY

μισθός, οῦ, ὁ	- wages, reward
μυστήριον, ου, τό	- mystery
οὔπω	- not yet
παράκλησις, εως, ἡ	- exhortation, consolation (Paraclete, the Comforter or Counselor)
πάσχα, τό	- (indeclinable) passover (paschal)
πλούσιος, α, ον	- rich (plutocrat)
πόθεν	- whence
ποτέ	- at some time, once, ever
προσκαλέομαι	- I summon
προφητεύω	- I prophesy
τελέω	- I finish
φίλος, η, ον	- loving; as a noun, friend (bibliophile)

Review the vocabulary in Lessons 1-6.

Principal parts of verbs:

Review the principal parts of verbs given in Lessons 20, 22 and 24.
Review the indicative forms of λύω.

EXPLANATION

The student has studied the different-looking second aorist forms of ἔγνων
developed from the second aorist base or stem of γινώσκω (see Lesson 34,
page 86). Another verb with a somewhat similar meaning and with
distinctive forms is οἶδα, I know. It is conjugated in only two tenses:
the perfect, which is to be translated as if it were a present form,
I know; and the pluperfect form, ἤδειν, which is to be translated simply
as past, I knew. The forms of this verb are as follows:

Perfect

	Indicative	Subjunctive	Imperative	Infinitive
1.	οἶδα	εἰδῶ		εἰδέναι
2.	οἶδας	εἰδῇς	ἴσθι[1]	
3.	οἶδε(ν)	εἰδῇ	ἴστω	

				Participle
1.	οἴδαμεν	εἰδῶμεν		εἰδώς
2.	οἴδατε	εἰδῆτε	ἴστε	εἰδυῖα
3.	οἴδασι(ν)	εἰδῶσι(ν)	ἴστωσαν	εἰδός

Pluperfect

	Indicative
1.	ἤδειν
2.	ἤδεις
3.	ἤδει

1.	ἤδειμεν
2.	ἤδειτε
3.	ἤδεισαν

---

[1]Compare the present imperative of εἰμί: ἴσθι, ἔστω, ἔστε, ἔστωσαν.

ἴνα clauses:

The student has learned that the introductory word ἴνα with the subjunctive is used to indicate purposes, as in the sentence, ὁ Ἰησοῦς εἶπε τοῖς μαθηταῖς ἴνα ἀκολουθήσωσιν αὐτῷ, Jesus spoke to the disciples in order that they might follow him.

It is now to be observed that ἴνα with the subjunctive can also be used as an object or as an appositional clause, often being an equivalent to a ὅτι clause. Examples:

John 6:40 - This is the will of my Father, ἴνα πᾶς ὁ θεωρῶν τὸν υἱόν...ἔχῃ ζωὴν αἰώνιον, that every one seeing the son....may have eternal life. (The ἴνα clause here is an appositional clause to "This is the will of my Father.")

Mark 7:26 - And she asked him that (ἴνα) he cast the demon out. (Here the ἴνα clause is the object of the verb ask.)

Variations of usage like this will be learned by practice.

Conditional Sentences:

The student has been presented with the essentials of Greek conditional sentences. A summary of the pattern of New Testament Greek conditional sentences is as follows:

CLASS	CONJUNCTION	PROTASIS[1]	APODOSIS[1]	EXAMPLES
First (Factual)	εἰ (sometimes ἐάν)	Indicative (any tense)	Generally Indicative (any tense)	John 15:20
Second (contrary to fact)	εἰ	Indicative Imperfect (for present time contrary to fact)	Indicative Impf. generally with ἄν (for present time contrary to fact)	John 14:28
		Aorist (for past time contrary to fact)	Aorist with ἄν (for past time contrary to fact)	Matt. 11:21
Third (probability, possibility)	ἐάν, ἄν (sometimes εἰ)	Subjunctive	Usually fut. or pres. indic. or impv. (great variety)	John 11:40; John 13:17 (both first and third class conditions present)
Fourth (less certain than ἐάν + subj.)	infrequent in N.T. and then fragmentary	Optative	Optative often with ἄν	Acts 17:27

[1]The term protasis is used to indicate a conditional or subordinate clause setting forth a supposed or assumed case. The apodosis is the conclusion, giving what follows if the condition is fulfilled.

For the optative forms of the verb, the student is to see the accompanying page with the paradigm of the optative. As was just noted above, the optative suggests less certainty than even the subjunctive. It may carry the idea of wish, potentiality, deliberation, etc. The student should study the optative mood as presented in the New Testament Greek Syntax Chart on page 199 in the Appendix.

EXERCISES

1. Learn the vocabulary set forth in Lesson 37.

2. Review the principal parts of the verbs given in the previous lessons and the indicative forms of λύω.

3. Study the uses of ἵνα and the conditional sentences.

4. Translate John 6:51-65.

5. Translate the following sentences from English to Greek (based on the material in this lesson and John 6:46-65).

   a. This is life eternal, that we believe (or, may believe) on the Son of God.
   b. Jesus asked them that they believe the Word which God gave to them.
   c. If we should (or, shall) not eat his flesh, we do not have life from God.
   d. Jesus knew that some were not believing in him.
   e. If we in fact believe in Christ and eat his flesh, we have life from God.
   f. If we were to believe (which, in fact, we do not) in Christ, we would have eternal life.

6. Parse the following verb forms.

1. ἐπορεύεσθε	21. ἔμενεν	41. ἐγνώκαμεν
2. ἐλύσατε	22. ἤλθετε	42. γεννήσαντα
3. ἔχομεν	23. ἐδιδάχθητε	43. ἐλήλυθα (ἔρχομαι)
4. λέγει	24. πέμπονται	44. πεπιστευκότας
5. γινώσκουσι(ν)	25. ἐπέμφθησαν	45. ἤκουσα
6. λέγετε	26. ἑτοιμασθήσεται	46. γεννηθείς
7. βλέπεις	27. εἰμί	47. εἴπωσιν
8. ἀνέβαινον	28. ἤμην	48. λέγητε
9. ἐσμέν	29. ἀποκτείνει	49. ἔχει
10. ἐκπορεύεται	30. ἔχουσι(ν)	50. ἀκούειν
11. ἕξει	31. ἐδωσεν	51. ἔλαβον
12. γενήσεσθε	32. ἐπίστευσαν	52. ποιήσεις
13. ὑπέστρεψας	33. ἐστίν	53. ἐζήτουν
14. ἐδέξασθε	34. διωκόμενοι	54. βληθῆναι
15. ἐδέξω	35. πιστεύοντες	55. ἔρχεσθαι
16. ἦσαν	36. ἀναβαινούσῃ	56. λάβητε (λαμβάνω)
17. συνηγάγετε	37. ἐξήλθομεν	57. σώσαντα
18. λέγετε	38. ἐπορεύεσθε	58. ὦμεν
19. ὀψόμεθα	39. σῷζον	59. πορευομένου
20. παρελάβετε	40. ἤγγικεν	60. εἶπον

NEW TESTAMENT OPTATIVE

λύω

Pres. Act.	Pres. M.P.	Aor. Act.	Aor. M.	Aor. Pass.
(λύοιμι)*	(λυοίμην)	(λύσαιμι)	λυσαίμην	(λυθείην)
(λύοις)	(λύοιο)	(λύσαις)	(λύσαιο)	(λυθείης)
λύοι	λύοιτο	λύσαι	(λύσαιτο)	λυθείη
(λύοιμεν)	(λυοίμεθα)	(λύσαιμεν)	(λυσαίμεθα)	(λυθείημεν)
λύοιτε	(λύοισθε)	(λύσαιτε)	(λύσαισθε)	(λυθείητε)
λύοιεν	(λύοιντο)	λύσειαν	(λύσαιντο)	(λυθείησαν)
		or		
		λύσαιεν		

λαμβάνω

2 Aor. Act.	2 Aor. M.
(λάβοιμι)	(λαβοίμην)
(λάβοις)	(λάβοιο)
(λάβοι)	λάβοιτο
(λάβοιμεν)	(λαβοίμεθα)
(λάβοιτε)	(λάβοισθε)
λάβοιεν	(λάβοιντο)

εἰμί

Pres. Opt.

εἴην
εἴης
εἴη

εἴημεν
εἴητε
εἴησαν

The present optative formation of εἰμί is identical to the aorist passive optative endings of λύω.

* The forms found in parentheses are practically non-existent in the New Testament.

The Greek Comparative and Superlative; Articular Infinitive
of Purpose; Two-ending Third Declension Adjectives

VOCABULARY

Review the Vocabulary in Lessons 7-20.

Principal parts of verbs: Review the principal parts of verbs given in
Lessons 26, 28, and 30.

Basic Verb Review:

1. The verb λύω in the subjunctive, imperative, participle, infinitive, and
    optative.

2. The present and imperfect tenses of the contract verbs in -εω, -αω, and -οω.

EXPLANATIONS

The comparison of adjectives: There are two basic ways in which the comparative and superlative forms of adjectives might be constructed. Some words, in
forming the comparative degree, use endings of the first and second declension
in -τερος, α, ον; and some, third declension endings, with the masculine and
feminine genders using the one ending type of -(ι)ων and the neuter using the
ending type -(ι)ον (cf. John 14:12; 15:13, 20; 2 Tim. 1:18).

The comparative forms ἰσχυρότερος, α, ον meaning stronger are as follows:
(ἰσχυρός, ἰσχυρά, ἰσχυρόν, the positive forms, masculine, feminine, neuter, mean
strong).

	MASCULINE	FEMININE	NEUTER
N.	ἰσχυρότερος	ἰσχυρότερα	ἰσχυρότερον
G.	ἰσχυροτέρου	ἰσχυροτέρας	ἰσχυροτέρου
D.	ἰσχυροτέρῳ	ἰσχυροτέρᾳ	ἰσχυροτέρῳ
A.	ἰσχυρότερον	ἰσχυρότεραν	ἰσχυρότερον
N.	ἰσχυρότεροι	ἰσχυρότεραι	ἰσχυρότερα
G.	ἰσχυροτέρων	ἰσχυροτέρων	ἰσχυροτέρων
D.	ἰσχυροτέροις	ἰσχυροτέραις	ἰσχυροτέροις
A.	ἰσχυροτέρους	ἰσχυροτέρας	ἰσχυρότερα

The positive forms of μέγας meaning great are as follows:

N.	μέγας	μεγάλη	μέγα
G.	μεγάλου	μεγάλης	μεγάλου
D.	μεγάλῳ	μεγάλῃ	μεγάλῳ
A.	μέγαν	μεγάλην	μέγα
V.	μέγαλε	μεγάλη	μέγα
N.	μεγάλοι	μεγάλαι	μεγάλα
G.	μεγάλων	μεγάλων	μεγάλων
D.	μεγάλοις	μεγάλαις	μεγάλοις
A.	μεγάλους	μεγάλας	μεγάλα
V.	μεγάλοι	μεγάλαι	μεγάλα

The comparative forms μείζων, μεῖζον meaning greater are as follows:

μείζων- comparative, great:

Masc. and Fem.	Neuter
N. μείζων	μεῖζον
G. μείζονος	μείζονος
D. μείζονι	μείζονι
A. μείζονα (μείζω)	μεῖζον
N. μείζονες	μείζονα (μείζω)
G. μειζόνων	μειζόνων
D. μείζοσι(ν)	μείζοσι(ν)
A. μείζονας (μείζους)	μείζονα (μείζω)

The Superlative Degree is formed in Greek by the endings -τατος, η, ον and -ιστος, η, ον. An example of the superlative (not frequently used in the New Testament) is as follows:

μικρός, ά, όν   - positive form, little
ἐλάσσων, ον   - comparative form, less
ἐλάχιστος, η, ον   - superlative form, least

The superlative forms ἐλάχιστος, η, ον meaning, least, are as follows:

Masculine	Feminine	Neuter
N. ἐλάχιστος	ἐλαχίστη	ἐλάχιστον
G. ἐλαχίστου	ἐλαχίστης	ἐλαχίστου
D. ἐλαχίστῳ	ἐλαχίστῃ	ἐλαχίστῳ
A. ἐλάχιστον	ἐλαχίστην	ἐλάχιστον
N. ἐλάχιστοι	ἐλάχισται	ἐλάχιστα
G. ἐλαχίστων	ἐλαχίστων	ἐλαχίστων
D. ἐλαχίστοις	ἐλαχίσταις	ἐλαχίστοις
A. ἐλαχίστους	ἐλαχίστας	ἐλάχιστα

The use of the comparative of the adjective: This type of concept can be expressed in one of two ways: using the comparative form of the adjective followed by a genitive, or using the two Greek words μᾶλλον (more) . . . . . ἤ (than). Examples:

Matt. 13:32 . . . μικρότερον . . . πάντων τῶν σπερμάτων,
    smaller than all the seeds.

Matt. 5:20 . . . πλεῖον τῶν γραμματέων,
    more than the scribes.

John 3:19 . . . ἠγάπησαν οἱ ἄνθρωποι μᾶλλον τὸ σκότος ἤ τὸ φῶς.
    men loved darkness rather than (they loved) the light (both
    σκότος and φῶς being accusative because they are the object of
    the verb, ἠγάπησαν).

Adverbs: Often the genitive plural form of adjectives like καλός, good, and κακός, bad, can be used to form the adverb by removing the final ν after the ω and substituting a final ς. Examples:

καλῶν, καλῶς - well
κακῶν, κακῶς - badly

The Articular Infinitive of Purpose:

Purpose can be expressed by just the use of the infinitive, as exampled by ἦλθον λῦσαι τὸν μαθητήν, They went <u>to loose</u> the disciple. But sometimes the genitive article is used with the infinitive to express purpose. A good example is Luke 2:27,.... the parents brought in Jesus in order that they might do (τοῦ ποιῆσαι) according to the custom of the law concerning him.

The two-ending third declension adjectives:

In the forms of this type of adjective the first forms in -ης (nominative), -ους (genitive), etc., serve for the masculine and feminine genders, and the second set of forms in -ες (nominative), -ους (genitive), etc., serves for the neuter gender. The adjective ἀληθής, true, will be used as an example of this type (cf. ἀληθινός, ή, όν, which has three genders of endings in the first and second declensions). The declension of ἀληθής is as follows:

SINGULAR

	Masculine and Feminine		Neuter
N.	ἀληθής		ἀληθές
G.		ἀληθοῦς	
D.		ἀληθεῖ	
A.	ἀληθῆ		ἀληθές
V.	ἀληθές		ἀληθές

PLURAL

N.	ἀληθεῖς		ἀληθῆ
G.		ἀληθῶν	
D.		ἀληθέσι(ν)	
A.	ἀληθεῖς		ἀληθῆ
V.	ἀληθεῖς		ἀληθῆ

EXERCISES

1. Practice on the review vocabulary and verb forms.

2. Learn the comparison of the adjective.

3. Translate from Greek to English, John 6:66 - 7:9.

Greek Numerals, and Coordinate and Subordinate Clauses

VOCABULARY

Review the vocabulary in Lessons 21 to 37.

Principal parts of verbs: Review the principal parts of verbs in
Lessons 32 and 35.

Basic Verb Review:

1. The liquid verbs whose bases or stems end in λ, μ, ν or ρ (see page 77).

2. The μι verb system (Lessons 32, 33 and 34); the second aorist active
   forms of γινώσκω (Lesson 34); other second aorist verb forms (Lessons
   14 and 34); the paradigm forms of εἰμί (Lessons 13 and 34); and the
   second perfect and second pluperfect forms of οἶδα (Lesson 37).

EXPLANATION

Numerals: In the student's reading of Greek several instances of Greek
numerals have occurred. The numerals one, three and four are declinable
as follows:

	εἷς, μία, ἕν, one					τρεῖς, τρία, three	
	SINGULAR					PLURAL	
	Masc.	Fem.	Neut.			Masc.-Fem.	Neut.
N.	εἷς	μία	ἕν		N.	τρεῖς	τρία
G.	ἑνός	μιᾶς	ἑνός		G.	τριῶν	τριῶν
D.	ἑνί	μιᾷ	ἑνί		D.	τρισί(ν)	τρισί(ν)
A.	ἕνα	μίαν	ἕν		A.	τρεῖς	τρία

	τέσσαρες, τέσσαρα, four	
	PLURAL	
	Masc.-Fem.	Neut.
N.	τέσσαρες	τέσσαρα
G.	τεσσάρων	τεσσάρων
D.	τέσσαρσι(ν)	τέσσαρσι(ν)
A.	τέσσαρας	τέσσαρα

The numbers δύο, two (except for the dative δυσίν), and from πέντε, five,
up to two hundred are indeclinable. The numerals 200, 300, etc. are then
declined as, for example, διακόσιοι, διακόσιαι, διακόσια, 200.

Coordinate and Subordinate Clauses: In a general way clauses may be
divided into two categories:

1. Those which are paratactic, or coordinate (clauses that are on a
   parallel with others of like nature and connected by such conjunctions as and, but, etc.);

2. Those which are hypotactic, or subordinate (clauses that are subordinate to another clause or clauses in the sentence; these are
   exampled by relative clauses, temporal clauses, the participle, etc.).

Common Greek conjunctions introducing <u>paratactic</u> clauses are:

<u>Copulative conjunctions</u>:
καί, and; καί....καί, both....and
τέ, and; τέ....τέ, both....and (Rom. 14:8)

<u>Adversative conjunctions</u>:
δέ, but (Matt. 5:21)
ἀλλά, but (Luke 1:60)

<u>Disjunctive conjunctions</u> as:
οὐδὲ....οὐδέ, neither....nor (Rev. 9:4)
οὔτε....οὔτε, neither....nor (Luke 20:35)
ἤ, or (Matt. 5:17)
ἤ....ἤ, either....or (Mark 13:35)

<u>Inferential conjunctions</u> as:
γάρ, for, indeed (Matt. 1:21; Matt. 27:23)
οὖν, then (John 12:1), therefore (Rom. 5:1)

Hypotactic sentences involve the relative pronouns; the temporal conjunctions such as ὅτε (when), etc.; causal conjunctions such as ὅτι (because); indirect discourse; uses of the infinitive, participle, etc.

EXERCISES

1. **Practice** on the review vocabulary and the verb forms.

2. Learn the declension of the numerals one, three and four.

3. Translate from Greek to English John 7:10-24.

SUPPLEMENTAL LIST OF GREEK VERBS FOR PARSING

1. ὀψόμεθα
2. ἐγίνεσθε
3. ἐδεξάμην
4. ἠκούσαμεν
5. ἐπέστρεφαν
6. ὑπέστρεψας
7. ἡτοίμασα
8. ἐδέξω
9. γίνεσθε
10. γινώσκομεν
11. πορεύῃ
12. ἀκούσομεν
13. εἴδομεν
14. ἐγένοντο
15. εἶπον
16. ἤγαγον
17. ὀρώμεθα
18. ἐπιστεύσαμεν
19. παρελάβετε
20. ἔμενεν
21. ἐγράφη
22. ἐγερήσονται
23. συνήχθησαν
24. ἐξέβαλεν
25. ἐπέμφθησαν
26. ἐβαπτίσθης
27. ἐπιστεύθη
28. δέξονται
29. ἐκηρύχθη
30. ἤκουσαν
31. ἐσώθην
32. ἤνεγκαν (φέρω)
33. ὄψεσθε
34. γινώσκομεν
35. ἀποκτείνει
36. ἦλθεν (ἔρχομαι)
37. ἠγέρθησαν
38. διωκόμενοι
39. προσευχόμεθα
40. πιστεύοντες
41. γραφόμεθα
42. ἄγοντες
43. λαμβάνοντας
44. σῷζον
45. πιστεύουσα
46. ἐπορεύεσθε
47. βαπτίζοντα

48. λαβόντες
49. δεξάμεναι
50. προσενεγκόντες (φέρω)
51. λεγόμενα
52. ἀκουσάντων
53. ὄντας
54. πορευθέντος
55. ἐπίστευσεν
56. θεραπευθεῖσι(ν)
57. διωχθέντας
58. ἐξέβαλον
59. ὄντες
60. προσενεγκοῦσι(ν)
61. εὐαγγελισώμεθα
62. διδάσκωμεν
63. σωθῶσιν
64. γενώμεθα
65. γεγραμμένα
66. εὐηγγελίσατο
67. ἤγγικεν
68. ἑωράκαμεν
69. ἀκηκόαμεν
70. λέγομεν
71. πιστεύσητε
72. γινώσκομεν
73. ἐγνώκαμεν
74. γεγεννημένον
75. γεγεννημένος
76. ἁμαρτάνει
77. γεννηθείς
78. γέγονεν
79. γέγραπται
80. ἐστίν
81. ἔλεγον
82. τεθεραπευμένῳ
83. ἔξεστιν
84. ἐλήλυθα
85. δέχεσθε
86. εἶπον
87. ἑωράκατε
88. πιστεύετε
89. φάγητε
90. λελάληκα
91. ἀπεκρίθη
92. ἀπελευσόμεθα
93. πεπιστεύκαμεν
94. εἶ

95. ἐπίστευσαν
96. ἤκουσα
97. ἐβαπτίσθησαν
98. πεπιστευκότας
99. ἐγνώκαμεν
100. ἐπορεύθη
101. εὐλογήσει
102. περιπατοῦντα
103. ἀγαπώμενοι
104. ἀκολουθοῦσιν
105. ἤρξατο
106. παρακαλεῖν
107. ἀπελθεῖν
108. λαλήσαντι
109. ζητήσωμεν
110. ἐλάλει
111. θεραπευθείς
112. ἀκολουθοῦντι
113. ἐθεώρουν
114. περιπατεῖν
115. ἔρχεσθαι
116. περιεπάτει
117. βληθῆναι
118. ἐζήτουν
119. ποιούμενα
120. φιλοῦσιν
121. ἐλάλησεν
122. καλέσαι
123. ἐποιεῖτε
124. ἀγαπᾶν
125. λαλήσαντι
126. κληθέντες
127. θεωρήσομεν
128. περιπατοῦντι
129. ἐθεώρουν
130. σταυρούμενον
131. κηρύσσομεν
132. ἐγείρας
133. ἐγερεῖ
134. ἀγαπᾶτε
135. ἔσεσθε
136. ἀποθανόντος
137. μετανοήσαντι
138. ἐκβαλοῦσιν
139. ἔμεινα
140. ἐπίστευσα
141. λαβεῖν

142. εἴπωμεν
143. φοβούμεθα
144. ἀποστελεῖ
145. φοβῶνται
146. δοξάζοντες
147. ἐφοβοῦντο
148. ἐροῦμεν
149. ἀποσταλεῖσι(ν)
150. κρινεῖτε
151. κρινῇ
152. κρίνομεν
153. κρινοῦμεν
154. ἀπεστείλαμεν
155. μείνωμεν
156. ἠγειράμην
157. ἀπεκτείνατε
158. πιστεύσετε
159. ἔχεις
160. ἦν
161. δίδωσι(ν)
162. διδόασι(ν)
163. δῷς
164. δός
165. ἔδωκαν
166. τίθης
167. τίθεται
168. τίθησι(ν)
169. τιθέασι(ν)
170. θῶ
171. θῇ
172. ἵστατε
173. ἵστησι(ν)
174. ἱστᾶσι(ν)
175. ἵστασο
176. ἵστασαν
177. ἔστη
178. ἔγνως
179. γνῶθι
180. στῆθι
181. ἱστάς
182. τιθέναι
183. θεῖναι
184. δούς
185. διδούς
186. δοῦ
187. ἔδου
188. λάβετε

SUPPLEMENTAL SENTENCES FOR PRACTICE IN TRANSLATING ENGLISH TO GREEK

Lesson Five:

a. I am a man in the world.
b. John believes and has a witness of the Word.
c. Man is being loosed by God.
d. I say, "I received the life and the light of God."

Lesson Six:

a. The men believe the Word of God.
b. Jesus says, "I am holy."
c. The heart of man is dead in sin.
d. The angel said, "The crowd receives the law."

Lesson Seven:

a. He comes as (even as) he said.
b. I see the road and I come to Jesus.

Lesson Eight:

a. I see him and he sends the people to me.
b. Jesus says, "I tell you the truth (verily, verily, I say to you), you hear my voice and you follow me."
c. The prophet himself was among the people and now you will hear him.
d. The other prophet is not the same prophet.

Lesson Nine:

a. I see the servant of the Lord whom he sends.
b. This (person, demonstrative masc.) is Jesus.
c. Jesus comes again from God.
d. I speak concerning Jesus who (nominative, masculine, singular, relative pronoun) is the Son of God.
e. I write concerning Jesus whom (accus. masc. relative pronoun) I will see in heaven.
f. Jesus is the prophet who (nom., masc., sing. relative pronoun) is the life from God.

Lesson Ten:

a. The church of the Lord remains in the truth.
b. My life remains in the Lord and I will not see death.
c. God judges his Church which is his house.
d. How do I remain in the truth and do not die?

Lesson Eleven:

a. I was departing in the way of life.
b. The Lord was bringing me to God and he saves me from death.
c. The hour comes when I will see the love of God.
d. He came unto his own world and he has authority in the world.

Lesson Twelve:

a. Jesus said, "You are my child. I loosed you from sin and you have the righteousness of God."
b. The Lord has his eye on (among) his people. They believed in him and they did not fear.
c. I was praying to God. He is the bread of life.
d. He comes before me and he does not cast me out. He has loosed me.

Lesson Thirteen:

a. He has loosed me from my sins.
b. He had loosed his people from their sin.
c. Another disciple is ready and he goes up to the place of the Lord.
d. Jesus is sitting there and I fall before him who is my Lord.

Lesson Fourteen:

a. John said, "I have the Gospel which saves men from their sins and I baptize with water in the name of Jesus."
b. Men were evil. Jesus' blood is for the sins of men.
c. The twelve disciples are there and they have faith in Jesus.
d. Jesus goes into the temple (area). He says, "This is my temple."

Lesson Fifteen:

a. This is the world of the Father who is the God of his people.
b. He comes down into the world, and the woman and the man find him.
c. The Spirit is here.
d. The hand of the Lord is upon me and he has peace and grace for me.

Lesson Sixteen:

a. When the fire of the Lord comes down into the world, the nations fear.
b. The water of life comes into my mouth.
c. I am an elder who seeks the Lord and worships him on the Sabbath Day.
d. Jesus is the beloved of God. The Gentiles come to him.

Lesson Seventeen:

a. I rejoice in the light which (relative pronoun) is the faithful word of God.
b. I preach in the night and in the day.
c. His people gather together and he has loosed them from their sins.
d. The Lord casts out the demon.

Lesson Eighteen:

a. This is the city of God and the throne of God is here.
b. No one comes to God's throne which is in heaven.
c. Jesus said, "I exist with God. The rest are evil."
d. I find the scribe of the Lord.

Lesson Nineteen:

a. The one loosing men from their sins is the Lord.
b. Jesus is the one who is in the Father.
c. The Lord goes into the synagogue.
d. Men glorify and receive the king and the high priest of God.

Lesson Twenty:

a. I preach the good news until the Lord comes.
b. The Scriptures are the promise of God concerning his salvation which comes to men.
c. Seeing the Lord, I will believe in God.
d. Jesus spoke in parables. Seeing him, they believed in him.

Lesson Twenty-One:

a. In the wisdom of God, I persuade men who have not believed.
b. Having seen (when I saw) the men who loosed the child, I believed in the Lord.
c. I received hope which is in God.
d. I became blessed, when I saw (having seen) the Lord.

Lesson Twenty-Two:

a. I am a sinner who is blessed.
b. I no longer sit in judgment.
c. I saw the Word of God on (in) the Third Day.
d. I will cast (throw) the word of God on the road (way). I taught men the commandment of God.

Lesson Twenty-Three:

a. The one being loosed from his sins in this year is blessed of the Lord.
b. He brings such a salvation to a man who is evil.
c. They who were loosed (having been loosed) from sin received the salvation of God.
d. I having been in need of the Lord (when I was in need), the man was there, announcing the truth of God.

Lesson Twenty-Four:

a. I was sinning. Since I had believed in Jesus (having believed, ●———),
   I marvelled at the grace of God.
b. The seed of God is in him.
c. When the man had loosed the child, the Lord went out into Galilee.
d. He pursued the wild beast who was like the evil one.

Lesson Twenty-Five:

a. Having been loosed (●———) from his sins, the man went into the temple.
b. He recognized Jesus and believed in him.
c. I know the Lord. Today is the day of salvation.
d. The one who healed will receive honor in the day of resurrection and the judgment.

Lesson Twenty-Six:

a. I preach the good news in order that he may loose men from their sins.
b. I am the door in order that people might pass through from death unto life.
c. I work that I may save men.
d. I, his sheep, will glorify God. I abound in him.

Lesson Twenty-Seven:

a. If I should prepare the good news, I will be keeping his commandment.
b. I suffer in order that God may be glorified.
c. Let us do the commandments of God.
d. This is sufficient, but I weep for my sins.

Lesson Twenty-Eight:

a. To marvel at the good news is blessed.
b. In his pursuing righteousness (while he was pursuing), the man was preaching the good news.
c. You love to sow the seed of God's Word.
d. I, a poor man, will return to see the ruler. I will not go after him. He is the devil.

Lesson Twenty-Nine:

a. Loose the man. Do not tempt him.
b. I ought to go out to see the Lord.
c. Let us pray. Do not wish to tempt the people of the Lord.
d. The anger of the Lord is a witness. Do not return to sin.

Lesson Thirty:

a. I am weak in sin. Ask the Lord to heal me.
b. They seek the Lord in order that he may bless them.
c. I was repenting and I was bearing witness to the truth of God.
d. Walk in the Lord. Live in his grace.

Lesson Thirty-One:

a. The one loving the Lord will receive his joy and grace.
b. I was wandering in my sin.
c. They were crucifying Jesus and God was justifying sinners who sinned against him.
d. I see the Lord. I will remain in him.

Lesson Thirty-Two:

a. The priest gives the Covenant of God to the people.
b. I do this in order that I may give glory to God.
c. I wish to give the book of life to the man.
d. I will follow (dative) God, who gives (the one giving) life to me.

Lesson Thirty-Three:

a. I was placing my feet in the way (road) of life so that I might guard my life from sin.
b. Have patience in the Lord.
c. The Lord has put his grace on me.
d. Let us put our faith in Jesus.

Lesson Thirty-Four:

a. Let us stand here. Let us worship the Lord.
b. When he stood (having stood) in the temple courts, he preached the good news.
c. I am a member of his body.
d. I knew him. He saved me.

Lesson Thirty-Five:

a. Let them come into the house of the Lord.
b. I was in darkness, but I was being cleansed from sin.
c. He will call. I will save him in order that he will praise my name.
d. The Lord who comes to his people is the Lamb of God.

Lesson Thirty-Six:

a. The Lord is strong. He will bring his judgment.
b. Turn _from_ your sin.
c. Worship the Lord _on_ his day.
d. He will save you by his Word. He will bring _you_ salvation.

Lesson Thirty-Seven:

a. If in fact you believe in the Lord, he will bless your life.
b. If you were to cause your brother to stumble, you would not be walking in the light of his Word.
c. If you should live according to God's Word, you will know that his promise is true.
d. Believe in the Lord, if you have (really) found him faithful.

A Simplified Greek Reader on

The Gospel of John

by W. Harold Mare

Chapter 1

Ἐν ἀρχῇ ἦν ὁ λόγος, καὶ ὁ λόγος ἦν πρὸς τὸν θεόν, καὶ θεὸς ἦν ὁ
λόγος. ²ἦν ἐν ἀρχῇ πρὸς τὸν θεόν. ³ἐποίησε πάντα τὸν κόσμον. ⁴ἐν αὐτῷ
ζωὴ ἦν, καὶ ἡ ζωὴ ἦν τὸ φῶς τῶν ἀνθρώπων. ⁵καὶ τὸ φῶς ἐν τῇ σκοτίᾳ
φαίνει, καὶ ἡ σκοτία τὸ φῶς οὐ καταλαμβάνει.

⁶Ἐγένετο ἄνθρωπος παρὰ θεοῦ, ὄνομα αὐτῷ ἦν Ἰωάννης. ⁷ἔχει
μαρτυρίαν περὶ τοῦ φωτός. ἄνθρωποι πιστεύουσι δι' Ἰωάννου. ⁸οὐκ ἦν
τὸ φῶς, ἀλλ' ἐμαρτύρησε περὶ τοῦ φωτός. ⁹ἦν τὸ φῶς τὸ ἀληθινόν. τὸ
φῶς φωτίζει ἀνθρώπους ἐν τῷ κόσμῳ. ¹⁰ἐν τῷ κόσμῳ ἦν, καὶ ἐποίησε τὸν
κόσμον καὶ ὁ κόσμος τὸ φῶς οὐ γινώσκει. ¹¹εἰς τὰ ἴδια ἦλθεν, καὶ οἱ
ἴδιοι τὸ φῶς οὐ λαμβάνουσιν. ¹²ἄνθρωποι λαμβάνουσι τὸ φῶς καὶ πιστεύσουσιν
εἰς τὸ ὄνομα αὐτοῦ. ¹³ὁ θεὸς ποιεῖ αὐτοὺς τέκνα θεοῦ. λαμβάνουσι
τὴν ζωὴν τοῦ θεοῦ καὶ βλέπουσι τὸ φῶς τοῦ θεοῦ.

¹⁴Καὶ ὁ λόγος σὰρξ ἐγένετο καὶ ἐσκήνωσεν ἐν τῷ κόσμῳ, καὶ βλέπομεν
τὴν δόξαν τοῦ λόγου. ἔχει δόξαν παρὰ θεοῦ καὶ ἦν πλήρης εἰρήνης καὶ
ἀληθείας. ¹⁵Ἰωάννης μαρτυρεῖ περὶ τοῦ λόγου καὶ λέγει λόγους τοῖς
ἀνθρώποις περὶ τοῦ υἱοῦ. ¹⁶Ἰωάννης λέγει, Ὁ λόγος ἦν ἐν ἀρχῇ.
λαμβάνομεν εἰρήνην ἐκ τοῦ λόγου καὶ τὰς ἐντολάς. ¹⁷Μωϋσῆς καὶ οἱ
ἄνθρωποι τοῦ θεοῦ γράφουσι τὰς ἐντολὰς ἐν ταῖς γραφαῖς καὶ Ἰησοῦς Χριστὸς

Greek Reader Text--John 1

λέγει τὴν ἀλήθειαν τοῖς ἀνθρώποις. ¹⁸θεὸν ἄνθρωποι οὐ γινώσκουσι
καὶ οὐ βλέπουσιν. ὁ μονογενὴς θεός ἐστιν εἰς τὸν κόλπον τοῦ θεοῦ καὶ
δεικνύει τὸν θεόν.

¹⁹καὶ ὁ Ἰωάννης ἔχει τὴν μαρτυρίαν ὅτε ἀποστέλλουσι πρὸς αὐτὸν οἱ
Ἰουδαῖοι ἐξ Ἱεροσολύμων ἱερεῖς καὶ Λευίτας ἵνα ἐρωτήσωσιν αὐτόν, Σὺ τίς
εἶ; ²⁰καὶ ὁμολογεῖ ὅτι Ἐγὼ οὐκ εἰμὶ ὁ Χριστός. ²¹καὶ ἐρωτῶσιν αὐτόν,
Τί οὖν; Ἡλίας εἶ σύ; καὶ λέγει, Οὐκ εἰμί. Ὁ προφήτης εἶ σύ; καὶ
ἀπεκρίθη, Οὔ. ²²λέγουσιν οὖν αὐτῷ, Τίς εἶ; δεῖ τοὺς Ἰουδαίους γινώσκειν.
Τί λέγεις περὶ σεαυτοῦ; ²³λέγει, Ἐγώ εἰμι φωνὴ ἐν τῇ ἐρήμῳ. Δεικνύω τὴν
ὁδὸν κυρίου, καθὼς εἶπεν Ἡσαΐας ὁ προφήτης. ²⁴καὶ οἱ Φαρισαῖοι ἀπέστειλαν
αὐτούς. ²⁵καὶ ἠρώτησαν αὐτόν, Τί οὖν βαπτίζεις εἰ σὺ οὐκ εἶ ὁ Χριστὸς οὐδὲ
Ἡλίας οὐδὲ ὁ προφήτης; ²⁶ἀπεκρίθη αὐτοῖς ὁ Ἰωάννης καὶ εἶπεν, Ἐγὼ
βαπτίζω ἐν ὕδατι· μέσος ὑμῶν στήκει ὃν ὑμεῖς οὐ γινώσκετε. ²⁷οὐκ εἰμὶ ἐγὼ
ἄξιος ἵνα λύσω αὐτοῦ τὸν ἱμάντα τοῦ ὑποδήματος. ²⁸ταῦτα ἐν Βηθανίᾳ γίνεται
πέραν τοῦ Ἰορδάνου, ὅπου ὁ Ἰωάννης ἐστὶ καὶ βαπτίζει.

²⁹Τῇ ἐπαύριον βλέπει τὸν Ἰησοῦν ὡς ἔρχεται πρὸς αὐτόν, καὶ λέγει,
Ἴδε ὁ ἀμνὸς τοῦ θεοῦ αἴρει τὴν ἁμαρτίαν τοῦ κόσμου. ³⁰Ἔστιν ὑπὲρ οὗ ἐγὼ
εἶπον, Ὀπίσω μου ἔρχεται ἀνήρ. πρῶτός μου ἦν. ³¹κἀγὼ οὐκ ἔγνων αὐτόν, ἀλλ'
ἐμαρτύρησα περὶ αὐτοῦ τῷ Ἰσραήλ. διὰ τοῦτο ἦλθον καὶ ἐγὼ ἐν ὕδατι βαπτίζω.
³²καὶ μαρτυρεῖ Ἰωάννης καὶ λέγει ὅτι θεάομαι τὸ πνεῦμα καταβαῖνον ὡς
περιστερὰν ἐξ οὐρανοῦ, καὶ μένει ἐπ' αὐτόν. ³³κἀγὼ οὐκ ἔγνων αὐτόν, ἀλλ'
ὁ θεὸς πέμπει με καὶ βαπτίζω ἐν ὕδατι καί μοι εἶπεν, Μέλλεις βλέπειν τὸ
πνεῦμα. Καταβαίνει καὶ μένει ἐπ' αὐτόν. Βαπτίζει ἐν πνεύματι ἁγίῳ. ³⁴κἀγὼ
βλέπω καὶ μαρτυρῶ ὅτι ἐστὶν ὁ υἱὸς τοῦ θεοῦ.

Greek Reader Text--John 1

³⁵Τῇ ἐπαύριον πάλιν στήκει ὁ Ἰωάννης καὶ ἐκ τῶν μαθητῶν αὐτοῦ δύο,
³⁶καὶ ἐμβλέπει τῷ Ἰησοῦ καὶ λέγει, Ἴδε ὁ ἀμνὸς τοῦ θεοῦ. ³⁷καὶ ἀκούουσιν
οἱ δύο μαθηταὶ αὐτοῦ καὶ ἀκολουθοῦσι τῷ Ἰησοῦ. ³⁸στρέφει δὲ ὁ Ἰησοῦς καὶ
βλέπει αὐτοὺς καὶ λέγει αὐτοῖς, Τί ζητεῖτε; οἱ δὲ εἶπον αὐτῷ, Ῥαββί
(μεθερμηνεύεται διδάσκαλε), ποῦ μένεις; ³⁹λέγει αὐτοῖς, Ἔρχεσθε καὶ βλέπετε.
ἔρχονται οὖν καὶ βλέπουσι ποῦ μένει, καὶ παρ' αὐτῷ μένουσι τὴν ἡμέραν
ἐκείνην· ὥρα ἦν ὡς δεκάτη. ⁴⁰ἦν Ἀνδρέας ὁ ἀδελφὸς Σίμωνος Πέτρου εἷς τῶν
δύο τῶν μαθητῶν τοῦ Ἰωάννου. ⁴¹εὑρίσκει πρῶτον τὸν ἀδελφὸν τὸν ἴδιον
Σίμωνα καὶ λέγει αὐτῷ, Ὧδέ ἐστιν ὁ Μεσσίας (μεθερμηνεύεται Χριστός).
⁴²φέρει αὐτὸν πρὸς τὸν Ἰησοῦν. ἐνέβλεψε καὶ εἶπεν, Σὺ εἶ Σίμων ὁ υἱὸς
Ἰωάννου· σὺ κληθήσῃ Κηφᾶς (μεθερμηνεύεται Πέτρος).

⁴³Τῇ ἐπαύριον ἐξέρχεται εἰς τὴν Γαλιλαίαν, καὶ εὑρίσκει Φίλιππον.
καὶ λέγει αὐτῷ ὁ Ἰησοῦς, Ἀκολούθει μοι. ⁴⁴ἦν δὲ ὁ Φίλιππος ἀπὸ Βηθσαϊδά,
ἐκ τῆς πόλεως Ἀνδρέου καὶ Πέτρου. ⁴⁵εὑρίσκει Φίλιππος τὸν Ναθαναὴλ
καὶ λέγει αὐτῷ, Τὸν Μεσσίαν ἔγραψε Μωϋσῆς ἐν τῷ νόμῳ καὶ οἱ προφῆται,
καὶ εὑρήκαμεν αὐτόν, Ἰησοῦν υἱὸν τοῦ Ἰωσὴφ τὸν ἀπὸ Ναζαρέτ. ⁴⁶καὶ εἶπεν
Ναθαναήλ, Ἐκ Ναζαρέτ τι ἀγαθόν ἐστιν; λέγει αὐτῷ Φίλιππος, Ἔρχου καὶ
ἴδε. ⁴⁷βλέπει ὁ Ἰησοῦς τὸν Ναθαναὴλ ὡς ἔρχεται πρὸς αὐτὸν καὶ λέγει περὶ
αὐτοῦ, Ἴδε ἀληθῶς Ἰσραηλίτης καὶ ἐν αὐτῷ δόλος οὐκ ἔστιν. ⁴⁸λέγει αὐτῷ
Ναθαναήλ, Πόθεν με γινώσκεις; ἀπεκρίθη Ἰησοῦς καὶ εἶπεν αὐτῷ, Σὺ ἦς
ὑπὸ τὴν συκῆν καὶ Φίλιππος ἐφώνησεν· τότε ἔβλεψά σε. ⁴⁹ἀπεκρίθη αὐτῷ
Ναθαναήλ, Ῥαββί, σὺ εἶ ὁ υἱὸς τοῦ θεοῦ, σὺ βασιλεὺς εἶ τοῦ Ἰσραήλ.
⁵⁰ἀπεκρίθη Ἰησοῦς καὶ εἶπεν αὐτῷ, Ὅτι εἶπόν σοι ὅτι ἔβλεψά σε ὑποκάτω
τῆς συκῆς, πιστεύεις; μείζονα βλέψεις. ⁵¹καὶ λέγει αὐτῷ, Ἀμὴν ἀμὴν
λέγω ὑμῖν, ὁ οὐρανὸς ἀνοίξει καὶ οἱ ἄγγελοι τοῦ θεοῦ ἀναβήσονται καὶ
καταβήσονται ἐπὶ τὸν υἱὸν τοῦ ἀνθρώπου καὶ ταῦτα βλέψετε.

Greek Reader Text--John 2

¹Καὶ τῇ ἡμέρᾳ τῇ τρίτῃ γάμος ἐγένετο ἐν Κανὰ τῆς Γαλιλαίας, καὶ ἦν ἡ μήτηρ τοῦ Ἰησοῦ ἐκεῖ. ²καλοῦσι δὲ τὸν Ἰησοῦν καὶ τοὺς μαθητὰς αὐτοῦ εἰς τὸν γάμον. ³οἶνος ὑστερεῖ καὶ λέγει ἡ μήτηρ τοῦ Ἰησοῦ πρὸς αὐτόν, Οἶνον οὐκ ἔχουσιν. ⁴καὶ λέγει αὐτῇ ὁ Ἰησοῦς, Πῶς μετέχομεν τούτου, γύναι; οὔπω ἥκει ἡ ὥρα μου. ⁵λέγει ἡ μήτηρ αὐτοῦ τοῖς διακόνοις, Τί λέγει ὑμῖν ποιήσατε. ⁶ἦσαν δὲ ἐκεῖ λίθιναι ὑδρίαι ἓξ κατὰ τὸν καθαρισμὸν τῶν Ἰουδαίων καὶ ἐχώρουν ἀνὰ μετρητὰς δύο ἢ τρεῖς. ⁷λέγει αὐτοῖς ὁ Ἰησοῦς, Γεμίσατε τὰς ὑδρίας ὕδατος. καὶ γεμίζουσιν αὐτὰς ἕως ἄνω. ⁸καὶ λέγει αὐτοῖς, Ἀντλήσατε νῦν καὶ φέρετε τῷ ἀρχιτρικλίνῳ. οἱ δὲ ἄνθρωποι φέρουσιν. ⁹ὁ δὲ ἀρχιτρίκλινος γεύεται τὸν οἶνον (οὗτος πρότερον ἦν τὸ ὕδωρ καὶ οὐκ ἐγίνωσκε πόθεν ἐστίν, οἱ δὲ διάκονοι ἐγίνωσκον ὅτι ἤντλησαν τὸ ὕδωρ). φωνεῖ τὸν νυμφίον ὁ ἀρχιτρίκλινος. ¹⁰καὶ λέγει αὐτῷ, ἄνθρωποι πρῶτον τὸν καλὸν οἶνον φέρουσιν καὶ μεθύσκονται. ἄνθρωποι τότε τὸν οἶνον τὸν ἐλάσσω φέρουσιν. σὺ τηρεῖς τὸν καλὸν οἶνον ἕως ἄρτι. ¹¹ταύτην ποιεῖ ἀρχὴν τῶν σημείων ὁ Ἰησοῦς ἐν Κανὰ τῆς Γαλιλαίας καὶ φανεροῖ τὴν δόξαν αὐτοῦ, καὶ ἐπίστευον εἰς αὐτὸν οἱ μαθηταὶ αὐτοῦ.

¹²Μετὰ τοῦτο καταβαίνει εἰς Καφαρναοὺμ αὐτὸς καὶ ἡ μήτηρ αὐτοῦ καὶ οἱ ἀδελφοὶ αὐτοῦ καὶ οἱ μαθηταὶ αὐτοῦ, καὶ ἐκεῖ μένουσιν οὐ πολλὰς ἡμέρας.

¹³Καὶ ἐγγὺς ἦν τὸ πάσχα τῶν Ἰουδαίων, καὶ ἀναβαίνει εἰς Ἱεροσόλυμα ὁ Ἰησοῦς. ¹⁴καὶ ἐν τῷ ἱερῷ ἄνθρωποι ἐπώλουν βόας καὶ πρόβατα καὶ περιστεράς, καὶ οἱ κερματισταὶ ἦσαν ἐκεῖ. ὁ Ἰησοῦς εὑρίσκει αὐτούς. ¹⁵ποιεῖ φραγέλλιον ἐκ σχοινίων καὶ πάντας ἐκβάλλει ἐκ τοῦ ἱεροῦ καὶ τὰ πρόβατα καὶ τοὺς βόας καὶ τῶν κολλυβιστῶν ἐκχεῖ τὸ κέρμα καὶ τὰς τραπέζας ἀνατρέπει. ¹⁶καὶ ἄνθρωποι τὰς περιστερὰς ἐπώλουν, καὶ αὐτοῖς εἶπεν, Ἄρατε ταῦτα ἐντεῦθεν. μὴ ποιεῖτε τὸν οἶκον τοῦ πατρός μου οἶκον ἐμπορίου. ¹⁷μιμνήσκονται οἱ μαθηταὶ

τῆς γραφῆς, Ὁ ζῆλος τοῦ οἴκου σου κατεσθίει με. [18]ἀπεκρίθησαν
οὖν οἱ Ἰουδαῖοι καὶ ἔλεγον αὐτῷ, Τί σημεῖον δεικνύεις ἡμῖν, ὅτι
ταῦτα ποιεῖς; [19]ἀπεκρίθη Ἰησοῦς καὶ εἶπεν αὐτοῖς, Λύσατε τὸν
ναὸν τοῦτον καὶ ἐν τρισὶν ἡμέραις ἐγείρω αὐτόν. [20]εἶπον οὖν οἱ
Ἰουδαῖοι, Τεσσαράκοντα καὶ ἒξ ἔτεσιν οἰκοδομεῖται ὁ ναὸς οὗτος, καὶ
σὺ ἐν τρισὶν ἡμέραις ἐγείρεις αὐτόν; [21]ἐκεῖνος δὲ ἔλεγεν περὶ τοῦ ναοῦ
τοῦ σώματος αὐτοῦ. [22]ὅτε οὖν ἠγέρθη ἐκ νεκρῶν, ἐμνήσθησαν οἱ μαθηταὶ
αὐτοῦ ὅτι τοῦτο ἔλεγεν, καὶ ἐπίστευον τῇ γραφῇ καὶ τῷ λόγῳ τοῦ Ἰησοῦ.

[23]Ὡς δὲ ἦν ἐν τοῖς Ἱεροσολύμοις ἐν τῇ ἑορτῇ, πολλοὶ
ἐπίστευον εἰς τὸ ὄνομα αὐτοῦ, ὅτι ἐθεώρουν αὐτοῦ τὰ σημεῖα. [24]αὐτὸς
δὲ Ἰησοῦς οὐκ ἐπίστευεν ἑαυτὸν αὐτοῖς ὅτι αὐτὸς ἐγίνωσκεν πάντας.
[25]καὶ οὐκ ἔδει αὐτοὺς μαρτυρεῖν περὶ τοῦ ἀνθρώπου· αὐτὸς γὰρ ἐγίνωσκεν
τί ἦν ἐν τῷ ἀνθρώπῳ.

John 3

[1]Ἦν δὲ ἄνθρωπος ἐκ τῶν Φαρισαίων, Νικόδημος ὄνομα αὐτοῦ, πρῶτος
ἄνθρωπος τῶν Ἰουδαίων· [2]οὗτος ἔρχεται πρὸς αὐτὸν μετὰ τὰς ὥρας τῆς
ἡμέρας καὶ εἶπεν αὐτῷ, Ῥαββί, γινώσκομεν ὅτι ἀπὸ θεοῦ ἔρχῃ ὡς διδάσκαλος.
σὺ γὰρ ταῦτα τὰ σημεῖα ποιεῖς, καὶ δεῖ τὸν θεὸν εἶναι μετ' ἀνθρώπου ἢ
ἄνθρωπος οὐ δύναται ποιεῖν ταῦτα. [3]ἀπεκρίθη Ἰησοῦς καὶ εἶπεν αὐτῷ,
Ἀμὴν ἀμὴν λέγω σοι, δεῖ ἄνθρωπον γεννηθῆναι ἄνωθεν ἢ οὐ δύναται ἰδεῖν
τὴν βασιλείαν τοῦ θεοῦ. [4]λέγει πρὸς αὐτὸν ὁ Νικόδημος, Πῶς δύναται
γέρων ἄνθρωπος γεννηθῆναι ἄνωθεν; μὴ δύναται εἰς τὴν κοιλίαν τῆς
μητρὸς αὐτοῦ δεύτερον εἰσελθεῖν καὶ γεννηθῆναι; [5]ἀπεκρίθη Ἰησοῦς,
Ἀμὴν ἀμὴν λέγω σοι, δεῖ ἄνθρωπον γεννηθῆναι ἐξ ὕδατος καὶ πνεύματος
ἢ οὐ δύναται εἰσελθεῖν εἰς τὴν βασιλείαν τοῦ θεοῦ. [6]ἡ γένεσις ἐκ τῆς

σαρκὸς σάρξ ἐστιν, καὶ ἡ γένεσις ἐκ τοῦ πνεύματος πνεῦμά ἐστιν. [7]οὐ
θαυμάζεις ὅτι εἶπόν σοι, Δεῖ ὑμᾶς γεννηθῆναι ἄνωθεν. [8]τὸ πνεῦμα
ὅπου θέλει πνεῖ, καὶ τὴν φωνὴν αὐτοῦ ἀκούεις ἀλλ' οὐ γινώσκεις πόθεν
ἔρχεται καὶ ποῦ πορεύεται. οὕτως ἐστὶν πᾶς ὁ ἄνθρωπος ὁ γεννηθεὶς
ἐκ τοῦ πνεύματος. [9]ἀπεκρίθη Νικόδημος καὶ εἶπεν αὐτῷ, Πῶς ἐστιν τοῦτο;
[10]ἀπεκρίθη Ἰησοῦς καὶ εἶπεν αὐτῷ, Σὺ εἶ ὁ διδάσκαλος τοῦ Ἰσραὴλ
καὶ ταῦτα οὐ γινώσκεις; [11]ἀμὴν ἀμὴν λέγω σοι ὅτι γινώσκομεν ταῦτα
καὶ λέγομεν. ἑωράκαμεν ταῦτα καὶ μαρτυροῦμεν, καὶ τὴν μαρτυρίαν ἡμῶν
οὐ λαμβάνετε. [12]τὰ ἐπίγεια εἶπον ὑμῖν, καὶ οὐ πιστεύετε. λέγω ὑμῖν
τὰ ἐπουράνια καὶ πιστεύσετε τὴν μαρτυρίαν μου; [13]καὶ ἄνθρωπος οὐκ
ἀναβαίνει εἰς τὸν οὐρανόν, ἀλλ' ὁ υἱὸς τοῦ ἀνθρώπου ἐκ τοῦ οὐρανοῦ
καταβαίνει. [14]καὶ καθὼς Μωϋσῆς ὕψωσεν τὸν ὄφιν ἐν τῇ ἐρήμῳ, οὕτως
ὑψωθῆναι δεῖ τὸν υἱὸν τοῦ ἀνθρώπου· [15]οὕτως γὰρ ἄνθρωποι πιστεύσουσιν
ἐν αὐτῷ καὶ ἕξουσι ζωὴν αἰώνιον.

[16]οὕτως γὰρ ἠγάπησεν ὁ θεὸς τὸν κόσμον, ὥστε τὸν υἱὸν τὸν μονογενῆ
ἔδωκεν καὶ οὕτως ἄνθρωποι πιστεύουσιν εἰς αὐτόν, καὶ οὖν οὐκ ἀπολλύονται
ἀλλ' ἔχουσι ζωὴν αἰώνιον. [17]οὐ γὰρ ἀπέστειλεν ὁ θεὸς τὸν υἱὸν εἰς
τὸν κόσμον κρῖναι τὸν κόσμον ἀλλὰ σωθῆναι τὸν κόσμον δι' αὐτοῦ. [18]εἷς
μὲν ἄνθρωπος πιστεύει εἰς αὐτὸν καὶ οὐ κρίνεται, ἕτερος δὲ οὐ πιστεύει
καὶ ἤδη κέκριται, ὅτι οὐ πεπίστευκεν εἰς τὸ ὄνομα τοῦ μονογενοῦς
υἱοῦ τοῦ θεοῦ. [19]αὕτη δέ ἐστιν ἡ κρίσις, ὅτι τὸ φῶς ἦλθεν εἰς τὸν
κόσμον καὶ ἠγάπησαν οἱ ἄνθρωποι μᾶλλον τὸ σκότος ἢ τὸ φῶς, ἦν γὰρ
αὐτῶν πονηρὰ τὰ ἔργα. [20]τινὲς γὰρ φαῦλα πράσσουσιν καὶ μισοῦσιν τὸ φῶς
καὶ οὐκ ἔρχονται πρὸς τὸ φῶς ὅτι οὐ θέλουσιν ἐλεγχθῆναι τὰ ἔργα
αὐτῶν. [21]τινὲς δὲ ποιοῦσι τὴν ἀλήθειαν καὶ ἔρχονται πρὸς τὸ φῶς ὅτι
θέλουσιν αὐτῶν τὰ ἔργα φανερωθῆναι ὅτι ἐν θεῷ ἐργάζονται.

²²Μετὰ ταῦτα ἦλθεν ὁ Ἰησοῦς καὶ οἱ μαθηταὶ αὐτοῦ εἰς τὴν Ἰουδαίαν γῆν, καὶ ἐκεῖ διέτριβεν μετ' αὐτῶν καὶ ἐβάπτιζεν. ²³ἐβάπτιζεν δὲ καὶ ὁ Ἰωάννης ἐν Αἰνὼν ἐγγὺς τοῦ Σαλείμ, ὅτι ὕδατα πολλὰ ἦν ἐκεῖ, καὶ παρεγίνοντο καὶ ἐβαπτίζοντο. ²⁴οὔπω γὰρ ἐβέβλητο εἰς τὴν φυλακὴν ὁ Ἰωάννης. ²⁵Ἐγένετο οὖν ζήτησις ἐκ τῶν μαθητῶν Ἰωάννου μετὰ Ἰουδαίου περὶ καθαρισμοῦ. ²⁶καὶ ἦλθον πρὸς τὸν Ἰωάννην καὶ εἶπον αὐτῷ, Ῥαββί, Ἰησοῦς ἦν μετὰ σοῦ πέραν τοῦ Ἰορδάνου καὶ αὐτῷ σὺ ἐμαρτύρεις. ἴδε οὗτος βαπτίζει καὶ πάντες ἔρχονται πρὸς αὐτόν. ²⁷ἀπεκρίθη Ἰωάννης καὶ εἶπεν, Δῶρα μόνα δίδοται ἐκ τοῦ οὐρανοῦ καὶ μόνα ἐκ τοῦ οὐρανοῦ δύναται ἄνθρωπος λαμβάνειν δῶρον. ²⁸αὐτοὶ ὑμεῖς μοι μαρτυρεῖτε ὅτι εἶπον ὅτι Οὐκ εἰμὶ ἐγὼ ὁ Χριστός, ἀλλ' ὅτι ἀπεστάλην ἔμπροσθεν ἐκείνου. ²⁹ὁ νυμφίος ἔχει τὴν νύμφην. ὁ δὲ φίλος τοῦ νυμφίου στήκει καὶ ἀκούει αὐτοῦ καὶ χαρᾷ χαίρει διὰ τὴν φωνὴν τοῦ νυμφίου. αὕτη οὖν ἡ χαρὰ ἡ ἐμὴ πληροῦται. ³⁰ἐκεῖνον δεῖ αὐξάνειν, ἐμὲ δὲ ἐλαττοῦσθαι. ³¹Ὁ υἱὸς ἄνωθεν ἔρχεται καὶ ἐπάνω πάντων ἐστίν. ὁ ἄνθρωπος ὁ ἐκ τῆς γῆς ἐκ τῆς γῆς ἐστιν καὶ ἐκ τῆς γῆς λαλεῖ. ὁ υἱὸς ἐκ τοῦ οὐρανοῦ ἔρχεται καὶ ἐπάνω πάντων ἐστίν. ³²τοῦτο εἶδεν καὶ ἤκουσεν καὶ μαρτυρεῖ, καὶ τὴν μαρτυρίαν αὐτοῦ ἄνθρωποι οὐ λαμβάνουσιν. ³³τινὲς δὲ ἔλαβον αὐτοῦ τὴν μαρτυρίαν καὶ ἐσφράγισαν ὅτι ὁ θεὸς ἀληθής ἐστιν. ³⁴τὸν γὰρ υἱὸν ἀπέστειλεν ὁ θεὸς καὶ τὰ ῥήματα τοῦ θεοῦ λαλεῖ, οὐ γὰρ ἐκ μέτρου δίδωσιν τὸ πνεῦμα. ³⁵ὁ πατὴρ ἀγαπᾷ τὸν υἱόν, καὶ πάντα δέδωκεν ἐν τῇ χειρὶ αὐτοῦ. ³⁶οἱ μὲν πιστεύουσιν εἰς τὸν υἱὸν καὶ ἔχουσι ζωὴν αἰώνιον. οἱ δὲ ἀπειθοῦσι τῷ υἱῷ καὶ οὐκ ὄψονται ζωήν, ἀλλ' ἡ ὀργὴ τοῦ θεοῦ μένει ἐπ' αὐτούς.

Greek Reader Text -- John 4

¹Ὡς οὖν ἔγνω ὁ Ἰησοῦς ὅτι ἤκουσαν οἱ Φαρισαῖοι ὅτι Ἰησοῦς πλείονας
μαθητὰς ποιεῖ καὶ βαπτίζει ἢ Ἰωάννης ²--Ἰησοῦς αὐτὸς οὐκ ἐβάπτιζεν
ἀλλ' οἱ μαθηταὶ αὐτοῦ--³ἐξῆλθεν ἐκ τῆς Ἰουδαίας καὶ ἀπῆλθεν πάλιν εἰς
τὴν Γαλιλαίαν. ⁴Ἔδει δὲ αὐτὸν διέρχεσθαι διὰ τῆς Σαμαρείας. ⁵Ἔρχεται
οὖν εἰς πόλιν τῆς Σαμαρείας καὶ ἐλέγετο Συχάρ. πλησίον ἦν χωρίον καὶ
αὐτὸ ἐδεδώκει Ἰακὼβ τῷ Ἰωσὴφ τῷ υἱῷ αὐτοῦ. ⁶ἦν δὲ ἐκεῖ πηγὴ τοῦ Ἰακώβ.
ὁ οὖν Ἰησοῦς ἐκοπίασεν ἐκ τῆς ὁδοιπορίας καὶ ἐκαθέζετο οὕτως ἐπὶ τῇ
πηγῇ. ὥρα ἦν ὡς ἕκτη.

⁷Ἔρχεται γυνὴ ἐκ τῆς Σαμαρείας ἀντλῆσαι ὕδωρ. λέγει αὐτῇ ὁ Ἰησοῦς,
Δώσεις μοι ὕδωρ; ⁸οἱ γὰρ μαθηταὶ αὐτοῦ πρότερον ἀπῆλθον εἰς τὴν πόλιν
καὶ τροφὰς ἠγόραζον. ⁹λέγει οὖν αὐτῷ ἡ γυνὴ ἡ Σαμαρῖτις, Σὺ εἶ
Ἰουδαῖος, καὶ πῶς πόσιν ὕδατος αἰτεῖς παρ' ἐμοῦ γυναικὸς Σαμαρίτιδος;
(οὐ γὰρ συγχρῶνται Ἰουδαῖοι Σαμαρίταις.) ¹⁰ἀπεκρίθη Ἰησοῦς καὶ εἶπεν
αὐτῇ, Οὐ γινώσκεις τὴν δωρεὰν τοῦ θεοῦ καὶ ἐμέ (ἐγὼ γὰρ ᾔτησα ὕδωρ
τῆς πηγῆς). σὺ οὖν οὐκ ᾔτησας αὐτόν (καὶ ἐμέ) ὕδωρ τῆς ζωῆς. αὐτὸς γὰρ
ἔδωκεν ἄν σοι αὐτό. ¹¹λέγει αὐτῷ ἡ γυνή, Κύριε, οὔτε ἄντλημα ἔχεις
καὶ τὸ φρέαρ ἐστὶ βαθύ. πόθεν οὖν ἔχεις τὸ ὕδωρ τῆς ζωῆς; ¹²μὴ σὺ μείζων
εἶ τοῦ πατρὸς ἡμῶν Ἰακώβ; ἔδωκεν ἡμῖν τὸ φρέαρ καὶ αὐτὸς ἐξ αὐτοῦ ἔπιεν
καὶ οἱ υἱοὶ αὐτοῦ καὶ τὰ θρέμματα αὐτοῦ. ¹³ἀπεκρίθη Ἰησοῦς καὶ εἶπεν
αὐτῇ, Ἄνθρωποι πίνουσιν ἐκ τοῦ ὕδατος τούτου καὶ διψῶσιν πάλιν.
¹⁴ὅτε δέ τις πίνει ἐκ τοῦ ὕδατος ἀπ' ἐμοῦ, καὶ οὐ μὴ διψήσει εἰς τὸν
αἰῶνα, ἀλλὰ τὸ ὕδωρ ἀπ' ἐμοῦ γενήσεται ἐν αὐτῷ πηγὴ ὕδατος καὶ τοῦτο
τὸ ὕδωρ ἅλλεται εἰς ζωὴν αἰώνιον. ¹⁵λέγει πρὸς αὐτὸν ἡ γυνή, Κύριε,
θέλω τοῦτο τὸ ὕδωρ. Τότε γὰρ οὐ διψήσω, οὐδὲ διελεύσομαι ἐνθάδε οὐδὲ
ἀντλήσω.

Greek Reader Text--John 4

¹⁶λέγει αὐτῇ, Ἔνεγκον τὸν ἄνδρα σου ἐνθάδε. ¹⁷ἀπεκρίθη ἡ γυνὴ
καὶ εἶπεν αὐτῷ, Οὐκ ἔχω ἄνδρα. λέγει αὐτῇ ὁ Ἰησοῦς, Καλῶς εἶπες
ὅτι Ἄνδρα οὐκ ἔχω. ¹⁸πέντε γὰρ ἄνδρας ἔσχες, καί σου ἀνὴρ νῦν οὐκ
ἔστιν σου ἀνήρ. τοῦτο ἀληθὲς εἶπες. ¹⁹λέγει αὐτῷ ἡ γυνή, Κύριε,
θεωρῶ ὅτι προφήτης εἶ σύ. ²⁰οἱ πατέρες ἡμῶν ἐν τῷ ὄρει τούτῳ προσεκύνησαν
καὶ ὑμεῖς λέγετε ὅτι ἐν Ἱεροσολύμοις ἐστὶν ὁ τόπος ὅπου προσκυνεῖν
δεῖ. ²¹λέγει αὐτῇ ὁ Ἰησοῦς, Ἰδού, ἔρχεται ὥρα ὅτε οὔτε ἐν τῷ ὄρει
τούτῳ οὔτε ἐν Ἱεροσολύμοις προσκυνήσετε τῷ πατρί. ²²ὑμεῖς προσκυνεῖτε
ἄνευ τῆς ἀληθινῆς γνώσεως· ἡμεῖς προσκυνοῦμεν μετὰ τῆς ἀληθινῆς γνώσεως,
ὅτι ἡ σωτηρία ἐκ τῶν Ἰουδαίων ἐστίν. ²³ἀλλὰ ἔρχεται ὥρα καὶ νῦν
ἐστίν, ὅτε οἱ ἀληθινοὶ προσκυνηταὶ προσκυνήσουσιν τῷ πατρὶ ἐν πνεύματι
καὶ ἀληθείᾳ. καὶ γὰρ ὁ πατὴρ τοιούτους ζητεῖ τοὺς προσκυνοῦντας αὐτῷ.
²⁴πνεῦμα ὁ θεός, καὶ τοὺς προσκυνοῦντας αὐτῷ ἐν πνεύματι καὶ ἀληθείᾳ
δεῖ προσκυνεῖν. ²⁵λέγει αὐτῷ ἡ γυνή, Γινώσκω ὅτι Μεσσίας ἔρχεται, ὁ
λεγόμενος Χριστός. ὅτε ἔρχεται ἐκεῖνος, λαλήσει ἡμῖν πάντα. ²⁶λέγει
αὐτῇ ὁ Ἰησοῦς, Ἐγώ εἰμι, ὁ λαλῶν σοι.

²⁷Καὶ ἐπὶ τούτῳ ἦλθον οἱ μαθηταὶ αὐτοῦ, καὶ ἐθαύμαζον ὅτι γυναικὶ
συνεχράτο. οἱ μέντοι μαθηταὶ οὐκ εἶπον, Τί ζητεῖς; ἤ, Τί λαλεῖς μετ'
αὐτῆς; ²⁸Ἔλιπεν οὖν τὴν ὑδρίαν αὐτῆς ἡ γυνὴ καὶ ἀπῆλθεν εἰς τὴν πόλιν
καὶ λέγει τοῖς ἀνθρώποις, ²⁹Δεῦτε καὶ βλέψετε ἄνθρωπον. οὗτος εἶπέν
μοι πάντα τῆς ζωῆς μου. μήτι οὗτός ἐστιν ὁ Χριστός; ³⁰ἐξῆλθον ἐκ τῆς
πόλεως καὶ ἤρχοντο πρὸς αὐτόν.

³¹Ἐν τῷ μεταξὺ ἠρώτησαν οἱ μαθηταὶ λέγοντες, Ῥαββί, φάγῃ σύ; ³²ὁ
δὲ εἶπεν αὐτοῖς, Ἐγὼ βρῶσιν ἔχω φαγεῖν καὶ περὶ αὐτῆς ὑμεῖς οὐ γινώσκετε.
³³ἔλεγον οὖν οἱ μαθηταὶ πρὸς ἀλλήλους, Μὴ ἄνθρωπος ἤνεγκεν αὐτῷ φαγεῖν;
³⁴λέγει αὐτοῖς ὁ Ἰησοῦς, Βρῶμά μού ἐστιν τὸ θέλημα τοῦ πέμψαντός με
καὶ ποιήσω αὐτὸ καὶ τελειώσω αὐτοῦ τὸ ἔργον. ³⁵οὐχ ὑμεῖς λέγετε ὅτι

Greek Reader Text--John 4

Ἔτι τετράμηνός ἐστιν καὶ ὁ θερισμὸς ἔρχεται; λέγω ὑμῖν, βλέψετε τὰς
χώρας, ὅτι λευκαί εἰσι πρὸς θερισμόν. ³⁶ἤδη ὁ θερίζων μισθὸν λαμβάνει.
καὶ συνάγει καρπὸν εἰς ζωὴν αἰώνιον. καὶ ὁ σπείρων καὶ ὁ θερίζων ὁμοῦ
χαίρουσιν. ³⁷ἐν γὰρ τούτῳ ὁ λόγος ἐστὶν ἀληθινὸς ὅτι ἄλλος ἐστὶν ὁ
σπείρων καὶ ἄλλος ὁ θερίζων. ³⁸ἐγὼ ἀπέστειλα ὑμᾶς, καὶ μὴ σπείραντες
θερίσετε. ἄλλοι ἐκοπίασαν καὶ ὑμεῖς εἰς τὸν κόπον αὐτῶν εἰσήλθετε.

³⁹Ἐκ δὲ τῆς πόλεως ἐκείνης πολλοὶ ἐπίστευσαν εἰς αὐτὸν τῶν
Σαμαριτῶν διὰ τὸν λόγον τῆς γυναικὸς μαρτυρούσης ὅτι Εἶπέν μοι περὶ πάσης
τῆς ζωῆς μου. ⁴⁰ἐλθόντες οὖν πρὸς αὐτὸν οἱ Σαμαρῖται ἠρώτησαν αὐτὸν
μεῖναι παρ' αὐτοῖς καὶ ἔμεινεν ἐκεῖ δύο ἡμέρας. ⁴¹καὶ πολλοὶ ἔτι
ἐπίστευσαν διὰ τὸν λόγον αὐτοῦ, ⁴²καὶ τῇ γυναικὶ ἔλεγον ὅτι Οὐκέτι διὰ τὸν
λόγον σου πιστεύομεν· αὐτοὶ γὰρ ἠκούσαμεν καὶ γινώσκομεν ὅτι οὗτός ἐστιν
ἀληθῶς ὁ σωτὴρ τοῦ κόσμου.

⁴³Μετὰ δὲ τὰς δύο ἡμέρας ἐξῆλθεν ἐκεῖθεν εἰς τὴν Γαλιλαίαν. ⁴⁴αὐτὸς
γὰρ Ἰησοῦς ἐμαρτύρησεν ὅτι προφήτης ἐν τῇ ἰδίᾳ πατρίδι τιμὴν οὐκ
ἔχει. ⁴⁵ὅτε οὖν ἦλθεν εἰς τὴν Γαλιλαίαν, ἐδέξαντο αὐτὸν οἱ Γαλιλαῖοι,
ἰδόντες πάντα τὰ ἔργα αὐτοῦ ἐν Ἰεροσολύμοις ἐν τῇ ἑορτῇ. καὶ αὐτοὶ γὰρ
ἦλθον εἰς τὴν ἑορτήν. ⁴⁶Ἦλθεν οὖν πάλιν εἰς τὴν Κανὰ τῆς Γαλιλαίας
ὅπου ἐποίησεν τὸ ὕδωρ οἶνον. καὶ ὁ υἱὸς βασιλικοῦ κακῶς εἶχεν ἐν Καφαρναούμ.
⁴⁷οὗτος ἀκούσας ὅτι Ἰησοῦς ἥκει ἐκ τῆς Ἰουδαίας εἰς τὴν Γαλιλαίαν,
ἀπῆλθεν πρὸς αὐτόν. ἠρώτησεν, Κατελεύσῃ καὶ θεραπεύσεις τὸν υἱόν μου;
ἀποθνήσκει. ⁴⁸εἶπεν οὖν ὁ Ἰησοῦς πρὸς αὐτόν, Πιστεύσετε σημεῖα καὶ
τέρατά μου; ⁴⁹λέγει πρὸς αὐτὸν ὁ βασιλικός, Κύριε, κατελεύσῃ; ἀποθνήσκει
τὸ παιδίον μου. ⁵⁰λέγει αὐτῷ ὁ Ἰησοῦς, Ὁ υἱός σου ἐθεραπεύθη. ἐπίστευσεν
ὁ ἄνθρωπος τῷ λόγῳ τοῦ Ἰησοῦ, καὶ ἐπορεύετο. ⁵¹ἤδη δὲ αὐτοῦ καταβαίνοντος
οἱ δοῦλοι ὑπήντησαν αὐτῷ λέγοντες ὅτι ὁ παῖς αὐτοῦ θεραπεύεται. ⁵²ἐπύθετο
οὖν παρ' αὐτῶν τὴν ὥραν τῆς ἰάσεως αὐτοῦ. εἶπον οὖν αὐτῷ ὅτι Ἐχθὲς ὥραν
ἑβδόμην ἀπῆλθεν ἀπ' αὐτοῦ ὁ πυρετός. ⁵³ὁ οὖν πατὴρ εἶπεν, Ὁ Ἰησοῦς

ἐθεράπευσεν αὐτὸν ἐν τῇ ὥρᾳ ἐκείνῃ. καὶ ἐπίστευσεν αὐτὸς καὶ ἡ οἰκία αὐτοῦ ὅλη. ⁵⁴τοῦτο δὲ πάλιν δεύτερον σημεῖον ἐποίησεν ὁ Ἰησοῦς ἐλθὼν ἐκ τῆς Ἰουδαίας εἰς τὴν Γαλιλαίαν.

John 5

¹Μετὰ ταῦτα ἦν ἑορτὴ τῶν Ἰουδαίων καὶ ἦλθεν Ἰησοῦς εἰς Ἱεροσόλυμα. ²ἔστιν δὲ ἐν τοῖς Ἱεροσολύμοις ἐπὶ τῇ προβατικῇ κολυμβήθρα, ἡ ἐπιλεγομένη Ἑβραϊστὶ Βηθζαθά, πέντε στοὰς ἔχουσα. ³ἐν ταύταις κατέκειτο πλῆθος τῶν ἀσθενούντων, τυφλῶν, χωλῶν, ξηρῶν. ⁵ἦν δέ τις ἄνθρωπος ἐκεῖ τριάκοντα καὶ ὀκτὼ ἔτη ἔχων ἐν τῇ ἀσθενείᾳ αὐτοῦ· ⁶ὁ Ἰησοῦς εἶδε τοῦτον κατακείμενον καὶ ἐγίνωσκεν ὅτι ἤδη μακρὸν χρόνον ἔχει. λέγει αὐτῷ, θεραπευθήσῃ; ⁷ἀπεκρίθη αὐτῷ ὁ ἀσθενῶν, Κύριε, ταραχθέντος τοῦ ὕδατος, ἄνθρωπος οὐκ βάλλει με εἰς τὴν κολυμβήθραν. ἐμοῦ δὲ ἐρχομένου, ἄλλος πρὸ ἐμοῦ καταβαίνει. ⁸λέγει αὐτῷ ὁ Ἰησοῦς, Ἀναλήμφῃ τὸν κράβαττόν σου καὶ περιπατήσεις. ⁹καὶ εὐθέως ἐγένετο ὑγιὴς ὁ ἄνθρωπος, καὶ ἦρεν τὸν κράβαττον αὐτοῦ καὶ περιεπάτησεν.

⁷Ἦν δὲ σάββατον ἐν ἐκείνῃ τῇ ἡμέρᾳ. ¹⁰ἔλεγον οὖν οἱ Ἰουδαῖοι τῷ θεραπευθέντι, Σάββατόν ἐστιν καὶ οὐκ ἔξεστίν σοι φέρειν τὸν κράβαττον. ¹¹ἀπεκρίθη δὲ αὐτοῖς, Ὁ ποιήσας με ὑγιῆ, ἐκεῖνός μοι εἶπεν, Ἀναλήμφῃ τὸν κράβαττόν σου καὶ περιπατήσεις. ¹²ἠρώτησαν αὐτόν, Τίς ἐστιν ὁ ἄνθρωπος ὁ εἰπών σοι, Ἀναλήμφῃ καὶ περιπατήσεις; ¹³ὁ δὲ ἰαθεὶς οὐκ ἐγίνωσκεν αὐτόν, ὁ γὰρ Ἰησοῦς ἐξένευσεν, ὄχλου ὄντος ἐν τῷ τόπῳ. ¹⁴μετὰ ταῦτα εὑρίσκει αὐτὸν ὁ Ἰησοῦς ἐν τῷ ἱερῷ καὶ εἶπεν αὐτῷ, θεραπεύῃ· οὐκέτι ἁμαρτήσεις καὶ χεῖρόν σοι οὐ γενήσεται. ¹⁵ἀπῆλθεν ὁ ἄνθρωπος καὶ εἶπεν τοῖς Ἰουδαίοις ὅτι Ἰησοῦς ἐστιν ὁ θεραπεύσας αὐτόν.

¹⁶καὶ διὰ τοῦτο ἐδίωκον οἱ Ἰουδαῖοι τὸν Ἰησοῦν, ὅτι ταῦτα ἐποίησεν ἐν σαββάτῳ. ¹⁷ὁ δὲ ἀπεκρίνατο αὐτοῖς, Ὁ πατήρ μου ἕως ἄρτι ἐργάζεται, κἀγὼ ἐργάζομαι. ¹⁸διὰ τοῦτο οὖν μᾶλλον ἐζήτησαν αὐτὸν οἱ Ἰουδαῖοι ἵνα ἀποκτείνωσιν αὐτόν, ὅτι οὐ μόνον ἔλυεν τὸ σάββατον, ἀλλὰ καὶ πατέρα ἴδιον

ἔλεγεν τὸν θεόν, ἴσον ἑαυτὸν ποιῶν τῷ θεῷ.

19Ἀπεκρίνατο οὖν ὁ Ἰησοῦς καὶ ἔλεγεν αὐτοῖς, Ἀμὴν ἀμὴν λέγω ὑμῖν, ὁ μὲν πατὴρ ποιεῖ ἔργα, ὁ δὲ υἱὸς καὶ ποιεῖ τὰ αὐτὰ ἔργα καθὼς ὁ πατὴρ ποιεῖ. 20ὁ γὰρ πατὴρ φιλεῖ τὸν υἱὸν καὶ δείκνυσιν αὐτῷ πάντα τὰ ἔργα αὐτοῦ, καὶ ἔτι δείξει αὐτῷ μεγάλα ἔργα, ἵνα ὑμεῖς θαυμάζητε. 21ὥσπερ γὰρ ὁ πατὴρ ἐγείρει τοὺς νεκροὺς καὶ ζωοποιεῖ οὕτως καὶ ὁ υἱὸς ζωοποιεῖ. 22οὐδὲ γὰρ ὁ πατὴρ κρίνει οὐδένα, ἀλλ' ὁ υἱὸς τὴν κρίσιν πᾶσαν ἔχει, 23ἵνα πάντες τιμῶσι τὸν υἱὸν καθὼς τιμῶσι τὸν πατέρα. ὁ μὴ τιμῶν τὸν υἱὸν οὐ τιμᾷ τὸν πατέρα τὸν πέμψαντα αὐτόν. 24Ἀμὴν ἀμὴν λέγω ὑμῖν ὅτι ὁ τὸν λόγον μου ἀκούων καὶ πιστεύων τῷ πέμψαντί με ἔχει ζωὴν αἰώνιον, καὶ εἰς κρίσιν οὐκ ἔρχεται ἀλλ' ἔχει τὴν ζωὴν καὶ οὐκ ἔστιν ἐν τῷ θανάτῳ. 25ἀμὴν ἀμὴν λέγω ὑμῖν ὅτι ἔρχεται ὥρα καὶ νῦν ἐστιν ὅτε οἱ νεκροὶ ἀκούσουσιν τῆς φωνῆς τοῦ υἱοῦ τοῦ θεοῦ καὶ οἱ ἀκούσαντες ζήσουσιν. 26ὥσπερ γὰρ ὁ πατὴρ ἔχει ζωὴν ἐν ἑαυτῷ, οὕτως καὶ ὁ υἱὸς ἔχει ζωὴν ἐν ἑαυτῷ. 27ὁ υἱὸς τῷ θελήματι τοῦ θεοῦ ποιεῖ κρίσιν ὅτι υἱὸς ἀνθρώπου ἐστίν. 28ἔρχεται ὥρα ὅτε οἱ ἐν τοῖς μνημείοις ἀκούσουσιν τῆς φωνῆς αὐτοῦ 29καὶ ἐκπορεύσονται, οἱ τὰ ἀγαθὰ ποιήσαντες εἰς ἀνάστασιν ζωῆς, οἱ τὰ φαῦλα πράξαντες εἰς ἀνάστασιν κρίσεως.

30Οὐ δύναμαι ἐγὼ ποιεῖν ἀπὸ τῆς ἐξουσίας μου οὐδέν. Καθὼς ἀκούω κρίνω καὶ ἡ κρίσις μου δικαία ἐστίν, ὅτι οὐ ζητῶ τὸ θέλημά μου ἀλλὰ τὸ θέλημα τοῦ πέμψαντός με.

31Ἡ μαρτυρία μού ἐστιν ἀλήθεια· 32ἄλλος γάρ ἐστιν ὁ μαρτυρῶν περὶ ἐμοῦ καὶ γινώσκω ὅτι μαρτυρεῖ τὴν ἀλήθειαν περὶ ἐμοῦ. 33ὑμεῖς ἐπέμψατε πρὸς Ἰωάννην καὶ ἐμαρτύρησεν τῇ ἀληθείᾳ. 34ἐγὼ δὲ οὐ παρὰ ἀνθρώπου τὴν μαρτυρίαν λαμβάνω ἀλλὰ ταῦτα λέγω ἵνα ὑμεῖς σωθῆτε. 35ἐκεῖνος ἦν ὁ λύχνος ὁ καιόμενος καὶ φαίνων, ὑμεῖς δὲ ἠθέλετε πρὸς ὥραν πρὸς τὸ φῶς αὐτοῦ. 36Ἰωάννης ἔχει μαρτυρίαν ἐγὼ δὲ ἔχω τὴν μεγάλην μαρτυρίαν. ὁ γὰρ πατὴρ ἔδωκέ μοι τὰ ἔργα καὶ τελειώσω αὐτά. ὁ γὰρ πατὴρ μαρτυρεῖ διὰ αὐτῶν τῶν ἔργων ὅτι με ἀπέστειλεν. 37καὶ ὁ πέμψας με ὁ πατὴρ ἐκεῖνος ἐμαρτύρησεν περὶ ἐμοῦ. οὔτε φωνὴν αὐτοῦ πώποτε ἠκούσατε οὔτε εἶδος αὐτοῦ εἴδετε, 38καὶ τὸν λόγον αὐτοῦ οὐκ ἔχετε ἐν ὑμῖν μένοντα ὅτι ὑμεῖς οὐ πιστεύετε τῷ ἀποσταλέντι ὑπὸ θεοῦ. 39ἐραυνᾶτε τὰς γραφάς, ὅτι ὑμεῖς δοκεῖτε ἐν αὐταῖς ζωὴν αἰώνιον ἔχειν· καὶ ἐκεῖναί εἰσιν αἱ μαρτυροῦσαι περὶ ἐμοῦ. 40καὶ οὐ θέλετε ἐλθεῖν πρός με ἵνα ζωὴν ἔχητε.

41Δόξαν παρὰ ἀνθρώπων οὐ λαμβάνω, 42ἀλλὰ γινώσκω ὑμᾶς ὅτι τὴν ἀγάπην τοῦ θεοῦ οὐκ ἔχετε ἐν ὑμῖν. 43ἐγὼ ἦλθον ἐν τῷ ὀνόματι τοῦ πατρός μου καὶ οὐ λαμβάνετέ με. ὅτε ἄλλος ἔρχεται ἐν τῷ ὀνόματι τῷ ἰδίῳ ἐκεῖνον λήμφεσθε. 44ὑμεῖς οὐ πιστεύετε. λαμβάνοντες δὲ δόξαν παρὰ ἀνθρώπων τὴν δόξαν τὴν παρὰ τοῦ μόνου θεοῦ οὐ ζητεῖτε. 45ἐγὼ οὐ κατηγορήσω ὑμῶν πρὸς τὸν πατέρα. Μωϋσῆς κατηγόρει ὑμῶν καὶ ὑμεῖς ἐλπίζετε εἰς αὐτόν. 46οὐκ ἐπιστεύσατε Μωϋσεῖ οὐδὲ πιστεύετε ἐμοί. καὶ περὶ ἐμοῦ ἐκεῖνος ἔγραψεν. 47εἰ δὲ τοῖς ἐκείνου γράμμασιν οὐ πιστεύετε, πῶς τοῖς ῥήμασίν μου πιστεύσετε;

SIMPLIFIED GREEK READER NOTES--JOHN 1

1:1   ἐν ἀρχῇ   -- in the beginning (prepositional phrase)

      ἦν   -- he, she, it was (past tense)

      ὁ λόγος   -- the word (ὁ is the article)

      καί   -- and

      πρὸς τὸν θεόν   -- to, in relationship with, with God (The word θεός, being a proper noun, may or may not have the article, the form of ὁ [here τόν] depending on the grammatical construction and the thoughts involved.)

1:3   ἐποίησε   -- He made (past tense, aorist)

      πάντα τὸν κόσμον   -- all the world (ὁ κόσμος here with object endings, τὸν κόσμου)

1:4   ἐν αὐτῷ   -- in him (αὐτῷ being in the dative form with the preposition ἐν)

      ζωή, ἡ   -- life, the life (The article is ἡ, not ὁ, because ζωή is feminine in gender.)

      τὸ φῶς τῶν ἀνθρώπων   -- the light of the men, or of men (The article is τό, not ὁ, because the noun φῶς is neuter in gender. The underscored endings in the words τῶν ἀνθρώπων indicate the plural "of" relationship conveyed in the English expression, "of [the] men.)

1:5   ἐν τῇ σκοτίᾳ   -- in the darkness (prepositional phrase)

      φαίνει   -- it shines (What does the "it" neuter subject refer to in this sentence? The verb φαίνει here has the present third person singular ει ending.)

      οὐ   -- not (Before words beginning with vowels it is written οὐκ, and before words beginning with vowels with rough breathing it is written οὐχ.)

      καταλαμβάνει   -- it (the darkness) did (not) overcome or comprehend (In the New Testament Greek the historical present is frequently used in narrative to describe a past event.)

1:6   ἐγένετο   -- there came (became)

        ἄνθρωπος   -- a man (There is no article ὁ, so here it is to be translated, "a" man.)

        παρὰ θεοῦ   -- from God

        ὄνομα   -- name (neuter noun; the article is τό)

        αὐτῷ   -- to him (Or, translate it here, his.) (third personal pronoun masculine)

        ᾽Ιωάννης   -- John

1:7   ἔχει   -- he had (has) (Compare the historical present in 1:5.)

        μαρτυρίαν   -- a witness (no article with this noun)

        περὶ τοῦ φωτός   -- concerning the light (The underscored endings of this expression, τοῦ φωτός, indicate the genitive singular, endings that are used here with the preposition περί.)

        πιστεύουσι   -- they believed (believe) (historical present)

        δι᾽ ᾽Ιωάννου   -- through John (prepositional phrase; διά shortened to δι᾽)

1:8   ἀλλά   -- but (conjunction)

        ἐμαρτύρησε   -- he bore witness (past tense, third singular)

1:9   τὸ φῶς τὸ ἀληθινόν   -- the light, the true one (or more fluently, the true light)

        φωτίζει   -- "it" lightens (Present tense third singular. What is the subject of this verb?)

        ἀνθρώπους   -- men (accusative plural, object case)

        ἐν τῷ κόσμῳ   -- in the world (The dative case is used here with ἐν.)

1:10   ἐποίησε   -- he made (past tense, third singular)

        γινώσκει   -- "it" did know (Historical present. What is the subject?)

        τὸ φῶς   -- the light (Here these words are the object of the verb.)

1:11   εἰς τὰ ἴδια ἦλθεν   -- He came (past tense, third singular) unto his own possessions (things).

1:11   οἱ ἴδιοι   -- his own people (This expression is mas-
                                          culine, whereas the τὰ ἴδια is neuter.)

        λαμβάνουσιν   -- they did receive (do receive; historical
                                            present; the final ν on the ending of
                                          third plural verbs is added after the
                                          ουσι before a following word beginning
                                          with a vowel or at the end of a sentence.
                                          This final ν moveable does not alter the
                                          meaning.)

1:12   πιστεύσουσιν εἰς   -- they will believe in his name (in the
        τὸ ὄνομα αὐτοῦ   name of him)

1:13   ποιεῖ αὐτοὺς τέκνα   -- he makes them children

        βλέπουσι   -- they see

1:14   σὰρξ ἐγένετο   -- he (it) became (past tense, third singu-
                                          lar) flesh (What is the subject?)

        ἐσκήνωσεν   -- he (it) dwelt (tented) (past tense,
                                          third singular)

        βλέπω   -- I see (Identify the μεν ending.)

        δόξα, ἡ   -- glory

        πλήρης   -- full of (indeclinable here; used with
                                          the genitive)

        εἰρήνη, ἡ   -- peace

        ἀλήθεια, ἡ   -- truth

1:15   περί   -- concerning (preposition here with the
                                          genitive)

        τοῖς ἀνθρώποις   -- to the men (dative of indirect object)

        υἱός, ὁ   -- son

1:16   λέγω   -- I say

        ἐκ   -- from (preposition with the genitive)

        ἐντολή, ἡ   -- commandment (object relationship here)

1:17   Μωῦσῆς, έως, ὁ   -- Moses

        γράφω   -- I write (What is the person and number here?)

        γραφή, ἡ   -- writing, Scripture

        Ἰησοῦς Χριστός   -- Jesus Christ

1:18	μονογενής, ές	-- unique, only (only one of its kind) (an adjective with ὁ θεός)
	ἐστιν	-- he is (present, third singular of the verb εἰμί, I am)
	κόλπος, ου, ὁ	-- bosom, chest
	δεικνύει	-- he shows (displays), reveals
1:19	μαρτυρία, ας, ἡ	-- witness, testimony
	ὅτε	-- when
	ἀποστέλλω	-- I send, send out or away
	πρὸς αὐτόν	-- to him (πρός, preposition here with the accusative)
	οἱ Ἰουδαῖοι	-- the Jews
	ἐξ Ἰεροσολύμων	-- out of, from Jerusalem (ἐκ before vowels is ἐξ)
	ἱερεῖς καὶ Λευίτας	-- priests and Levites (accusative objects)
	ἵνα ἐρωτήσωσιν	-- in order that they might ask (In verse 25 translate the form there, they asked.)
	Σὺ τίς εἶ;	-- You, who are you? (Σύ, you, is emphatic since the idea of "you" is carried also in the verb form εἶ, which in form is the present indicative, second singular of εἰμί, I am.)
1:20	ὁμολογέω	-- I confess, declare, say plainly
	ὅτι	-- This word here need not be translated, as it just introduces a direct quotation. (Compare quotation marks in English.)
	ἐγώ	-- I
	εἰμί	-- I am (present indicative, first person singular)
1:21	ἐρωτάω	-- I ask (a question), request
	Τί οὖν	-- What then?
	Ἡλίας, ου, ὁ	-- Elias (Elijah)
	προφήτης, ου, ὁ	-- prophet (masculine gender, first declension noun)
	ἀπεκρίθη	-- he answered (past tense passive, third singular of the deponent verb, ἀποκρίνομαι)

1:22	δεῖ	-- it is necessary (that or for) (impersonal verb, present indicative, 3rd singular)
	γινώσκειν	-- to know (present, active, infinitive)
	περὶ σεαυτοῦ	-- concerning yourself. (Preposition with the genitive)
1:23	φωνή, ἡ	-- voice
	ἐν	-- in, among, with, etc. (preposition with the dative)
	ἔρημος, ἡ	-- desert (Both this and the next word are feminine nouns of the 2nd declension; there are just a few of these.)
	ὁδός, ἡ	-- way
	κύριος, ὁ	-- Lord
	καθώς	-- just as
	εἶπεν	-- he said (past tense, λέγω)
	Ἠσαΐας	-- Isaiah
1:24	οἱ Φαρισαῖοι	-- the Pharisees
	ἀπέστειλαν	-- they sent (past tense, 3rd plural, ἀποστέλλω)
	αὐτούς	-- them (accusative, plural object)
1:25	τί	-- why (sometimes, in context, it means what)
	βαπτίζω	-- I baptize
	εἰ	-- if
	οὐδέ	-- nor (conjunction)
1:26	ἀπεκρίθη	-- he answered them
	ὕδωρ, τό	-- water (dative singular, ὕδατι)
	μέσος ὑμῶν	-- in the midst of you
	στήκει ὅν	-- there stands one whom (ὅν means, one whom)
	ὑμεῖς	-- you (nominative plural)
1:27	ἄξιος	-- worthy (adjective, nominative singular after the verb, to be)

1:27	ἵνα λύσω	-- that I might loose
	ἱμάς, ὁ	-- leather strap, thong, latchet (of a sandal) (ἱμάντα, accusative singular third declension noun; object of the verb)
	ὑπόδημα, τό	-- sandal, sole bound to the foot (ὑποδήματος, genitive singular of a third declension noun)
1:28	ταῦτα	-- these things
	Βηθανία, ἡ	-- Bethany
	γίνεται	-- they came about (historical present, third singular. A neuter plural subject, like ταῦτα, may take a singular verb.)
	πέραν	-- on the other side, across (preposition with the genitive)
	Ἰορδάνης, ου, ὁ	-- Jordan
	ὅπου	-- where (adverb)
1:29	τῇ ἐπαύριον	-- on the next day
	ὡς	-- as (adverb)
	ἴδε	-- Look! See! Listen!
	ἀμνός, ὁ	-- lamb
	αἴρω	-- I take up (and away)
	ἁμαρτία, ας, ἡ	-- sin (failure; earlier it meant, "missing the mark")
1:30	ὑπὲρ οὗ	-- in the behalf of whom
	εἶπον	-- I said (past tense)
	ὀπίσω μου	-- after (preposition with the genitive)
	ἀνήρ, ὁ	-- man, husband
	πρῶτός μου	-- before me
1:31	κἀγώ	-- and I (crasis; a coalescing of καί and ἐγώ)
	οὐκ ἔγνων	-- I did not know (past tense first singular of γινώσκω)
	ἀλλά	-- but (conjunction; the second α of ἀλλά is elided because the word following it begins with a vowel)

1:31 &ἐμαρτύρησα   -- I witnessed (past tense, 1st singular
                              of μαρτυρέω)

     Ἰσραήλ   -- Israel

     διὰ τοῦτο   -- on account of this

     ἦλθον   -- I came (past tense, 1st singular of
                              ἔρχομαι)

1:32 ὅτι   -- do not translate here; it introduces a
                              direct quotation

     θεάομαι   -- I saw (historical present, deponent)

     πνεῦμα, τό   -- spirit, wind

     καταβαῖνον   -- descending

     περιστερά, ἡ   -- dove

     οὐρανός, ὁ   -- heaven

     μένω   -- I remain

     ἐπ' αὐτόν   -- (up)on him (ἐπί, preposition with the
                              accusative)

1:33 πέμπει με   -- he sent me (historical present)

     βαπτίζω   -- I baptize

     μοι   -- to me

     μέλλω   -- I am about to (with infinitive)

     μένω   -- I remain

     ἐν πνεύματι ἁγίῳ   -- with the Holy Spirit

1:34 μαρτυρῶ   -- I witness, am witnessing

     ὅτι   -- that

1:35 τῇ ἐπαύριον   -- on the next day

     πάλιν   -- again (adverb)

     στήκω   -- I stand

     μαθητής, ὁ   -- disciple

     αὐτοῦ   -- of him, his

     δύο   -- two

1:36	ἐμβλέπω	-- I look on (with the dative case following the verb) (historical present)
1:37	ἀκούω	-- I hear
	ἀκολουθέω	-- I follow (with the dative case after the verb: I follow him, etc.)
1:38	στρέφω	-- I turn
	δέ	-- but, and (conjunction)
	αὐτοῖς	-- to them (dative plural of the personal pronoun, αὐτός, etc., he, she, it, they)
	τί	-- what?
	ζητέω	-- I seek
	οἱ δέ	-- and they (οἱ with the conjunction δέ has the force of the pronoun, they.)
	εἶπον	-- they said (Also this form could mean, I said; what the form means in each case is determined by the context.)
	Ῥαββί	-- Rabbi, Master
	μεθερμηνεύω	-- I interpret, translate (The form here is present passive, third singular, It is interpreted, translated.)
	διδάσκαλος, ὁ	-- teacher
	ποῦ	-- where? (interrogative)
1:39	ἔρχεσθε	-- (you) come (plural)
	παρ' αὐτῷ	-- with him (preposition; with the dative it means, with, being by the side of)
	τὴν ἡμέραν ἐκείνην	-- for that day (accusative of extension of time)
	ὥρα, ἡ	-- hour
	ὡς δεκάτη	-- about ten
1:40	Ἀνδρέας, ὁ	-- Andrew
	Σίμων, ὁ	-- Simon
	Πέτρος, ὁ	-- Peter (rock)
	εἷς	-- one (numeral)

1:41   εὑρίσκω   -- I find (historical present here)

       πρῶτον   -- first (used as an adverb here)

       ὧδε   -- here (adverb of place)

       Μεσσίας, ὁ   -- Messiah

1:42   φέρω   -- I bring, bear

       πρός   -- to (preposition with the accusative)

       ἐνέβλεψε   -- he looked on (him, understood) (past tense, third singular of ἐμβλέπω)

       κληθήσῃ   -- you shall be called (future passive, second person singular of καλέω, I call)

       Κηφᾶς, ὁ   -- Cephas (rock)

1:43   ἐξέρχεται   -- he goes out (historical present, third singular)

       εἰς   -- into, to, unto (preposition with the accusative)

       Φίλιππος, ὁ   -- Philip

       ἀκολούθει μοι   -- (you, singular) follow me (present active imperative)

1:44   ἀπό   -- from (preposition with the genitive)

       Βηθσαϊδά   -- Bethsaida (a city in the vicinity of the Sea of Galilee)

       ἐκ   -- out of, from (preposition with the genitive)

1:45   Ναθαναήλ, ὁ   -- Nathanael

       ἔγραψεν   -- he wrote (past tense, third person singular of γράφω, I write)

       νόμος, ὁ   -- law

       εὑρήκαμεν   -- we have found (perfect tense, first person plural of εὑρίσκω, I find)

       'Ιωσήφ, ὁ   -- Joseph

       Ναζαρέτ   -- Nazareth

1:46	τι ἀγαθόν ἐστιν;	-- Is there anything good?
	Ἔρχου καὶ ἴδε	-- (You, singular) come and see.
1:47	ὡς	-- as
	περί	-- concerning (preposition with the genitive)
	ἴδε	-- behold, lo, see (an interjection)
	ἀληθῶς	-- truly (adverb, with an --ως ending)
	Ἰσραηλίτης, ὁ	-- Israelite
	δόλος, ὁ	-- cunning, deceit, treachery
1:48	πόθεν	-- whence, from where? (interrogative adverb)
	συκῆ, ῆς, ἡ	-- fig tree
	ἐφώνησε	-- he called (past tense, third singular of φωνέω, I call)
	τότε	-- then (adverb)
	ἔβλεψα	-- I saw (past tense, first singular of βλέπω)
1:49	βασιλεύς, ὁ	-- king
1:50	Ὅτι	-- because (Here; sometimes it means, that; the context determines the meaning.)
	ὑποκάτω	-- below, under (preposition with the genitive)
	πιστεύω	-- I believe
	μείζονα	-- greater things (neuter accusative plural)
	βλέψεις	-- you will see (future, second singular)
1:51	ἀμήν	-- truly, of a truth, verily (with λέγω, I tell you the truth.)
	ἀνοίξει	-- it will open (future, third singular, ἀνοίγω)
	ἄγγελος, ὁ	-- angel, messenger
	ἀναβήσονται καὶ καταβήσονται	-- they will go up and down (future middle deponent [middle or passive forms with an active meaning], third plural of ἀναβαίνω and καταβαίνω)

1:51	ἐπί	-- on (preposition with the accusative means on or upon; it takes other cases)
	ταῦτα	-- these things
	βλέψετε	-- you shall see

GREEK READER NOTES--JOHN 2

2:1	τῇ ἡμέρᾳ τῇ τρίτῃ	-- on the third day; dative of time when (the Greek does not have a preposition in such a situation)
	γάμος, ὁ	-- wedding
	ἐγένετο	-- (there) came to be, came about
	Κανά	-- Cana
	μήτηρ, ἡ	-- mother
	ἐκεῖ	-- there (an adverb)
2:2	καλέω	-- I call (οὗσι--3rd plural)
	δέ	-- but, and
	εἰς	-- preposition with the accusative--unto
2:3	οἶνος, ὁ	-- wine (often of the grape)(among the Greeks, customarily mixed with water); see Liddell and Scott.
	ὑστερέω	-- I am lacking, fall short
2:4	πῶς	-- how (interrogative)
	μετέχω	-- I share, partake of (with the genitive of the thing shared, τούτου)
	γύναι	-- vocative singular of γυνή, ἡ--woman (in the vocative, often as a term of respect or affection, mistress, lady)
	οὔπω	-- not yet (an adverb)
	ἥκω	-- I come, am present
	ὥρα	-- hour
2:5	διάκονος, ὁ	-- servant, deacon
	τί	-- what
	ποιήσατε	-- you (plural) do (it) (imperative)

2:6	ἦσαν	-- they (there) were (past tense, third plural)
	λίθινος	-- made of stone
	ὑδρία, ἡ	-- water pot, pitcher, vessel
	ἔξ	-- six
	κατά	-- according to (preposition with the accusative here)
	καθαρισμός, ὁ	-- purification, cleansing
	χωρέω	-- I hold, contain
	ἀνά	-- up to
	μετρητής, ὁ	-- measure (about nine gallons)
	δύο	-- two
	ἤ	-- or
	τρεῖς	-- three
2:7	Γεμίσατε	-- fill up (imperative, second plural, γεμίζω)
	ὕδατος	-- with water (genitive singular of ὕδωρ. Verbs of filling take the genitive of the thing with which something is filled.)
	ἔως ἄνω	-- up to the top (an adverbial expression)
2:8	ἀντλήσατε	-- draw (imperative, second plural of ἀντλέω)
	ἀρχιτρίκλινος, ὁ	-- head or chief of the feast (τρίκλινος means "three couches" or, "a dining room with three couches." So the ἄρχων would be the ruler or head of the dining room activities, the maître d' hôtel.)
2:9	γεύεται	-- he tasted (tastes) (present middle and passive, deponent, third singular)
	πρότερον	-- formerly, before (adverb)
	ἐγίνωσκε	-- he was not knowledgeable (past tense, third singular, continuous action)
	πόθεν	-- from where? whence?
	διάκονος, ὁ	-- servant, deacon
	ἐγίνωσκον	-- they were knowledgeable (they had a continuing knowledge) (past tense, third plural, continuous action)

ὅτι	-- because (sometimes ὅτι means that; the context determines the meaning)
ἤντλησαν	-- they drew (past tense, 3rd plural)
φωνεῖ	-- he called (calls)
νυμφίος, ου, ὁ	-- bridegroom
2:10 μεθύσκω	-- to make drunk; passive as here, they drink freely or get drunk.
τότε	-- then (adverb)
ἐλάσσω	-- less, worse (comparative adjective)
τηρεῖς	-- you keep (are keeping)
ἕως ἄρτι	-- until now (adverbial expression)
2:11 ποιεῖ	-- he did (does)
ἀρχή, ἡ	-- beginning
σημεῖον, τό	-- sign
φανεροῖ	-- he manifested, showed (historical present)
ἐπίστευον	-- they were believing (past tense continuous, third plural). πιστεύω εἰς means, I believe on (or, in).
2:12 μετὰ τοῦτο	-- after this
καταβαίνω	-- I come down
Καφαρναούμ	-- Capernaum
αὐτός	-- he
ἐκεῖ	-- there (adverb)
πολλάς	-- many (feminine accusative plural). It agrees with the feminine noun, ἡμέρας.
2:13 ἐγγύς	-- near
πάσχα, τό	-- Passover
ἀναβαίνω	-- I go up
2:14 ἱερόν, οῦ, τό	-- temple, temple courts
πωλέω	-- I sell; ἐπώλουν -- they were selling (imperfect past tense, active, 3rd plural)
βοῦς, ὁ, ἡ	-- bull, ox, cow; βόας, accusative plural
πρόβατον, τό	-- sheep

2:14	περιστερά, ἡ	-- dove, pigeon
	κερματιστής, ὁ	-- money changer (κέρμα, small coin, small change)
2:15	ποιέω	-- I make, do
	φραγέλλιον, τό	-- whip
	σχοινίον, τό	-- rope, cord
	πάντας	-- all (individuals; masculine accusative plural)
	ἐκβάλλω	-- I cast out
	κολλυβιστής, ὁ	-- money changer (κόλλυβος, a small coin or, rate of exchange)
	ἐκχέω	-- I pour out
	κέρμα, τό	-- small change, money
	τράπεζα, ἡ	-- table
	ἀνατρέπω	-- I turn (up and) over
2:16	ἄρατε	-- take up (aorist imperative, second plural of αἴρω)
	ταῦτα	-- these things
	ἐντεῦθεν	-- from here (adverb)
	μὴ ποιεῖτε	-- do not be making (present imperative, second plural with the negative, μή)
	ἐμπόριον, τό	-- trading place, mart, merchandise place
2:17	μιμνῄσκονται	-- they remembered (historical present, middle and passive deponent)
	ζῆλος, ὁ	-- zeal
	κατεσθίω	-- I eat up
2:18	ἀπεκρίθησαν	-- they answered (past tense, passive, deponent, third person plural)
	οὖν	-- therefore, then
	τί	-- what
	σημεῖον, τό	-- sign, miraculous sign, miracle
	δείκνυμι (δεικνύω)	-- I show

2:19	ναός, ὁ	-- temple, the temple building itself
	τρισίν	-- three (dative plural)
2:20	τεσσαράκοντα καὶ ἕξ	-- forty-six (forty and six)
	οἰκοδομέω	-- I build. This is the present passive 3rd singular here.
2:21	ἔλεγεν	-- imperfect active indicative, 3rd singular of λέγω. How would you translate this?
	περί	-- with the genitive--concerning
	τοῦ σώματος	-- of the body
2:22	ὅτε	-- when
	ἠγέρθη	-- he was raised
	νεκρός	-- dead
	ἐμνήσθησαν	-- they remembered (past tense passive, 3rd plural. See 2:17).
	ἐπίστευον τῇ γραφῇ	-- they were believing the Scripture (this is different from believing on [εἰς] a person).
2:23	Ὡς	-- when (this word also means, "as" or "about," sometimes)
	ἑορτή, ἡ	-- feast
	θεωρέω	-- I behold, view; how do you translate the imperfect, active, indicative, 3rd plural, ἐθεώρουν, here?
2:24	οὐκ ἐπίστευεν ἑαυτόν	-- he was not entrusting himself
2:25	οὐκ ἔδει	-- "it was not necessary for" --- δεῖ is an impersonal verb.
	μαρτυρεῖν	-- to witness, bear witness--What does περί with the genitive mean? See 2:21.
	γάρ	-- for, indeed (conjunctive particle)
	ἐγίνωσκεν	-- is imperfect -- "He continually knew."
	τί	-- what
	τῷ ἀνθρώπῳ	-- the article here is used to emphasize man as the generic man, mankind.

3:1	Φαρισαῖος	-- Pharisee (member of one of the important religious parties of the Jews)
	Νικόδημος, ὁ	-- Nicodemos (an important Jewish ruler)
	ὄνομα, τό	-- name
3:2	μετά	-- after (with the accusative)
	'Ραββί	-- Master, my Master (a recognized Jewish leader and teacher)
	διδάσκαλος, ὁ	-- teacher
	σημεῖον, τό	-- sign, miraculous sign, miracle
	ποιέω	-- I do, make
	δεῖ	-- it is necessary (for) (an impersonal verb "taking" an accusative subject and an infinitive; here τὸν θεὸν εἶναι, "for God to be")
	ἤ	-- or (a particle; distinguish from ἡ, the)
	δύναμαι	-- I am able (a deponent verb "taking" an infinitive; here ποιεῖν, "to do")
3:3	δεῖ	-- (see 3:2)
	γεννηθῆναι	-- to be born (passive infinitive form from γεννάω)
	ἄνωθεν	-- from above, again (adverb)
	ἰδεῖν	-- to see (second aorist infinitive from εἶδον, ὁράω)
3:4	πῶς	-- how? (interrogative particle)
	γέρων, ὁ	-- old man
	μή	-- not (negative adverb; at the beginning of a question it expects a negative answer; He is not able....is he? οὐ at the beginning of a question expects a positive answer; He is able....isn't he?)
	κοιλία, ἡ	-- belly, bowels, hollow, womb
	μήτηρ, μητρός, ἡ	-- mother
	δεύτερον	-- second time
	εἰσελθεῖν	-- to enter into (second aorist infinitive of εἰσέρχομαι)

3:5   ἐξ ὕδατος (gen.) καὶ   -- of or from (the source of) water, even
        πνεύματος (gen.)   the Spirit

        πνεῦμα, τό   -- Spirit, wind

        ἤ   -- or

3:6   γένεσις, ἡ   -- birth

        σάρξ, ἡ   -- flesh (human nature and/or man's sinful
                               nature; such is the use with reference
                               to man in the N.T.)

        ἐκ τῆς σαρκός   -- from (the source of) the flesh

3:7   θαυμάζω   -- marvel, wonder

3:8   πνέω   -- blow

        ὅπου   -- where (adverb)

        θέλω   -- I will, wish, desire

        πόθεν   -- from where, whence (interrogative adverb)

        ποῦ   -- where (interrogative adverb)

        πορεύομαι   -- I go

        οὕτως   -- thus (adverb)

        πᾶς ἄνθρωπος   -- every man

        ὁ γεννηθείς   -- the one (the man) who was (or has been
                               born)

3:9   πῶς   -- how? (interrogative adverb)

3:10   Σύ   -- is emphatic

3:11   ἑωράκαμεν   -- we have seen (perfect tense of the verb,
                               from ὁράω, I see)

        μαρτυρέω   -- I witness, bear witness (present active
                                 indicative, first plural form here; compare
                               μαρτυρία)

3:12   τὰ ἐπίγεια   -- the earthly things (γῆ--earth; ἐπί--upon);
                                ἐπίγεια (neuter), things upon the earth

3:13   ἄνθρωπος   -- translate, "man," not "a man" here

        ἀναβαίνω   -- I go up

	καταβαίνω	-- I come (go) down
3:14	καθώς	-- just as
	Μωῦσῆς	-- Moses
	ὕψωσεν	-- he lifted up (aorist active indicative, third singular of ὑψόω)
	ὄφις, εως, ὁ	-- serpent, snake
	ὑψωθῆναι	-- to be lifted up (aorist passive infinitive, used with the impersonal verb, δεῖ, it is necessary)
3:15	ἕξουσι	-- they will have (future active indicative, third plural of ἔχω)
	αἰώνιος, ον	-- (adjective) eternal
3:16	οὕτως	-- thus
	ἠγάπησεν	-- (he) loved (aorist active indicative, third singular of ἀγαπάω)
	κόσμος, ὁ	-- world
	ὥστε	-- that, so that, to the end that
	ἔδωκεν	-- he gave (aorist active indicative, third singular of δίδωμι)
	μονογενής, ές	-- only one of its kind, unique
	πιστεύω εἰς	-- I believe on or in
	οὖν	-- therefore
	ἀπολλύονται	-- they are perishing, are being lost
3:17	ἀπέστειλεν	-- (he) sent (aorist active indicative, third singular of ἀποστέλλω)
	κρῖναι	-- to judge (past tense active infinitive of κρίνω)
	σωθῆναι	-- to be saved (past tense passive infinitive of σῴζω)
3:18	εἷς μὲν ἄνθρωπος	-- one man on the one hand (εἷς means "one"; compare εἰς, "unto")
	ἕτερος δέ	-- but another one (of a different kind) on the other hand
	ἤδη	-- already

	κέκριται	-- he stands judged (perfect passive indicative, third singular of κρίνω)
	μή	-- not
	πεπίστευκεν	-- he has believed (perfect active indicative, third singular of πιστεύω)
	ὄνομα, τό	-- name
	μονογενοῦς	-- unique (genitive singular of μονογενής)
3:19	κρίσις	-- judgment
	μᾶλλον ἤ	-- rather than
	σκότος, τό	-- darkness
	πονηρός, ά, όν	-- evil, wicked
	ἔργον, τό	-- work, deed (Observe in this verse the application of the Greek grammatical principle that a neuter plural subject may take a singular verb.)
3:20	τινές	-- some (people) (enclitic pronoun and adjective)
	φαῦλος, η, ον	-- bad, mean, worthless
	πράσσω	-- I practice
	μισέω	-- I hate
	θέλω	-- I wish, desire
	ἐλεγχθῆναι	-- to be reproved (aorist passive infinitive of ἐλέγχω)
3:21	ποιέω	-- I do, make
	ἀλήθεια, ἡ	-- truth
	φανερωθῆναι	-- to be manifested, be made known (aorist passive infinitive of φανερόω)
	ἐργάζομαι	-- I work, perform
3:22	Ἰουδαῖος, α, ον	-- a Jew, Jewish, Judean
	γῆ, γῆς, ἡ	-- land, earth, region, soil
	διατρίβω	-- I spend time, remain, stay
3:23	Αἰνών, ἡ	-- Aenon (Springs) (A place near Salem, on the west side of the Jordan River. The site is uncertain.)
	ἐγγύς	-- near, close to (with the genitive)

3:23 Σαλείμ

-- Salem (a city near Aenon, possibly the Salim about 8 miles south of Beisan (Bethshan--Scythopolis) or a Salim east of Nablus (cf. Gen. 14:18b)

παραγίνομαι

-- (deponent) I come (what is the tense used here?)

3:24 ούπω

-- not yet (an adverb)

γάρ

-- indeed, for

ἐβέβλητο

-- he had been cast, thrown (pluperfect passive indicative, 3rd singular, βάλλω)

φυλακή, ἡ

-- watch, guard, prison

3:25 ἐγένετο

-- there came to be, or about (aorist middle indicative, 3rd singular, γίνομαι, deponent)

ζήτησις, ἡ

-- questioning

καθαρισμός, ὁ

-- purification, cleansing

3:26 'Ραββί

-- Rabbi, Master

πέραν

-- across (with genitive here)

μαρτυρέω

-- I bear witness

ίδε

-- behold

πάντες (nom., plural, πᾶς) -- all (men, people)

3:27 μόνον

-- only (adverbial use)

δίδοται

-- is (here, are) given (present passive indicative, third singular, δίδωμι)

δῶρον, ου, τό (δῶρα, nominative plural)

-- gift

λαμβάνειν

-- to receive (pres., act., infin.)

3:28 ἀπεστάλην

-- I was sent (aor., pass., ind., 1 sing., ἀποστέλλω)

ἔμπροσθεν

-- (adverb, with the gen. here) before

3:29 νυμφίος, ὁ

-- bridegroom

νύμφη, ἡ

-- bride

φίλος, ὁ

-- friend

στήκω

-- I stand

3:29	ἀκούει	-- he hears (This verb takes a genitive object here.)
	χαρά, ἡ	-- joy
	χαίρω	-- I rejoice
	οὖν	-- therefore, then (inferential particle)
	ἐμός, ἡ, όν	-- my (possessive adjective)
	πληρόω	-- I fill, fulfill; passive, be full
3:30	δεῖ	-- it is necessary (impersonal verb)
	αὐξάνω	-- I grow, increase
	ἐλαττόω	-- I make less; passive, become smaller
3:31	ἄνωθεν	-- from above, again (adverb)
	ἐπάνω	-- above (preposition with the genitive here)
	λαλέω	-- I speak
3:32	εἶδον	-- I saw (second aorist active indicative of ὁράω)
	μαρτυρία, ἡ	-- witness
3:33	τινὲς δέ	-- but some (in contrast to men who did not receive the witness; τινές, an indefinite enclitic pronoun and adjective)
	σφραγίζω	-- I set a seal upon, accredit
	ἀληθής, ές	-- true, truthful, genuine (adjective)
3:34	ῥῆμα, τό	-- word, what is said
	μέτρον, τό	-- measure
	δίδωσιν	-- he gives (present active indicative, third singular of δίδωμι)
	πνεῦμα, τό	-- spirit, wind
3:35	πατήρ, ὁ	-- father
	ἀγαπάω	-- I love
	δέδωκεν	-- he has given (perfect active indicative, third singular of δίδωμι)
	χείρ, ἡ	-- hand (χειρί is dative singular)

3:36 οἱ μὲν...οἱ δέ   -- some (on the one hand) but some (on
                               the other hand)

     πιστεύω εἰς   -- I believe in (or, on)

     ζωή, ἡ   -- life

     αἰώνιος, -ον   -- eternal, everlasting

     ἀπειθέω   -- I disobey (this verb takes a dative object
                               or complement)

     ὄψονται   -- they shall see (fut. mid. deponent ind. 3
                               plural, ὁράω)

     ὀργή, ἡ   -- wrath

     μένω   -- I remain, abide, stay

     ἐπί   -- upon, on

GREEK READER NOTES--JOHN 4

4:1 ὡς   -- when

     οὖν   -- therefore

     ἔγνω   -- he knew (second aorist active
                               indicative, 3rd singular, γινώσκω)

     πλείονας   -- more (accusative plural); modifies μαθητάς;
                               πλείονας goes with ἤ and means "more...than")

4:2 ἐβάπτιζεν   -- notice the force of the imperfect of
                               βαπτίζω (baptize) here.

4:3 πάλιν   -- again (adverb)

4:4 ἔδει   -- it was necessary (imperfect, act., ind.,
                               3rd sing., impersonal of δεῖ); this verb
                               takes the inf. (here διέρχεσθαι--to go
                               through)

     αὐτὸν διέρχεσθαι   -- for him to go through (αὐτόν, here, is the
                               subject accusative with the infinitive)

4:5 πόλιν   -- city (accus. of πόλις)

     Σαμαρεία   -- Samaria

     ἐλέγετο   -- it was called

     Συχάρ   -- Sychar

     πλησίον   -- near

     χωρίον, τό   -- piece of ground, place

4:5	ἐδεδώκει	— (he) had given (pluperfect active indicative, third singular, δίδωμι, give)
	Ἰακώβ, ὁ	— Jacob (James)
	Ἰωσήφ, ὁ	— Joseph
4:6	ἐκεῖ	— there (adverb)
	πηγή, ἡ	— well, spring
	κοπιάω	— I toil, am tired, grow weary
	ὁδοιπορία, ἡ	— journey, day's journey
	καθέζομαι	— I set myself down, sit down (Note the imperfect. How would you translate it?)
	οὕτως	— thus (adverb)
	ἐπί	— on, at (preposition here with the dative)
	ὡς	— about (adverb)
	ἕκτος, η, ον	— sixth (12 o'clock if Jewish reckoning is employed)
4:7	γυνή, ἡ	— woman
	ἀντλῆσαι	— to draw (aorist active infinitive of ἀντλέω)
	ὕδωρ, ὕδατος, τό	— water (As a neuter noun the nominative and accusative forms ὕδωρ are the same.)
	δώσεις	— Will you give? (future active indicative, second singular of δίδωμι)
4:8	γάρ	— for
	πρότερον	— earlier, before (adverb)
	τροφή, ἡ	— nourishment, food
	ἀγοράζω	— I am in the ἀγορά (marketplace), buy, sell (Note the imperfect.)
4:9	πῶς	— how (is it)? (interrogative particle)
	πόσις, πόσεως, ἡ	— drink, a drinking
	αἰτέω	— I ask
	παρά	— from (preposition with the genitive here)
	συγχράομαι	— I associate on friendly terms; use dishes in common (with someone else)

4:10	δωρεά, ᾶς, ἡ	-- gift, present
	ᾔτησα	-- I asked (aorist active indicative, first person singular of αἰτέω)
	καί	-- How should this be translated here?
	ἔδωκεν ἄν	-- he would (ἄν) have given
	αὐτό	-- To what does this neuter pronoun refer?
4:11	Κύριε	-- Here in this context the meaning is, Sir (with a tone of respect).
	ἄντλημα, ατος, τό	-- bucket, vessel (for drawing water)
	φρέαρ, ατος, τό	-- well, pit shaft, cistern, reservoir
	βαθύς, βαθεῖα, βαθύ	-- deep
	πόθεν	-- from where? where? how? why? (interrogative adverb)
4:12	μή	-- not (Before a question this adverb expects a negative response, "You are not....are you?)
	μείζων, ον	-- greater than (with a following genitive)
	πατήρ, πατρός, ὁ	-- father
	ἔδωκεν	-- he gave (aorist active indicative, third person singular of δίδωμι)
	τὸ φρέαρ	-- the well (Here this neuter noun, which has the same form in the accusative as the nominative, is the object of the verb.)
	ἔπιεν	-- he drank (second aorist active indicative, third singular of πίνω)
	θρέμμα, ατος, τό	-- domesticated animal (related to τρέφω, nourish); whatever is fed; plural, cattle, flocks
4:13	διψάω	-- I thirst (present active indicative, third plural, with the form διψῶσιν instead of having the ending -ουσιν)
	πάλιν	-- again, once more, back (adverb)
4:14	ὅτε	-- when (conjunction)
	τις, τι	-- someone, anyone (enclitic pronoun and adjective)
	πίνει	-- he (someone) drinks (present active indicative, third person singular of πίνω)

4:14	οὐ μὴ διψήσει	-- he shall not at all thirst (the double negative intensifies the negation)
	εἰς τὸν αἰῶνα	-- forever
	γενήσεται	-- (it) shall become (future middle, deponent, indicative, 3rd singular, γίνομαι)
	πηγή, ἡ	-- well
	ἅλλεται	-- (it) springs (bounds) up (present middle-passive, deponent, indicative, ἅλλομαι)
	αἰώνιον	-- eternal
4:15	θέλω	-- I wish, desire
	τότε	-- then
	γάρ	-- for, indeed (conjunction, particle)
	διελεύσομαι	-- I will come (future middle deponent, διέρχομαι)
	ἐνθάδε	-- here (adverb)
	ἀντλέω	-- I draw (note the future tense)
4:16	ἔνεγκον	-- (you, sing.) bring (2 aor., act., imperative, 2 sing. of φέρω)
	ἀνήρ, ἀνδρός, ἀνδρί, ἄνδρα, ὁ	-- man (as opposed to woman, youth), husband
4:17	καλῶς	-- well (adverb)
4:18	πέντε	-- five
	ἔσχες	-- you (sing.) had (2 aor., act., indic., 2 sing. of ἔχω)
	νῦν	-- now (adverb)
	ἀληθής, ἀληθές	-- true (second declension adjective, ἀληθής for the masculine and feminine, and ἀληθές for the neuter)
4:19	θεωρῶ	-- I behold, observe, see
4:20	πατήρ, ὁ	-- father (3rd declension, masc.)
	ὄρος, ους, τό	-- mountain (3rd declen., neuter)
	προσκυνέω	-- worship
	ἐν Ἱεροσολύμοις	-- in Jerusalem (sometimes the names of cities are in the plural)
	τόπος, ὁ	-- place
	ὅπου	-- where (adverb)

4:20	δεῖ	-- it is necessary (pres., act., indic., 3 sing., impersonal verb. It takes the infinitive here προσκυνεῖν, to worship).
4:21	ἰδού	-- behold, remember, consider (demonstrative particle)
	οὔτε...οὔτε	-- neither...nor
4:22	ἄνευ	-- without (prep. with the genitive)
	ἀληθινός, ή, όν	-- true, real, genuine (adjective)
	γνῶσις, γνώσεως, ἡ	-- knowledge (3rd decl. fem.)
	σωτηρία, ας, ἡ	-- salvation
4:23	ἀλλά	-- but (conjunction; here the second α is not elided before ἔρχεται).
	νῦν	-- now (adverb)
	προσκυνητής, οῦ, ὁ	-- worshipper
	πνεῦμα, -ατος, τό	-- spirit (wind) (3rd declen. neuter)
	ἀλήθεια, ας, ἡ	-- truth
	τοιοῦτος, η, ον	-- of such (a quality)
	ζητέω	-- seek
	τοιούτους τοὺς προσ- κυνοῦντας	-- such who are worshipping (him) (note the present participle here)
4:25	γυνή, -αικός, ἡ	-- woman, lady (3rd declen., fem.)
	ὁ λεγόμενος	-- the one called (pres. participle)
	λαλέω	-- speak
	πάντα	-- all things
4:26	ὁ λαλῶν	-- the one speaking (present participle)
4:27	ἐπὶ τούτῳ	-- at this
	θαυμάζω	-- marvel, wonder (observe the imperfect tense)
	συνεχρᾶτο	-- he was having dealings or contact with (uses the dative)
	μέντοι	-- nevertheless, indeed (particle)
	τί ζητεῖς;	-- what do you seek?

4:27   ἤ   -- or

        τί λαλεῖς;   -- Why do you speak?

4:28   λείπω   -- I leave (ἔλιπον, second aorist)

        οὖν   -- therefore

        ὑδρία, ας, ἡ   -- water jar

        πόλις, πόλεως, ἡ   -- city (third declension noun, feminine)

4:29   Δεῦτε   -- Come! Come on! (adverb)

        βλέπω   -- I see

        μήτι   -- particle in questions which expect
                                   a negative answer (He is not....
                                   is he? etc.)

4:30   ἐξῆλθον   -- They went out (second aorist of
                                   ἐξέρχομαι)

        ἤρχοντο   -- This form is imperfect (Note the difference
                                   in the kind of action between these last
                                   two verbs.)

4:31   ἐν τῷ μεταξύ   -- in the meantime

        ἐρωτάω   -- I ask (the aorist tense here)

        'Ραββί   -- Master (term of honor for outstanding
                                   teachers)

        φάγῃ σύ;   -- Will you eat? (φάγῃ is an irregular future
                                   middle, deponent, second singular of ἐσθίω)

4:32   βρῶσις, βρώσεως, ἡ   -- food

        φαγεῖν   -- to eat (second aorist active infinitive
                                   of ἐσθίω)

4:33   πρὸς ἀλλήλους   -- to one another (reciprocal pronoun)

        μή   -- (a man) did not, did he? (a negative in
                                   questions expecting a negative answer)

        ἤνεγκεν   -- second aorist of φέρω (Parse this form.)

4:34   βρῶμα, ατος, τό   -- that which is eaten, food, meat

        θέλημα, ατος, τό   -- will

        πέμψαντος   -- Parse this participle.

        ποιήσω   -- future active of ποιέω, I do, make

4:34	τελειώσω	-- I will complete, accomplish (the future of τελειόω)
	ἔργον, τό	-- work
4:35	τετράμηνος, ου, ἡ	-- period of four months
	θερισμός, ὁ	-- harvest
	χώρα, ας, ἡ	-- land, field, region, country
	λευκός, ή, όν	-- white
4:36	ἤδη	-- already, now (adverb)
	θερίζω	-- I harvest, reap
	μισθός, ὁ	-- pay, wages
	συνάγω	-- I gather together
	καρπός, ὁ	-- fruit
	σπείρω	-- I sow (Notice the participial use here.)
	ὁμοῦ	-- together (adverb)
	χαίρω	-- I rejoice
4:37	ἀληθινός, ή, όν	-- true, real, genuine (adjective)
	ἄλλος, η, ο	-- another, other
4:38	ἀπέστειλα	-- I sent (first aorist active indicative of ἀποστέλλω)
	σπείραντες	-- having sown (aorist participle, masculine nominative plural of σπείρω)
	ἐκοπίασαν	-- they toiled, labored (aorist of κοπιάω)
	κόπος, ὁ	-- labor, toil
4:39	Σαμαρίτης, ου, ὁ	-- Samaritan
	πολλοί	-- many (masculine nominative plural)
	γυνή, γυναικός, ἡ	-- woman
	μαρτυρούσης	-- witnessing (present active participle, feminine genitive singular of μαρτυρέω)
	πάσης	-- all (feminine genitive singular of πᾶς)

4:40	ἠρώτησαν	-- they asked (a request) (aorist of ἐρωτάω)
	μεῖναι	-- to remain (aorist active infinitive of μένω)
	παρά	-- with (preposition with the dative here)
	ἔμεινεν	-- he remained (aorist active of μένω)
	ἐκεῖ	-- there, at that place (adverb)
4:41	ἔτι	-- still, yet, further (adverb)
4:42	τῇ γυναικί	-- to the woman (dative singular of ἡ γυνή)
	γάρ	-- for, indeed, then (conjunction)
	ἀληθῶς	-- truly (adverb) (compare ἀλήθεια, truth)
	σωτήρ, ῆρος, ὁ	-- savior
	κόσμος, ὁ	-- world
4:43	δύο	-- two
	ἐκεῖθεν	-- from there (adverb)
4:44	ἐμαρτύρησεν	-- he bore witness (aorist active of μαρτυρέω)
	ἴδιος, α, ον	-- one's own, personal (adjective)
	πατρίς, ίδος, ἡ	-- homeland, home town
	τιμή, ῆς, ἡ	-- honor
4:45	δέχομαι	-- I receive (deponent)
	ἰδόντες	-- having seen (second aorist participle of εἶδον [ὁράω])
	ἔργον, τό	-- work
	πάντα	-- all (neuter accusative plural of πᾶς)
	ἑορτή, ἡ	-- feast, festival
4:46	πάλιν	-- again (adverb)
	Κανά, ἡ	-- Cana (name of a city in Galilee)
	ὅπου	-- where (adverb)
	ἐποίησεν	-- he made (aorist active indicative of ποιέω)
	ὕδωρ, ὕδατος, τό	-- water
	οἶνος, ὁ	-- wine

4:46	βασιλικός, ή, όν	-- royal; as a noun, royal official
	κακῶς ἔχω	-- I am sick (I have it bad) (εἶχεν, imperfect active, third singular)
	Καφαρναούμ, ἡ	-- Capernaum
4:47	ἥκω	-- I have come, am present
	ἠρώτησεν	-- I ask (aorist active indicative of ἐρωτάω)
	κατέρχομαι	-- I come down (deponent)
	θεραπεύω	-- I heal
	ἀποθνῄσκω	-- I die
4:48	οὖν	-- therefore, then, thus
	σημεῖον, τό	-- sign, miraculous sign, miracle
	τέρας, ατος, τό	-- wonder, object of wonder, omen
4:49	παιδίον, τό	-- young child, infant, child
4:50	ἐθεραπεύθη	-- he has been healed (aorist passive indicative)
	πιστεύω	-- I believe (in something; using the dative)
	πορεύομαι	-- I go, depart (deponent)
4:51	ἤδη	-- now, already (adverb)
	καταβαίνω	-- I go down (the genitive absolute here, with the pronoun and the participle both in the genitive)
	ὑπήντησαν	-- they met (aorist active indicative of ὑπαντάω, with the dative)
	θεραπεύεται	-- he is healed (In an indirect quotation the Greek keeps the same tense of the direct quotation after a past main verb.)
4:52	ἐπύθετο	-- he inquired (aorist middle indicative deponent of πυνθάνομαι)
	παρά	-- from (preposition with the genitive here)
	ἴασις, εως, ἡ	-- healing
	ἐχθές	-- yesterday (adverb)
	ἕβδομος, η, ον	-- seventh

4:52	πυρετός, οῦ, ὁ	-- fever
4:53	ὅλος, η, ον	-- whole, entire, complete (adjective)
4:54	πάλιν	-- again (adverb)
	δεύτερος, α, ον	-- second

GREEK READER NOTES--JOHN 5

5:1	ἑορτή, ῆς, ἡ	-- feast, festival
	Ἱεροσόλυμα, τά and ἡ, and Ἱερουσαλήμ, ἡ	-- Jerusalem
5:2	προβατικός, ή, όν	-- pertaining to sheep
	κολυμβήθρα, ας, ἡ	-- pool
	ἐπιλέγω	-- I call, name (middle, I choose)
	Ἑβραϊστί	-- in Hebrew, or better, in Aramaic
	Βηθζαθά, ἡ	-- (indeclinable) Bethzatha (the name of the northern extension of Jerusalem)
	πέντε	-- five
	στοά, ᾶς, ἡ	-- (roofed) colonnade or cloister, portico
5:3	κατάκειμαι	-- I lie down
	πλῆθος, ους, τό	-- multitude
	ἀσθενέω	-- I am weak, powerless, sick (here the form is a participle)
	τυφλός, ή, όν	-- blind
	χωλός, ή, όν	-- lame
	ξηρός, ά, όν	-- dry, dried (up), withered, paralyzed
5:4	This verse is not in the best Greek manuscripts.	
5:5	τριάκοντα καὶ ὀκτώ	-- 38 (thirty and eight)
	ἔτος, ους, τό	-- year (ἔτη is the neuter accusative plural form for this noun.)
	ἀσθένεια, ας, ἡ	-- sickness, disease

5:6	μακρός, ά, όν	— long
	χρόνος, ου, ὁ	— time
	θεραπεύω	— I heal
5:7	ὁ ἀσθενῶν	— the sick one (man) (the present participle with the article, nominative, masculine, singular)
	ταράσσω	— I trouble, stir up (The aorist passive participle in a genitive absolute is used here.)
	ὕδωρ, ὕδατος, τό	— water
	ἄλλος, η, ο	— another, other
	καταβαίνω	— I come or go down
5:8	ἀναλήμφῃ	— you will take up (future middle, deponent, of ἀναλαμβάνω)
	κράβαττος (or κράβατος), ου, ὁ	— mattress, pallet (the poor man's bed)
	περιπατέω	— I walk; περιπατήσω, future active indicative
5:9	εὐθέως	— immediately (adverb)
	ὑγιής, ές	— healthy, sound
	ὑγιὴς γίνεται	— he gets well
	αἴρω	— I lift up, take up (ἦρον, second aorist)
	σάββατον, ου, τό	— Sabbath
5:10	θεραπευθέντι	— aorist passive participle, dative, masculine, singular of θεραπεύω, I heal
	οὐκ ἔξεστιν	— it is not lawful (with a dative and an infinitive; here, φέρειν, to bear, carry)
5:11	ποιέω	— I make, do
	ὑγιῆ	— healthy, well (accusative singular of ὑγιής)
5:12	ἠρώτησαν	— they asked (aorist active indicative of ἐρωτάω)
	τίς	— who (interrogative)

5:13   ἰαθείς   -- having been healed (aorist passive participle, masculine nominative singular of ἰάομαι)

       ἐξένευσεν   -- he withdrew (aorist active indicative)

       ὄχλου ὄντος   -- This is a genitive absolute.

       τόπος, ὁ   -- place, location, region

5:14   εὑρίσκω   -- I find

       ἱερόν, τό   -- temple

       θεραπεύῃ   -- you are healed (present passive indicative, second singular)

       οὐκέτι   -- no longer (adverb)

       ἁμαρτήσω   -- I will sin (future active indicative)
       χεῖρον   -- worse (thing) (comparative neuter)
       γενήσεται   -- it will come (future middle indicative)

5:15   θεραπεύσας   -- having healed (aorist active participle)

5:16   διώκω   -- I pursue, persecute

       ἐποίησεν   -- he did (aorist active indicative)

       σάββατον, τό   -- Sabbath

5:17   ὁ δέ   -- and he

       ἀποκρίνομαι   -- I answer (present middle-passive deponent)

       ἕως   -- until

       ἄρτι   -- now, at the present time (adverb)

       ἐργάζομαι   -- I work (deponent)

       κἀγώ (καί + ἐγώ)   -- and I

5:18   οὖν   -- therefore, then

       μᾶλλον   -- more (adverb)

       ἐζήτησαν   -- they sought (aorist active indicative)

       ἵνα   -- in order that (conjunction) (purpose clause with the subjunctive here)

       ἴσος, η, ον   -- equal, the same (takes the dative here, "equal to, or with, God")

5:19   ἀμήν   -- truly, verily (with λέγω, I tell you the truth)

       ἔργον, τό   -- work

       καθώς   -- just as, as (adverb)

5:20   φιλεῖ   -- he loves (present active indicative, third singular)

       δείκνυσιν   -- he shows, points out

       δείξει   -- he will show (future active indicative of δείκνυμι)

       μεγάλα ἔργα   -- great works

       θαυμάζω   -- I marvel, wonder

5:21   ὥσπερ   -- just as, even as

       ἐγείρω   -- I raise

       τοὺς νεκρούς   -- the dead (ones)

       ζωοποιεῖ   -- he makes alive

5:22   οὐδέ   -- neither

       οὐδένα   -- no one (Greek uses double negatives; we change the second one here to, anyone)

       κρίσις, εως, ἡ   -- judgment

       τὴν κρίσιν πᾶσαν   -- all judgment

5:23   πάντες   -- all (nominative masculine plural)

       τιμῶσι   -- they may honor (present active subjunctive with ἵνα. Notice that the second use of τιμῶσι in this verse is indicative, they honor.)

       καθώς   -- according to, just as

       πατήρ, ὁ   -- father (πατέρα, the accusative singular)

       ὁ τιμῶν   -- the one honoring (Observe the negative μή.)

       τιμᾷ   -- he honors (Observe the ᾳ instead of the ει in this contract verb, τιμάω.)

       πέμπω   -- I send (The aorist active participle of this verb is used here.)

5:24   ὁ....πιστεύων τῷ   -- the one believing the one who sent me
       πέμφαντί με   (Note that εἰς and the accusative are
                                  not used after πιστεύω here.)

       αἰώνιος, ον   -- eternal, unending

       θάνατος, ὁ   -- death

5:25   ζήσουσιν   -- they will live (future active indicative,
                                third plural of ζάω)

5:26   ὥσπερ   -- just as, as

       ἐν ἑαυτῷ   -- in himself

5:27   θέλημα, τό   -- will

5:28   ὅτε   -- when (conjunction)

       οἱ ἐν τοῖς μνημείοις -- the ones (those) in the tombs

5:29   ἐκπορεύομαι   -- I come out (deponent) (The future middle
                                indicative form is used here.)

       τὰ ἀγαθά   -- the good things

       οἱ ποιήσαντες   -- the ones having done (The aorist active
                                participle is used here.)

       ἀνάστασις, εως, ἡ   -- resurrection

       τὰ φαῦλα   -- bad (foul, evil) things

       οἱ πράξαντες   -- the ones who have practiced (The aorist
                                active participle is used again here.)

5:30   δύναμαι   -- I am able (deponent) (present middle
                                and passive, first singular)

       ποιεῖν   -- to do (present active infinitive of ποιέω)

       ἐξουσία, ας, ἡ   -- authority, right

       καθώς   -- just as

       κρίνω   -- I judge

       κρίσις, εως, ἡ   -- judgment, judging

       δίκαιος, α, ον   -- just, right (adjective)

       ζητέω   -- I seek

       θέλημα, τό   -- will, wish, desire

       πέμπω   -- I send (The aorist active participle is
                                used here.)

5:31   μαρτυρία, ας, ἡ   -- witness

         ἀλήθεια, ας, ἡ   -- truth

5:32   ἄλλος, η, ο   -- another, other

         μαρτυρέω   -- I bear witness

5:34   παρά   -- from (preposition with the genitive here)

         σωθῆτε   -- you might be saved (aorist passive subjunctive with ἵνα)

5:35   λύχνος, ὁ   -- lamp (a portable lamp requiring a lampstand on which to be set)

         καίω   -- I light, burn (passive, be lit, burn)

         φαίνω   -- I shine, give light, appear

         φῶς, φωτός, τό   -- light

5:36   μέγας, μεγάλη, μέγα   -- great (adjective)

         ἔδωκε   -- he gave (the κ aorist active indicative of δίδωμι)

         ἔργον, τό   -- work

         τελειώσω   -- I will complete, finish (future active indicative, first singular of τελειόω)

         πατήρ, πατρός, ὁ   -- father

         ἀπέστειλεν   -- he sent (This is the aorist active indicative, third singular of a liquid verb [ἀποστέλλω]. The liquid verb will be taken up in Lesson Thirty-one.)

5:37   περὶ ἐμοῦ   -- concerning me (preposition with the genitive. Notice here that περί is used with the emphatic form of the personal pronoun, ἐγώ.)

         οὔτε....οὔτε   -- neither....nor (adverb)

         πώποτε   -- ever, at any time (adverb)

         εἶδος, ους, τό   -- visible form, outward appearance (third declension σ-stem noun)

         εἴδετε   -- you (plural) have seen (second aorist active indicative, second plural of εἶδον from ὁράω)

5:38   μένοντα   -- What is the form of this participle of μένω?

         πιστεύω   -- with the dative this verb means, believe someone or something.

5:39	ἐραυνᾶτε	-- you (plural) search, examine (present active indicative of ἐραυνάω)
	τὰς γραφάς	-- the writings, Scriptures, here referring to the Old Testament
	δοκεῖτε	-- you (plural) think, suppose (from the verb, δοκέω)
	αἰώνιος, ον	-- eternal, unending, everlasting
	ἔχειν	-- to have (present active infinitive of ἔχω)
	μαρτυροῦσαι	-- witnessing (present active participle, feminine nominative plural of μαρτυρέω)
5:40	θέλω	-- I wish, want
	ἐλθεῖν	-- to come (second aorist active infinitive of ἔρχομαι)
	ἵνα	-- in order that (here a purpose clause; ἵνα uses the subjunctive.)
5:42	ἀγάπη, ἡ	-- love
5:43	ὄνομα, ατος, τό	-- name
	ἴδιος, α, ον	-- one's own, belonging to one (adjective)
	λήμψεσθε	-- you (plural) will receive (future middle, deponent, indicative, second person plural of λαμβάνω)
5:44	μόνος, η, ον	-- only, alone (adjective)
	ζητέω	-- I seek
5:45	κατηγορήσω	-- I will accuse, bring charges against (future active indicative, first singular of κατηγορέω)
	ἐλπίζω	-- I hope, have hope
5:47	εἰ	-- if (usually with the indicative)
	γράμμα, ατος, τό	-- writing, letter, Scripture
	πῶς	-- how? in what way? (interrogative particle)
	ῥῆμα, ατος, τό	-- word, what is said

PART II

LESSON PLANS FOR
THE INTERMEDIATE GREEK
STUDENT

INTERMEDIATE GREEK LESSON PLANS
(two lessons each week)

MNTG is an abbreviation for <u>Mastering New Testament Greek</u>, and D.M. for Dana and Mantey, <u>A Manual Grammar of the Greek New Testament</u>.[1] In the passages for translation in these lesson plans, the vocabulary words that are new to the student should be acquired as a part of the student's vocabulary, with the exception of infrequently used words.

FIRST WEEK

<u>Review</u> the three Greek declensions set forth in MNTG, Lessons three, six, fifteen, sixteen and eighteen.
<u>Translate</u> John 9:1-12.

SECOND WEEK

<u>Review</u> the λύω verb, indicative and subjunctive, given in MNTG, Lessons two, four, five, ten to thirteen and twenty-six.
<u>Translate</u> John 9:13-24.

THIRD WEEK

<u>Review</u> the λύω verb, participle, infinitive and imperative, set forth in MNTG, Lessons nineteen, twenty-one to twenty-five, twenty-eight and twenty-nine.
<u>Translate</u> John 9:24-34.
<u>Quiz</u> on the three declensions and the λύω verb.

FOURTH WEEK

<u>Review</u> the contract and liquid verbs given in MNTG, Lessons thirty and thirty-one.
<u>Translate</u> John 9:35-10:6.

FIFTH WEEK

<u>Review</u> the μι verbs given in MNTG, Lessons thirty-two to thirty-four.
<u>Translate</u> John 10:7-18.

SIXTH WEEK

<u>Translate</u> John 10:19-30.
<u>Review</u> for test.
<u>Test</u> over material covered in the first six weeks.

SEVENTH WEEK

<u>Study the relative clauses</u> and the uses of the nominative, vocative and accusative <u>cases</u>, set forth in MNTG, pages 89-90, and/or D.M., pages 270-273, 65-72, 91-92.
<u>Translate</u> John 10:31-42.

---

[1]For fuller references, see page 17, footnote 1.

EIGHTH WEEK

Study the functional uses of the genitive, ablative and dative cases.
MNTG, pages 91-92, and/or D.M., pages 72-75, 81-84.
Translate John 11:1-16.

NINTH WEEK

Study the types of New Testament Greek conditional sentences. MNTG, page 95,
and/or D.M., pages 286-291.
Translate John 11:17-37.

TENTH WEEK

Study the forms of the Greek comparative and superlative and their uses.
MNTG, pages 98-99.
Translate John 11:38-57.

ELEVENTH WEEK

Study the declension of Greek numerals and the basic elements in the Greek
coordinate and subordinate clauses. MNTG, pages 101-102.
Translate John 12:1-19.

TWELFTH WEEK

Translate John 12:20-43.
Parse 60 of the practice verbs included at the end of the lessons for the
Beginning Greek students. MNTG, pages 103-104.
Study the forms of the optative given in the chart in the appendix of MNTG,
page 178.

THIRTEENTH WEEK

Translate John 12:44-13:20.
Parse 60 more of the practice verbs included in MNTG.

FOURTEENTH WEEK

Translate John 13:21-35.
Parse 60 more of the practice verbs included in the MNTG.

FIFTEENTH WEEK

Translate John 14:1-14.
Review for the final examination.

PART III

LESSON PLANS

FOR THE

ADVANCED GREEK STUDENT

PART III

WEEKLY OUTLINE STUDY FOR ADVANCED GREEK

Advanced Greek:

A. This level of New Testament Greek study builds on the basic foundation of the materials studied in the Beginning and Intermediate Sections of this book.

B. This course in Advanced Greek meets several hours each week, with the following divisions of work:

1. One day a week will be devoted in general to the study of advanced Greek Grammar.
2. The other days will be spent in translating and exegeting, as there is opportunity, of a considerable portion of the Gospel of Luke.

C. The book, Mastering New Testament Greek, by W. H. Mare, and selected readings in A. T. Robertson, Dana and Mantey, R. W. Funk's A Beginning Intermediate Grammar of Hellenistic Greek, etc., are required reading. This is in addition to the translation from the Greek New Testament. At the end of the semester you will be required to indicate in writing that you have read the assigned materials.

D. The following are the symbols together with the authors and books they represent from which you are to accomplish your reading and study:

D.M. - Dana and Mantey, A Manual Grammar of the Greek New Testament (1923, 1955)
R.   - A. T. Robertson, A Grammar of the Greek New Testament in the Light of Historical Research (1931)
R.D. - A. T. Robertson and W. H. Davis, A New Short Grammar of the Greek Testament (1933)
B.D. - F. Blass and A. Debrunner, A Greek Grammar of the New Testament (1961)
S.   - H. W. Smyth, Greek Grammar (1963)
M.   - W. H. Mare, "New Testament Greek Syntax Chart" in Mastering New Testament Greek (1979)
F.   - R. W. Funk, A Beginning Intermediate Grammar of Hellenistic Greek (1973)

E. The basic text for translation and exegesis will be the Greek of the Gospel of Luke, c. forty verses a week.

F. Two hours of study for every hour of class are expected.

G. In the passages for translation in these lesson plans, the vocabulary words that are new to the student should be acquired as part of the student's vocabulary with the exception of infrequently used words.

H. The assignments week by week are as follows. (This schedule is an approximation. It will be followed as closely as possible.)

FIRST WEEK:

Introduction to Syntax
Funk Pt. II; 377-394

Cases
Funk Pt. I; 68-77

Translate: Luke 1:1-25

SECOND WEEK

Nominative and Vocative Cases and their Functions
M., Syntax Chart, 191.
D.M., 68-72; R., 456-466; R.D., 212-215; B.D., 79-82; S., 312-313; F., II 709-711.
Study Examples: Nominative

Matt. 16:18	Mark 8:2
Luke 19:2	Rom. 7:24
Acts 5:1	Matt. 15:22
John 13:13	Acts 1:1
1 Cor. 1:1	Matt. 1:20

Translate: Luke 1:26-56 and identify the appropriate functional uses of
the nominatives and vocatives in Luke 1:26-33.

THIRD WEEK

Study the Genitive case with its Genitive and Ablative functions from the
Syntax Chart: M., Syntax Chart 192f; D.M., 72-83; R., 491-520; R.D., 224-235;
B.D., 89-100; S., 313-332; F., II 711-717.

Look up in the following passages examples of the Genitive and Ablative and
their functions:

2 Cor. 5:14	Rom. 6:6	Mark 1:10
Phil. 4:7	Matt. 6:29	Luke 2:37
Mark 11:22	Luke 2:27	Matt. 10:31
Luke 24:10	Mark 9:28	
John 2:21	Eph. 2:12	

Translate: Luke 1:57-2:7, and identify pertinent genitival and ablatival
functions of the genitive case in Luke 1:76-2:7.

FOURTH WEEK

Study the Dative case in its associative, instrumental and locative
functions from the Syntax Chart: M., Syntax Chart 193; D.M., 86-91;
R., 520-535; R.D., 235-242; B.D., 103-109; S., 351-355, 346-351; F., II 720-723.

Look up in the following passages the examples of the locative and
instrumental functions of the dative case:

Mark 1:18	Eph. 2:3	John 21:8
Matt. 20:12	Gal. 2:13	Mark 14:12
Luke 7:38	Matt. 7:4	John 19:31
Luke 1:56	Luke 2:5	

Study the Dative case in its dative personal interest function from Syntax Chart:
M., Syntax Chart 194; D.M., 83-86; R., 535-543; R.D., 242-245; B.D., 100-103;
S., 337-346; F., II 718-720.

Look up in the following passages examples of the dative of personal interest:

        Matt. 7:6   Rom. 8:8
        Rev. 2:15-16   Matt. 11:29
        Phil. 1:21   Rom. 6:2
        Matt. 18:12

Translate Luke 2:8-52 and identify pertinent functions of the locative and
instrumental dative and the dative of personal interest in Luke 2:36-40; 48-52.

FIFTH WEEK

Study the accusative case and its functions from the Syntax Chart: M., Syntax
Chart 191; D.M., 91-95; R., 466-491; R.D., 215-224; B.D., 82-89; S., 353-365; F.,
II 724-726.

Look up in the following passages examples of the accusative case and identify:

        Luke 2:44   Luke 2:27
        Luke 15:29   Acts 18:25
        Matt. 2:10   John 15:15
        John 6:10   Gal. 5:2

Translate Luke 3:1-4:7 and identify pertinent functions of the accusative case
in Luke 4:1-6.

SIXTH WEEK

Study the introduction to the verb in F., II 419-426.

Study the examples of diagramming Greek sentences (see examples in the appendix,
pages 185-190).

Study the subject of the tense of the Greek verb: M., Syntax Chart 194; D.M., 176-
180; R., 821-829; R.D., 293-295; B.D., 166, 167; S., 412-421; F., II 611-612.

Study the present tense and its functions from the Syntax Chart: M., Syntax Chart
195; D.M., 181-186; R., 864-869; R.D., 297-300; B.D., 164-169; S., 421-423;
F., II 611-619.

Look up in the following passages functional uses of the present tense:

        Matt. 8:25   John 10:32   2 Cor. 5:1
        Luke 15:29   Acts 26:28   Matt. 6:2
        John 15:27   John 1:29
        Luke 18:12   Matt. 3:15

Translate Luke 4:8-5:11 and practice diagramming the sentences in Luke 5:1-2 and
identify the functional uses of the present tense in Luke 4:21, 22, 24, 34, 36, 41.

SEVENTH WEEK:

Study imperfect tense and its functional uses in the Syntax Chart: M., Syntax Chart 196; D.M., 186-191; R., 882-888; R.D., 300-301; B.D., 169-171; S., 423-427; F., II 623-626.

Look up in the following passages examples of the functional uses of imperfect tense:

Luke 3:18	Luke 9:49	Matt. 5:2
Luke 17:27	Matt. 26:9	
Mark 7:26	Matt. 7:29	

Translate Luke 5:12-6:19 and identify the functional uses of the imperfect tense in Luke 5:30; 6:1, 7, 11, 18-19.

EIGHTH WEEK:

Study the future and aorist tenses and functions in the Syntax Chart: M., Syntax Chart 196; D.M., 191-200; R., 870-879, 888-889, 830-864; R.D., 295-299, 301; B.D., 178-179, 171-175; S., 427-434; F., II 634-635, 620-621.

Look up in the following examples the functional uses of the future and aorist:

Matt. 20:21	Matt. 27:24	Luke 3:22
Luke 21:33	John 2:20	Matt. 9:18
Matt. 5:27	2 Cor. 8:9	Philem. 19
Matt. 18:21	Matt. 7:28	

Translate Luke 6:20-7:10 and identify the functional uses of the aorist and future in Luke 6:37-40; 7:1-3.

NINTH WEEK:

Study the perfect tense system and its functional uses in the Syntax Chart: M., Syntax Chart 197; D.M., 200-208; R., 892-907; R.D., 301-305; B.D., 175-180; S., 434-437; F., II 626-634.

Look up in the following passages examples of functional uses of the perfect, pluperfect, and future perfect:

2 Tim. 4:7	John 5:37	John 19:11
John 19:30	John 6:17	Matt. 16:19
Matt. 4:7	John 1:31	Matt. 18:18
Matt. 6:8		

Translate Luke 7:11-8:3 and identify the functional uses of the perfect and pluperfect in Luke 7:47-50; 8:2.

TENTH WEEK:

Study summary statement on mood in the Syntax Chart: M., Syntax Chart 198; F., II 637.

Study subjunctive mood in its functional uses: M., Syntax Chart 198f; D.M., 170–172; F., II 637–651.

Look up in the following passages examples of the functional uses of the subjunctive:

Matt. 1:20	Rom. 11:11
Matt. 26:46	Matt. 5:29
Luke 3:10	Rom. 15:24
Matt. 1:22	2 Cor. 12:20

Translate Luke 8:4–48 and identify the functional uses of the subjunctive mood in Luke 8:10, 12–13, 16–18.

ELEVENTH WEEK:

Study the imperative and its functional uses in the Syntax Chart: M., Syntax Chart 199; D.M., 174–176; F., II 637–647.

Look up in the following passages examples of functional uses of the imperative:

Matt. 5:44	John 2:19
John 6:20	Luke 6:37
Mark 9:22	Matt. 26:45

Study the optative and its functional uses in the Syntax Chart: M., Syntax Chart 199; D.M., 172–174; F., II 651–653.

Look up in the following passages examples of the functional uses of the optative mood:

Acts 26:29	Rom. 6:2
Luke 6:11	Luke 3:15
Mark 11:14	

Translate Luke 8:49–9:36 and identify the functional uses of the imperative mood in Luke 8:49–54; 9:23.

TWELFTH WEEK:

Study the conditional sentences in the Syntax Chart: M., Syntax Chart 203–204; D.M., 286–291; F., II 679–688.

Look up in the following passages examples of functional uses of conditional sentences:

Matt. 12:27	John 13:17
John 15:20	John 8:51
Luke 7:39	Acts 8:31
John 11:21	

Translate Luke 9:37-10:20 and identify the functional uses of conditional sentences in Luke 9:48; 10:5-6, 10.

THIRTEENTH WEEK:

Study the participle and its functional uses in the Syntax Chart: M., Syntax Chart 200 f; D.M., 220-233; F., II 597-610, 667-677.

Translate Luke 10:21-11:23 and identify the functional uses of the participial mood in Luke 10:23, 25, 29-30.

FOURTEENTH WEEK:

Study the infinitive and its functional uses in the Syntax Chart: M., Syntax Chart 201f; D.M., 208-220; F., II 655-665.

Translate Luke 11:24-12:12 and identify the functional uses of the infinitive mood in Luke 11:31, 37, 42; 12:1, 4-5.

APPENDIX

GREEK VERBAL PREFIXES AND SUFFIXES — PAGE 1

System	TENSE	AUGMENT	REDUPLI-CATION	BASE	EXTRA TENSE SIGN	VARIABLE OR THEMATIC VOWEL	ENDING
PRES. SYSTEM	PRESENT AMP			λυ		o/ε¹	PRIM.
	IMPERFECT AMP	ἐ²		λυ		o/ε	SEC.
FUTURE SYSTEM	FUTURE AM			λυ	σ	o/ε	PRIM.
1 AOR. SYSTEM	1 AORIST AM	ἐ		λυ	σα		SEC.
1 PF. ACT.	1 PERFECT A		λε³	λυ	κ	α/ε	PRIM.
SYSTEM	PLUPERFECT A	ἐ	λε	λυ	κ	ει	SEC.
PERF. MP	PERFECT MP		λε	λυ			PRIM.
SYSTEM	PLUPERFECT MP	ἐ	λε	λυ			SEC.
	FUTURE PF. MP		λε	λυ	σ	o/ε	PRIM.
1 PASSIVE	FUTURE			λυ	θησ	o/ε	PRIM.
SYSTEM	AORIST P	ἐ		λυ	θη		SEC.

VERBAL PREFIXES AND SUFFIXES - PAGE 2

1. a. In connection with the variable or thematic vowel o/ε (present
   and future systems and future perfect and future passive tenses)
   o is used before μ and ν; ε is used elsewhere.

   b. The subjunctive lengthens the thematic vowel from o to ω and from
   ε to η.

   c. The optative combines its mood suffix ι or ιη with the variable
   vowel o/ε to form οι, or with (σ)α of the aorist to form αι, or
   with (ϑ)η or with the forms of εἰμί to form ει, so that the optative
   mood suffix signs are:

   -οι
   -αι
   -ει

2. ἐ is a syllabic augment which is prefixed in the secondary tenses
   (imperfect, aorist and pluperfect) indicative to verbs beginning with
   a consonant. The second kind of augment is called temporal and
   lengthens the first syllable of verbs beginning with a vowel or
   diphthong. So:

   Unaugmented becomes augmented

α or ε	-------	η
ι	-------	ι
o	-------	ω
υ	-------	υ
αι or ᾳ	-------	ῃ
οι	-------	ῳ

3. There are two kinds of reduplication: syllabic and temporal.

   a. Syllabic reduplication means the reduplication of the initial consonant
   as a prefix in connection with verbs beginning with a single consonant
   (except ρ) and placing an ε after the reduplicated consonant; or in the
   case of verbs beginning with two consonants or a double consonant
   (ξ, ψ or ζ) or with ρ, reduplication is a simple ε prefixed. If the
   verb begins with a rough consonant, the reduplication is a smooth or
   voiceless consonant of the same class.

   b. Temporal reduplication: in most verbs beginning with vowels or
   diphthongs the reduplication is like the augment.

PRIMARY ENDINGS active		SECONDARY ENDINGS active	
-μι, -ω	-μεν	-ν	-μεν
-ς	-τε	-ς	-τε
-σι, -ι	-ωσι, ουσι	-	-ν, -σαν
middle and passive		**middle and passive**	
-μαι	-μεθα	-μην	-μεθα
-σαι, -ι	-σθε	-σο, -ο	-σθε
-ται	-νται	-το	-ντο

GREEK PARSING NUMBER SYSTEM

TENSE	VOICE	MOOD	PERSON AND NUMBER	
I – Present	a – active	Indicative	1 – 1st sing.	4 – 1st plu.
II – Imperfect	m – middle		2 – 2nd sing.	5 – 2nd plu.
1 & 2 III – Future	p – passive		3 – 3rd sing.	6 – 3rd plu.
1 & 2 IV – Aorist				
1 & 2 V – Perfect				
VI – Pluperfect				
VII – Future Perfect		Subjunctive	11 – 1st sing.	14 – 1st plu.
			12 – 2nd sing.	15 – 2nd plu.
			13 – 3rd sing.	16 – 3rd plu.
		Imperative	--	--
			22 –.2nd sing.	25 – 2nd plu.
			23 – 3rd sing.	26 – 3rd plu.
		Infinitive	31	
		Participle	33 – sing.	36 – plu.
		Optative	41 – 1st sing.	44 – 1st plu.
			42 – 2nd sing.	45 – 2nd plu.
			43 – 3rd sing.	46 – 3rd plu.

EXAMPLES

λύεται	– I, mp., 3
λύων	– I, a., 33 nom. masc.
λύσετε	– III, a., 5
λύοι	– I, a., 43
λῦσον	– 1-IV, a., 22
λελυκέναι	– V, a., 31
λυθῶμεν	– 1-IV, p., 14

NEW TESTAMENT GREEK   1ST DECLENSION:

Case	FEMININE — After ε, ι, and ρ (α continues in Gen./Dat.)		SHORT α	LONG	MASCULINE — ας	ης
N.	ἀσθένεια	χώρα	γλῶσσα	φωνή	νεανίας	προφήτης
G.	ἀσθενείας	χώρας	γλώσσης	φωνῆς	νεανίου	προφήτου
D.	ἀσθενείᾳ	χώρᾳ	γλώσσῃ	φωνῇ	νεανίᾳ	προφήτῃ
A.	ἀσθένειαν	χώραν	γλῶσσαν	φωνήν	νεανίαν	προφήτην
V.	ἀσθένεια	χώρα	γλῶσσα	φωνή	νεανία	προφῆτα
N.	ἀσθένειαι	χῶραι	γλῶσσαι	φωναί	νεανίαι	προφῆται
G.	ἀσθενειῶν	χωρῶν	γλωσσῶν	φωνῶν	νεανιῶν	προφητῶν
D.	ἀσθενείαις	χώραις	γλώσσαις	φωναῖς	νεανίαις	προφήταις
A.	ἀσθενείας	χώρας	γλώσσας	φωνάς	νεανίας	προφήτας
V.	ἀσθένειαι	χῶραι	γλῶσσαι	φωναί	νεανίαι	προφῆται

2nd Declension

Case	Masculine	Feminine	Neuter
N.	νόμος	ἡ ὁδός	τὸ δῶρον
G.	νόμου	ὁδοῦ	δώρου
D.	νόμῳ	ὁδῷ	δώρῳ
A.	νόμον	ὁδόν	δῶρον
V.	νόμε	ὁδέ	δῶρον
N.	νόμοι	ὁδοί	δῶρα
G.	νόμων	ὁδῶν	δώρων
D.	νόμοις	ὁδοῖς	δώροις
A.	νόμους	ὁδούς	δῶρα
V.	νόμοι	ὁδοί	δῶρα

Types of 1st Declension Nouns:

Case	FEMININE — α in all of sing.	(short) α	η	MASCULINE — ας	ης
N.	-α	-α	-η	-ας	-ης
G.	-ας	-ης	-ης	-ου	-ου
D.	-ᾳ	-ῃ	-ῃ	-ᾳ	-ῃ
A.	-αν	-αν	-ην	-αν	-ην
V.	-α	-α	-η	-α	-α
N.	-αι			-αι	
G.	-ων			-ων	
D.	-αις	the same		-αις	the same
A.	-ας			-ας	
V.	-αι			-αι	

Types of 2nd Declension Nouns

Case	Masc. and Fem.	Neuter
N.	-ος	-ον
G.	-ου	-ου
D.	-ῳ	-ῳ
A.	-ον	-ον
V.	-ε	-ον
N.	-οι	-α
G.	-ων	-ων
D.	-οις	-οις
A.	-ους	-α
V.	-οι	-α

NEW TESTMENT GREEK
THIRD DECLENSION

(All stems ending in consonants
and in the semi-vowels ι and υ)

THREE TYPES OF THIRD DECLENSION ENDINGS (in general):

	I		II	III	
	Masculine-Feminine	Neuter			*Monosyllabic third declension nouns generally
N.	---	---	-ς	---	have the accent on the
G.	-ος	-ος	-ους	-ως	ultima in the genitive
D.	-ι	-ι	-ει	-ει	and dative, singular and
A.	-α (short), ν	---	-ς	-ν(α)	plural.
N.	-ες	-α (short)	-η	-εις(ες)	
G.	-ων	-ων	-ων	-ων	
D.	-σι(ψ,ξ)(ν)	-σι(ν)	-εσι(ν)	-σι(ν)	
A.	-ας (short)	-α (short)	-η	-εις(ας)	

TYPE I

	MUTE STEMS			-ντ STEMS	NEUTER STEMS IN -τ- and -ας	
	Labial πβφ	Palatal κγχ	Lingual τδθ		-τ-	-ας
N.	λαῖλαψ	σάρξ	ἐλπίς	ἄρχων	σῶμα	πέρας
G.	λαίλαπος	σαρκός	ἐλπίδος	ἄρχοντος	σώματος	πέρατος
D.	λαίλαπι	σαρκί	ἐλπίδι	ἄρχοντι	σώματι	πέρατι
A.	λαίλαπα	σάρκα	ἐλπίδα	ἄρχοντα	σῶμα	πέρας
N.	λαίλαπες	σάρκες	ἐλπίδες	ἄρχοντες	σώματα	πέρατα
G.	λαιλάπων	σαρκῶν	ἐλπίδων	ἀρχόντων	σωμάτων	περάτων
D.	λαίλαψι(ν)	σαρξί(ν)	ἐλπίσι(ν)	ἄρχουσι(ν)	σώμασι(ν)	πέρασι(ν)
A.	λαίλαπας	σάρκας	ἐλπίδας	ἄρχοντας	σώματα	πέρατα
N.			χάρις			
G.			χάριτος			
D.			χάριτι			
A.			χάριν			
N.			χάριτες			
G.			χαρίτων			
D.			χάρισι(ν)			
A.			χάριτας			

STEMS IN -ρ-			-ν- STEMS		-ς-STEMS
Vowel Gradation	Little or no Vowel Gradation		Vowel Gradation	No Vowel Gradation	(ἐθνεσ-)
πατήρ	σωτήρ	μάρτυς	ποιμήν	αἰών	ἔθνος
πατρός	σωτῆρος	μάρτυρος	ποιμένος	αἰῶνος	ἔθνους
πατρί	σωτῆρι	μάρτυρι	ποιμένι	αἰῶνι	ἔθνει
πατέρα	σωτῆρα	μάρτυρα	ποιμένα	αἰῶνα	ἔθνος
πάτερ					
πατέρες	σωτῆρες	μάρτυρες	ποιμένες	αἰῶνες	ἔθνη
πατέρων	σωτήρων	μαρτύρων	ποιμένων	αἰώνων	ἐθνῶν
πατράσι(ν)	σωτῆρσι(ν)	μάρτυσι(ν)	ποιμέσι(ν)	αἰῶσι(ν)	ἔθνεσι(ν)
πατέρας	σωτῆρας	μάρτυρας	ποιμένας	αἰῶνας	ἔθνη
πατέρες					
ἀνήρ					ἔλεος
ἀνδρός					ἐλέους
ἀνδρί					ἐλέει
ἄνδρα					ἔλεος
ἄνερ					
ἄνδρες					
ἀνδρῶν					
ἀνδράσι(ν)					
ἄνδρας					

TYPE III

STEMS IN SEMI-VOWELS

-ι- and -υ-

ει & ι	ευ & υ	υ	ευ	ου	οι
πόλις	πῆχυς	ἰχθῦς	βασιλεύς	βοῦς	ἠχώ (or -ῷ)
πόλεως	πήχεως, εος	ἰχθύος	βασιλέως	βοός	ἠχοῦς
πόλει	πήχει	ἰχθύι	βασιλεῖ	βοΐ	ἠχοῖ
πόλιν	πῆχυν	ἰχθύν	βασιλέα	βοῦν	ἠχώ
			βασιλεῦ		
πόλεις	πήχεις	ἰχθύες	βασιλεῖς	βόες	
πόλεων	πήχεων	ἰχθύων	βασιλέων	βοῶν	
πόλεσι(ν)	πήχεσι(ν)	ἰχθύσι(ν)	βασιλεῦσι(ν)	βουσί(ν)	
πόλεις	πήχεις	ἰχθύας	βασιλεῖς	βόας	
		ὀσφῦς			
		ὀσφύος			
		ὀσφύι			
		ὀσφύν			
		ὀσφύες			
		ὀσφύων			
		ὀσφύσι(ν)			
		ὀσφύας			

VARIATIONS IN VERBS OTHER THAN THE λύω VERB:

A. Contract verbs:

These verbs have the same basic endings as are listed for the λύω verb
(see pages 168 and 169). Only in tenses I and II[1] does the end vowel of
the verb stem contract with the thematic vowel (e.g., φιλέω becomes φιλῶ).
Many times the accent becomes circumflex. Study the contract chart. The
stem-ending vowel outside of tenses I and II generally lengthens and then
doesn't contract (e.g., φιλήσω).

B. Liquid verbs:

1. These are verbs whose stems end in λ, μ, ν or ρ (e.g., μένω) and they
    are regular in formation in tenses I and II, but in tense III they act
    like present tense (I) -ε contract verbs in their formation.

2. In tense IV (aorist) the liquid verbs, instead of adding σ after the
    stem, make an internal change and generally take the regular endings
    (e.g., ἔμεινα), or sometimes 2 IV endings (e.g., ἔβαλον).

C. μι verbs:

1. General rules: they

    a. are regular (like λύω) in tenses III, V and VI.

    b. reduplicate the first letter of the stem in tenses I and II.

    c. do not reduplicate the first letter of the stem in tense IV.

2. δίδωμι. This verb has

    a. the ο/ω type vowels as a part of the verb stem.

    b. ω as the stem vowel in I act. singular, but ο in I act. plural.

    c. ου as the stem vowel in II act. singular, but ο in II act. plural.

    d. ω throughout I a.m.p. and IV a.m. subjunctive.

    e. κ (instead of σ) as a suffix to the stem in IV act. indicative
        only.

3. τίθημι. This verb has

    a. the ε/η type vowels as a part of the verb stem.

    b. η as the stem vowel in I act. sing., but ε in I act. plural.

    c. η and ει as the stem vowels in II act. 1 and II act. 2, 3, respec-
        tively, but ε in II act. plural.

    d. κ (instead of σ) in IV act. indicative only.

---

[1]See the Greek Parsing Number System on page 170.

(Principles of the New Testament Greek Verb continued)

4. ἵστημι

    a. Has the α/η type vowels as a part of the verb stem.

    b. Has ἱ as reduplication in I and II.

    c. Has α as the stem vowel in most forms of I and II.

    d. Has η in I and II active in the singular but α in I and II active in the plural.

    e. Has 1IV and 2IV forms as well.

RULES FOR CONTRACT VERBS:

There are certain verbs which have an α, ε or o before the suffix endings in the present and imperfect, active, middle and passive (i.e., I and II, a.m.p.). This vowel contracts with the variable vowel before the consonant suffix endings. If the α, ε or o is accented, the contraction receives the circumflex accent (this occurs most of the time and will help the student recognize a contract verb). Find out from what vowels or diphthong the contraction comes; then look for this vowel or diphthong in the chart below. Note that α and ᾳ contractions come from combinations which have an α as the first vowel of the combination.

Note that ει contractions come from ε-ε or ε-ει combinations.

Note that η contractions come from combinations of ε-η and ε-ῃ (the latter contracting to ῃ).

Observe that οι, ου and ω contractions come from combinations which contain an o, ου or ω vowel.

If the contracted vowel on the end of the word is	Then it comes from	
α	α+ε	τιμᾶτε
α	α+ει	τιμᾶν (I a 31)
α	α+η	τιμᾶτε
ᾳ	α+ει	τιμᾷ
ᾳ	α+ῃ	τιμᾷς
ει	ε+ε	ἐφίλει
ει	ε+ει	φιλεῖ
η	ε+η	φιλῆτε
ῃ	ε+ῃ	φιλῇ
οι	o+ει	δηλοῖ
οι	o+ῃ	δηλοῖ
ου	o+ε	δηλοῦτε
ου	o+ει	δηλοῦν (I a 31)
ου	o+o	ἐδήλουν
ου	o+ου	δηλοῦσα
ου	ε+o	φιλοῦμεν
ου	ε+ου	φιλοῦσα
ω	α+o	τιμῶμεν
ω	α+ου	τιμῶσα
ω	α+ω	τιμῶν
ω	ε+ω	φιλῶ
ω	o+η	δηλῶτε
ω	o+ω	δηλῶ

GREEK TENSES

The Verb, Its Time and Kind of Action

	Present System		Future	Aorist	Perfect	Pluperfect
	Present	Imperf.				
Time:					Present Completed	Past Completed
Kind of Action:	Pres.	Past	Future	Past		
	▬ ●	▬	▬ ●	●	▬▬▬● ●▬▬▬	▬▬▬● ●▬▬▬
	I am writing, I write.	I was writ-ing.	I will be writ-ing, I will write.	I wrote.	I have writ-ten and it stands so.	I had writ-ten and it stood so.

FORMATION OF THE PERFECT TENSE

The Perfect:

Prefix

If the stem or base begins in:	Then
(1) *Consonant	Reduplicate the consonant.
(2) An aspirated mute consonant (see page 2)	Reduplicate with the unaspirated voiceless conso-nant.
(3) A vowel or diphthong	Lengthen the vowel or first letter of diphthong.
(4) A consonant cluster	Reduplicate the first consonant or prefix an ε before the clus-ter.

* The regular λύω verb situation.

Suffix

If	Then
(1) *The verb is like λύω,	Add κ
(2) The stem ends in a vowel,	Lengthen the vowel; then add κ
(3) The stem ends in τ, δ, θ,	Drop τ, δ, θ before κ
(4) It is a 2 perfect,	Do not add κ

MIDDLE AND PASSIVE

If	Then
(5) The stem ends in one of the mute consonants	In the middle-passive there is likely to be assimila-tion or accom-modation to the initial consonant of the middle-pas-sive ending (e.g., γέγραμμαι, γεγραμμένος, δεδίωγμαι)

NEW TESTAMENT OPTATIVE

λύω

PRESENT ACTIVE	PRESENT MIDDLE-PASSIVE	AORIST ACTIVE	AORIST MIDDLE	AORIST PASSIVE
(λύοιμι)*	(λυοίμην)	(λύσαιμι)	λυσαίμην	(λυθείην)
(λύοις)	(λύοιο)	(λύσαις)	(λύσαιο)	(λυθείης)
λύοι	λύοιτο	λύσαι	(λύσαιτο)	λυθείη
(λύοιμεν)	(λυοίμεθα)	(λύσαιμεν)	(λυσαίμεθα)	(λυθείημεν)
λύοιτε	(λύοισθε)	(λύσαιτε)	(λύσαισθε)	(λυθείητε)
λύοιεν	(λύοιντο)	λύσειαν	(λύσαιντο)	(λυθείησαν)
		or		
		λύσαιεν		

λαμβάνω

2 AORIST ACTIVE	2 AORIST MIDDLE
(λάβοιμι)	(λαβοίμην)
(λάβοις)	(λάβοιο)
(λάβοι)	λάβοιτο
(λάβοιμεν)	(λαβοίμεθα)
(λάβοιτε)	(λάβοισθε)
λάβοιεν	(λάβοιντο)

εἰμί

PRESENT OPTATIVE

εἴην
εἴης
εἴη

εἴημεν
εἴητε
εἴησαν

The present optative formation of εἰμί is identical to the aorist passive optative endings of λύω.

*The forms found in parentheses are practically non-existent in the New Testament.

(See R.D., pages 172-174)

ABSTRACTS	AGENT	ACTION	RESULT	INSTRUMENT or MEANS	PLACE	QUALITY (from adj. stems)	DIMINUTIVE
A. -α, -η	A. -ευ-ς (nom. -ευ-ς)	A. -τι-ς	A. -ματ (nom. -μα)	A. -τρο (nom. -τρον; Latin -trum)	A. -τηρι (nom. -τήριον)	A. -τητ (nom. -της)	A. -ιο (nom. -ιον)
χαρ-ά (χαίρ-ω), joy	γον-εύ-ς, parent (γέγονα)	πίσ-τι-ς, faith (πείθ-ω) (πιθ-)	γράμ-μα, letter (γράφ-ω)	ἄρο-τρον, plow (ἀρό-ω)	ἀκροα-τήριον, auditorium (ἀκροά-ομαι)	ἁγιό-της, holiness (ἅγι-ος)	παιδ-ίον, little child (παῖς)
	γραμματ-εύ-ς, scribe (γραμματ-)	B. -σι-ς (τ becomes σ)	πνεῦ-μα, spirit (πνέ-ω)	λύ-τρον, ransom (λύ-ω)	κρι-τήριον, judgment seat (κρίν-ω)	νεό-της, youth (νέ-ος)	θυγάτρ-ιον, little daughter (θυγάτηρ)
B. -ο (nom. -ο-ς)	B. -τηρ	γνῶ-σι-ς, knowledge (γι-γνώ-σκω)	κήρυγ-μα, preaching (κηρύσσ-ω)	B. -τηριο (nom. -τήριον)	B. -ειο (nom. -εῖον in denominatives)	B. -συνα (nom. -σύνη)	B. -αριο (nom. -άριον)
λόγ-ο-ς, speech, word (λέγ-ω)	σω-τήρ, Savior	κρί-σι-ς, judging (κρίν-ω)	B. -σμα (with -άζω, -ίζω and with verbs with perfect passive in -σμαι)	ἱλασ-τήριον, means by which sins are forgiven (ἱλά-σκομαι)	πανδοχ-εῖον, inn (παν-δοχ-εύς)	δικαιο-σύνη, righteousness (δίκαιος)	παιδ-άριον, little child (παῖς)
τρόπ-ο-ς, turn (τρέπ-ω)	C. -τορ (masc.) (nom. -τωρ)	C. -σια	βάπτισ-μα, baptism (βαπτ-ίζω)	αἰσθη-τήριον, organ or power of discernment (αἰσθάν-ομαι)	ἀγγ-εῖον, vessel (ἄγγ-ος)	σωφρο-σύνη, sound judgment (σώφρων)	γυναικ-άριον, morally weak woman (γυνή)
	πράκ-τωρ, exactor, officer (πράσσ-ω)	δοκιμα-σία, testing (δοκιμ-άζω)	χρῖσ-μα, anointing (χρί-ω)		C. -ων (nom. -ών)	C. -ια (nom. -ια)	C. -διο (nom. -ίδιον)
	D. -την-ς (used most)	ἐκκλη-σία, church (ἐκ-καλ-έω)	C. -ες (nom. -ος)		ἐλαι-ών, olive orchard (ἐλαί-α)	ἀληθε-ια, truth (ἀληθής)	κλιν-ίδιον, small bed
	μαθη-τής, learner (μανθάν-ω)	D. -μο-ς	γέν-ος, offspring (γι-γέν-ομαι)		ἀμπελ-ών, vineyard (ἄμπελ-ος)	σοφ-ία, wisdom (σοφός)	D. -ισκο (nom. -ίσκος, -ίσκη)
	ἀκροα-τής, hearer (ἀκροά-ομαι)	βαπτισ-μός, baptism	ἔθος, custom (ἔθ-ω)				νεαν-ίσκος, young man (νεαν-ίας)
	ποιη-τής, doer (ποι-έω)	E. -εια					παιδ-ίσκη (παῖς), young girl
		βασιλ-εία, kingdom (βασιλ-εύω)					

SUFFIXES FOR ADJECTIVES

(See R.D., pages 175-177)

THAT WHICH PERTAINS TO A SUBSTANTIVE	ABILITY OR FITNESS	MATERIAL	TEMPORAL	COMPARATIVE RELATIONSHIP	VERBAL ADJECTIVE	LESS DEFINITE MEANINGS
A. -ιο	A. -ικό-ς	A. -ινος	-ινο-ς	-τερος	-τος	A. -ο-ς
οὐράν-ιος (heavenly)	λογ-ικός (rational)	λίθ-ινος (made of stone)	due to locatives or adverbs in ι	relationship ἡμέ-τερος (ours)	ἄ-πισ-τος (unfaithful)	καλ-ός φίλος
τίμ-ιο-ς (precious)	πνευματ-ικός (spiritual)	σάρκ-ινος (made of flesh)	πρω-ινός (pertaining to morning)	ὑμέ-τερος (yours)	κλη-τός (called)	B. -λο-ς
φυσ-ι-κός (natural) φύσις	σαρκ-ικός (fleshly)		ὀρθρ-ινός (early)		-τεος (once)	δοῦ-λος (δέω) τυφ-λός (τύφω)
	B. -τικό-ς	B. -εος (-οῦς)		comparison ἕ-τερος (another)	βλη-τέον	C. -ιλος
B. -ιακό-ς	αἱρε-τικός (capable of choosing)	χρυσ-οῦς (made of gold)		δεύ-τερος (second)	Luke 5:38 (must be put)	ποικ-ίλος (many colored)
κυρ-ιακός (relating to the Lord)	διδακ-τικός (apt at teaching)					D. -ωλος
						ἁμαρτ-ωλός (devoted to sin)
					G. -μος	E. -νος, -νη, -νον
					ἄ-μω-μος (spotless)	σεμ-νός (to be revered)
						F. -ανος
					H. -ρος	ἱκ-ανός (fit)
					αἰσχ-ρός (shameful)	
					I. -ης, -ες	
					ἀληθ-ής (true)	

WORD FORMATION - COMPOUND WORDS
(see R.D., pp. 180-182)
(the κοινή is fond of compound words)

Inseparable Prefixes	Prepositions (We will see these in detail later.)	Objective Compounds	Descriptive Determinative Compounds	Possessive Compounds	Denominative Compound Verbs
a) ἀ - (ἀν-) privative ἀ-γνοέω (be ignorant) ἀ-κατάκριτος (uncondemned)	παρά - κλησις compound verbs ἀντι - παρ -ῆλθεν (Luke 10:31f)	(the first part is related to the other as a sort of case relationship or grammatical object) a) Accusative θεο-μάχος (God-fighter, fighting God)	(the first element describes the second) ἀγρι-έλαιος (wild olive) συν-πρεσβύτερος (fellow elder)	(first part qualifies the second part like an adjective or adverb and the whole has notion of belonging to something or having something) ὀλιγό-πιστος (having little faith) σκληρο-τράχηλος (stiffnecked)	εἰρηνο-ποιέω (make peace) λιθο-βολέω (throw stones)
b) ἀρχι-(chief) (arch-) ἀρχιερεύς (chief priest)		b) Genitive οἰκο-νόμος (manager of a house)			
c) δυσ- δυσ-εντέριον (dysentery) δυσ-ερμήνευτος (hard to interpret)		c) Ablative θεο-δίδακτος (taught by God)			
d) ἡμι- (Latin, semi) ἡμί-ωρον (half an hour)		d) Locative ἀκρο-γωνιαῖος (at the extreme corner)			
e) νη- νή-πιος (infant) νη-πιάζω (νή, ἔπος) (speak as an infant)		e) Instrumental θεό-πνευστος (inspired by God) αἰχμ-άλωτος (captured by a spear) f) Dative ἀνθρωπ-άρεσκος (man-pleaser)			

GREEK WORD FORMATION

A. Roots

1. Roots involve original elements from which words came into being.

2. Robertson and Davis say that apparently about 400 roots of Greek words are known for about 90,000 words in Liddell and Scott's <u>A GREEK-ENGLISH LEXICON</u> (R.D., 172).

3. Two ultimate kinds of words were verbs and pronouns; e.g., φη-μί, "Says I."

4. The oldest parts of speech were verbs, substantives and pronouns.

5. Words formed directly from:

   a. Verb stems are called <u>verbals</u>, like ἀρχ-ή, beginning.

   b. Noun stems are called <u>demonstratives</u>, like ἀρχα-ῖος, of the beginning.

B. <u>Suffixes for substantives</u>

We are dealing here with <u>formative suffixes</u> by which is meant case suffixes for nouns (<u>personal suffixes</u> have to do with verbs).

1. <u>Abstracts</u> (verbals):

Mainly primitives:

α and η exampled in χαρ-ά (χαίρ-ω), joy,
         ἀρχ-ή (ἄρχ-ω), beginning

ο, nom. -ο-ς, exampled in λόγ-ο-ς (λέγ-ω), speech
                         τρόπ-ο-ς (τρέπ-ω), turn

2. <u>Agent:</u>
   a. -εύ-ς

   1) In verbals it indicates the one who does an action, like γον-εύ-ς, parent (γέγονα).

   2) In demonstratives it indicates one who is involved with something, e.g. γραμματ-εύ-ς, scribe (γραμματ-).

Other suffixes for the agent are:

   b. -τηρ, like masculine σω-τήρ, Savior (σῴζ-ω), feminine μαθή-τρια, woman disciple (Acts 9:36)

   c. -τορ, masculine, nom.-τωρ, like πράκτωρ, exactor (πράσσ-ω)

   d. -τα, masculine, nom. -τη-ς, like μαθη-τής, learner (μανθάν-ω). This is the suffix which is mainly used for the agent, <u>formed from many</u> kinds of verbs, such as:

-άω, ἀκροα-τής, hearer	-έω, ποιη-τής, doer
-όω, ζηλω-τής, zealot	-ευω, βουλευ-τής, councilor
-άζω, δικασ-τής, judge	-ίζω, εὐαγγελισ-τής, evangelist

3. Action:

-τι-ς

    πίσ-τι-ς (from πείθ-ω [πιθ-]) faith

-σι-ς   (in which τ has changed to ς)

    γνῶ-σι-ς   knowledge
    κρί-σι-ς   judging
    λύτρω-σι-ς   redemption

-σια

    θυ-σία   sacrifice
    δοκιμα-σία   proving
    ἐκκλη-σία   assembly, church

-μος   from verbs like ψάλλ-ω: ψαλ-μό-ς, twanging a chord or psalm

    from derivative verbs:

    ιζω, βαπτισ-μός baptism
    αζω, ἁγιασ-μός sanctification
    υζω, γογγυσ-μός murmuring

-εια   from verbs in ευω

    βασιλ-εία (βασιλεύ-ω) kingdom

4. Result:

a. -ματ, nominative -μα, is added
        1. to primary verb stems like:

        γράμ-μα (γράφω) letter
        πνεῦ-μα (πνέ-ω) spirit
        2. to denominative verbal stems like:

        κήρυγ-μα (κήρυξ, κηρύσσω) preaching
        πλήρω-μα (πληρ-όω)   fulness

b. -σμα with dental stems like αζω, ιζω, e.g., βάπτισ-μα; or with verbs
    with perfect passive in -σμαι, e.g., χρίσ-μα (χρί-ω), anointing

c. -ες, nominative -ος, e.g., γένος (γι-γέν-ομαι), ἔθος (root ἔθ-ω)

5. Instrument or means:

a. -τρο, nominative -τρον (Latin, trum)

    ἄρο-τρον (ἀρό-ω) plow
    λύ-τρον (λύ-ω)   ransom

b. -τηριο, nominative -τήριον

    ἱλασ-τήριον (ἱλά-σκομαι) means by which sins are forgiven

6. <u>Place</u>:

    a. <u>-τηρι</u>, nominative, -τήριον   only in verbals like:
         ἀκροα-τήριον(ἀκροά-ομαι)   auditorium
         κρι-τήριον (κρίν-ω)   judgment seat

    b. <u>-ειο</u>, nominative, -εῖον   in denominatives like:
         πανδοχ-εῖον(παν-δοχ-εύς)   inn

    c. <u>-ων</u> denominatives
         ἀμπελ-ών (ἄμπελ-ος)   vineyard
         ἐλαι-ών (ἐλαί-α)   olive orchard

7. <u>Quality</u> - from adj. stems:

    a. <u>-τητ</u>, nominative, -της
         ἁγιό-της (ἅγι-ος)   holiness
         νεό-της (νέ-ος)   youth

    b. <u>-συνα</u>, nominative, -σύνη
         δικαιο-σύνη (δίκαι-ος)   righteousness
         σωφρο-σύνη (σώφρων)   soundness of mind

    c. <u>-ια</u>
         ἀλήθε-ια (ἀληθής)   truth
         σοφ-ία (σοφός)   wisdom

8. <u>Diminutives</u>:

    a. <u>-ιο</u>, nominative, -ιον
         θυγάτρ-ιον   little daughter
         παιδ-ίον   little child

    b. <u>-αριον</u>
         παιδ-άριον   little child

    c. <u>-διο</u>, nominative, -ίδιον
         κλιν-ίδιον   small bed

    d. <u>-ισκο</u>, nominative, -ισκος (masc.), ίσκη (fem.)
         νεαν-ίσκος   young man
         παιδ-ίσκη   young girl

9. <u>Patronymics</u>:

Express descent - suffixes added to proper noun:

<u>-δα</u>
    -δης masc. noun
    -ς   fem. noun
    Ἡρωδίας (-δς = ς)   daughter of Herod

10. <u>Ethnic</u> - designating a people or country:

    <u>-ευ</u>, nominative, -εύς
      Ἀλεξανδρ-εύς   an Alexandrian
    <u>-ικος</u>, Γαλιτ-ικός   Galatian
    <u>-ιος</u>, Ἀθηνα-ῖος   Athenian

DIAGRAMMING

1. Subject and predicate:
   John 11:35

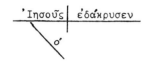

2. With predicate complements:

   a. Predicate nominative
      John 1:1b

   b. Direct object
      John 4:36a

      Genitive of the direct object:
      1 Cor. 9:12a

      | μετέχουσιν | ἐξουσίας |

      Dative of the direct object
      1 Cor. 9:12b

      | ἐχρησάμεθα | ἐξουσίᾳ |

   c. Two accusatives

      1. Direct object (person) and pred. acc.
         John 15:15a

      2. Accusative of person and thing
         John 14:26

3. Modifiers (words, indirect object, etc.)
   Lk. 15:29

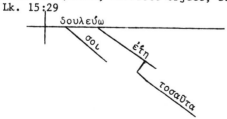

(3. Modifiers [words, indirect objects, etc.] continued)

John 11:49

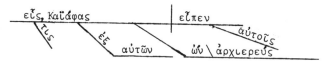

4. Relative dependent clauses
    a. As an adjective
        John 13:23

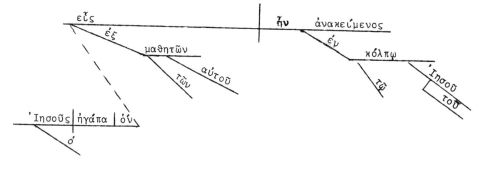

    b. As a substantive
        Matt. 10:38

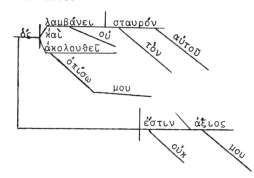

5. Adverbial dependent clauses (since, when, if, etc.)
   Matt. 24:33

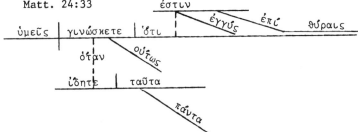

6. Genitive absolute
   Matt. 2:1

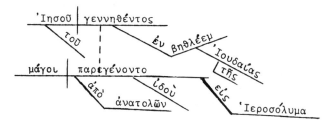

7. Infinitive phrases
   a. As subject
      Matt. 18:8

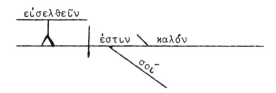

   b. As object or complement
      Luke 16:3

   c. Purpose or result
      Matt. 5:17

8. Noun clauses (subject, object, appositional)
   a. Subject
      Matt. 5:29

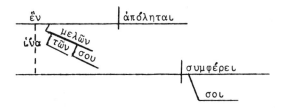

b . Object
   John 11:53

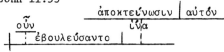

c. Apposition
   John 15:12

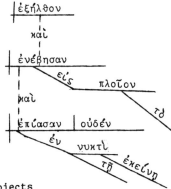

9. Compound elements
   a. Sentences
      John 21:3

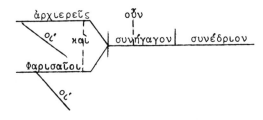

   b. Subjects
      John 11:47

   c. Predicates
      John 20:1

d. Predicate nominatives and direct objects
    1 Cor. 2:12

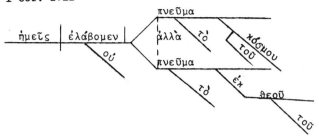

e. Prepositional phrases
    1 Cor. 2:3

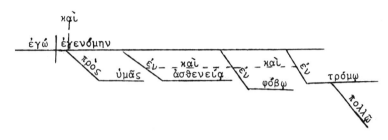

10. Interjections, vocatives and conjunctions
    a. Vocatives
        Acts 2:29

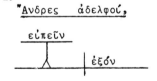

    b. Conjunctions
        Rom. 4:1

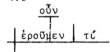

11. Quotations and questions
    a. Direct quotation
        John 11:4

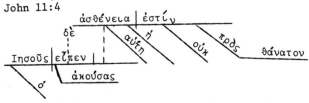

b. Indirect quotation or statement or thought
   1. ὅτι   clause
      John 11:20

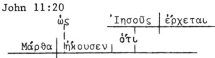

   2. Infinitive-
      Lk. 24:23

   3. Participle
      Lk. 10:18

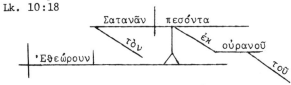

c. Indirect question
   Mk. 9:6

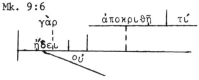

NEW TESTAMENT GREEK SYNTAX CHART

A. CASE CHART

CASE	KIND	USAGE	EXAMPLES	REF. TO GRAMMARS
1. _Nominative_	1. Subject		Matt. 4:1	
	2. Predicate		Luke 19:2	G., [1] Sec. 900
	3. Appositional		Acts 5:1	R., [2] p. 458
	4. Unaltered		John 13:13	M., [3] p. 69
				R., 459; M., 69
	5. Nominative Absolute		1 Cor. 1:1	R., 460; M., 69–70
	6. Parenthetic (or, Suspended)		Mark 8:2	
	7. Exclamatory		Rom. 7:24	R., 461; G., #1043; D.M., [4] 68–71
2. _Vocative_	1. Direct Address	a. the nominative form b. the mere stem c. ὦ (interjection) with the noun d. with the article	Matt. 1:20 Matt. 7:5 Acts 1:1 Luke 8:54	D.M., 71–72

3. _Accusative_*
(Idea of extension)
G., #1044–1079
	1. Extent of space
	2. Extent of time
	3. Direct object of the verb
	  a. Also accus. after pass. verbs (transl. by "with," "in," etc.)
	4. Cognate
	5. Double accusative
	  a. Predicate accusative
	  b. Accusative of the person and thing
			Luke 2:44
			Matt. 20:6
			Luke 4:20
			
			Acts 18:25
			
			Matt. 2:10
			
			John 15:15
			Gal. 5:2
				R., 469; G., #1061
				R., 469
				R., 471ff.
				
				R., 477
				R., 479ff.

[1] W. W. Goodwin, _Greek Grammar_, revised by C. B. Gulick (Boston: Ginn and Company, 1930).

[2] A. T. Robertson, _A Grammar of the Greek New Testament in the Light of Historical Research_, fifth ed. (New York: Harper and Brothers, 1931).

[3] J. H. Moulton, _A Grammar of the New Testament_, vol. I, Prolegomena (Edinburgh: T. and T. Clark, 1908).

[4] H. E. Dana and J. R. Mantey, _A Manual Grammar of the Greek New Testament_ (New York: Macmillan Co., 1948).

*The more infrequent and less important usages are starred, such as the Accusative, numbers 9 and 10, page 192.

New Testament Greek Syntax Chart – 2

CASE	KIND	USAGE	EXAMPLES	REF. TO GRAMMARS
	6. Adverbial			
	7. Subject of the infinitive (accusative of general reference)		John 6:10	R., 486; G., #1059
			Luke 2:27	R., 489
	8. Object of the prep.		(ἀνά)----Mark 7:31	R., 491
			(διά)----John 7:13	
			(εἰς)----Matt. 26:18	
			(ἐπί)----Matt. 15:35	
	*9. Inverse attraction accusative		1 Cor. 10:16	R., 488; D.M., 91-95
	*10. Accusative absolute		Acts 26:3	R., 490, 491
4. Genitive Ending a. Genitive function (idea of specification) G., #1080 -1156.	1. Time (time within which)		Matt. 24:20	
	2. Subjective		Phil. 4:7	R., 499
	3. Objective		Mark 11:22	R., 499
	4. Possessive (and gen. of relationship)	Following Substantives (i.e., nouns or noun equivalents)	Luke 2:30	
			Luke 24:10	
	5. Descriptive (or qualitative or attributive)		Rom. 6:6	R., 496
	6. Appositional (or gen. of definition)		John 2:21	R., 498
	7. Partitive			
	8. Simple object or complement	Following: a. adjectives b. adverbs and preps. c. verbs (of sensation, emotion, sharing, partaking, ruling, buying, selling)	Matt. 6:29	R., 502
			Matt. 3:8	R., 503-505
			Matt. 20:28	
			Luke 17:32	
			Mark 10:42	
	9. Purpose use of the gen. of the infin.		Luke 2:27	R., 512
	10. Gen. absolute			
	11. Price (cf. direct object verbs of buying)		1 Pet. 3:20	R., 513
			John 6:7	G., #1133
	12. Comparison		Matt. 6:25	G., #1147
	*13. Attraction of the relative into gen.		Luke 3:19	R., 512
	*14. Local (place)		Luke 19:4	R., 494; M., 73; D.M., 72-81

New Testament Greek Syntax Chart - 3

CASE	KIND	USAGE	EXAMPLES	REF. TO GRAMMARS
b. Ablative function G. #1117-1125	1. Source, origin, or separation	Following: a. adjectives b. prepositions c. verbs of: departure, removal, ceasing, abstaining, missing, lacking, despairing, differing, asking, hearing, partitive idea d. *substantive (rare)	Eph. 2:12 John 11:55 1 Tim. 4:1 Jas. 1:5 2 Cor. 1:8 Matt. 10:31 Acts 27:36 Rom. 10:12	R., 515 R., 516 D.M., 81-83 R., 514
5. Dative Ending a. Locative function (place idea) G., #1191-1196	1. Place of rest 2. Time when; point of time 3. Object (or complement)	Following: a. adjectives b. verbs c. substantives d. prepositions (ἐν, ἐπί, παρά, etc.)	John 21:8 Mark 14:12 Matt. 5:3 Acts 9:31 1 Cor. 14:20 John 20:11	R., 521 R., 522 R., 523-524 D.M., 86-88
b. Instrumental and Association G., #1180-1190	1. Association 2. Object (or complement) 3. Manner 4. Means 5. Degree of difference (measure) 6. Cause (motive or occasion)	Following verbs (mostly) and adjectives Following: a. words of likeness or identity b. prepositions, ἅμα, σύν There is a closeness between manner and means.	Mark 1:18 Acts 9:7 Luke 6:48 Luke 1:56 Matt. 13:29 Eph. 2:3 Gal. 2:13 Matt. 7:11 Rom. 11:20	R., 528 R., 530 R., 534 R., 530 R., 532 R., 532 R., 532 D.M., 88-91

New Testament Greek Syntax Chart – 4

CASE	KIND	USAGE	EXAMPLES	REF. TO GRAMMARS
c. Dative (idea of personal interest in the one for whom anything is done) G. #1157–1179.	1. Indirect Object	Following verbs.	Matt. 7:6	R., 538; G., #1158
	2. Advantage and Disadvantage (ethical)		1 Tim. 1:9	R., 538; G., #1165
	3. Possession		Matt. 18:12	R., 541; G., #1173
	*4. Agent (of persons) (rare)		Luke 23:15	R., 542; G., #1174a
	5. Object (or complement)	Following: a. verbs (transitive, intransitive and compound verbs) b. substantives c. adjectives d. adverbs and prepositions	Rom. 8:8 Matt. 11:29 Matt. 18:8 Matt. 18:7	R., 539, 541 G., #1159, 1179 R., 536; G., #1175 R., 537; G., #1175 R., 537; G., #1175
	6. Relation (or respect)		Rom. 6:2	G., #1172
				D.M., 83–86

B. THE VERB

1. The Tenses:

There are two ideas to keep in mind:
1) <u>Time is of primary importance in the indicative</u> (in the other moods time is secondary and relative).
2) <u>Kind of action is important.</u> There are three kinds of action: Punctiliar ●
Linear or durative ————,
State of completion ●————

2. Verb Chart of the Tenses:5

5Only the indicative is given here. Compare D.M., pages 176–180.

New Testament Greek Syntax Chart — 5

TENSE	KIND OF ACTION	DESCRIPTION OF USAGE	EXAMPLES	REFERENCE TO GRAMMARS
1. Present G., 1252-1258	a. Linear or durative (This is the more frequent usage for the present.)	1. Descriptive (continuous durative action at the time of writing or speaking)	Matt. 25:8	R., 879; B., 6 #8
		2. Progressive (the present of past action still in progress)	Luke 15:29	R., 879; B., #17
		3. Iterative or customary	Luke 18:12	R., 880
		4. Inchoative (begin) or conative (try)	John 10:32 Acts 26:28	R., 880; B., #11
		5. Historical pres. (sometimes linear)	John 6:19	R., 880; B., #14
		*6 Deliberative present (rhetorical question may be expressed in the present indicative)	John 11:47	R., 880
		*7. Periphrastic pres. (rare in N.T.)	Matt. 3:15	R., 880; B., #20
		*8. Futuristic pres. (sometimes linear)	Mark 10:33 2 Cor. 5:1	R., 869; B., #15
		9. Presents as perfects	Matt. 3:10 Luke 15:27	R., 881
	b. punctiliar (aoristic pres.)	1. Gnomic (timeless, true of all time)	Matt. 6:2	R., 866; B., #12
		2. Historical (usually punctiliar)	Matt. 3:1	R., 866; B., #14
		3. Futuristic present (usually punctiliar)	John 10:15	R., 869, 881; B., #15; D.M., 181-186

6 Burton, E.D., Syntax of Moods and Tenses in N.T. Greek (Edinburgh: T. and T. Clark, 1894).

7 The more infrequent or less important usages are starred.*

New Testament Greek Syntax Chart – 6

TENSE	KIND OF ACTION	DESCRIPTION OF USAGE	EXAMPLES	REF. TO GRAMMARS
2. Imperfect G., 1259–1260	Linear or durative action in past time	1. Progressive impf. 2. Iterative or customary (.....) 3. Inchoative 4. Conative 5. Potential (be on the point of) 6. Periphrastic impf.	Luke 17:27 Mark 7:26 Mark 15:6 Matt. 5:2 Luke 9:49 Matt. 26:9 Matt. 7:29	B., #21 R., 884; B., #24 R., 885 R., 885; B., #23 R., 885; B., #33 R., 887; B., #34 D.M., 186–191
3. Future	Punctiliar (mostly) and linear (sometimes)	1. Futuristic (like our uses of shall and will in older English) 2. Volitive 3. Deliberative 4. Imperative future 5. Gnomic future	Matt. 1:21 Matt. 5:21 Matt. 18:21 Matt. 27:24 Gal. 6:5	R., 872; B., #58–65 R., 872, 888; B., 58–65 R., 888; B., #70 B., #67 B., #69 D.M., 191–193
4. Aorist G., 1262–1264	Punctiliar Three kinds of punctiliar action in the Aorist. (As a narrative or historical tense, this is the one to use unless there is reason to use another.)	1. Constative (or indefinite or historical) (treats the act as a single whole) 2. Ingressive (or inceptive or inchoative) 3. Effective (or resultative) (emphasis on the end of a point action).[8] 4. Gnomic The following are adaptations of 1–3: 1. Dramatic (of actions which have just happened) 2. Epistolary ("the writer looks at the letter as the recipient will.")	John 2:20 2 Cor. 8:9 Matt. 3:8 Luke 3:22 Matt. 9:18 Philem. 19	R., 831; B., #35, 38 R., 834; B., #35, 41 R., 834; B., #35–42 R., 836; B., #43 R., 841; B., #45 R., 845; B., #44 D.M., 193–200

[8]These three uses are present in all the moods.

New Testament Greek Syntax Chart – 7

TENSE	KIND OF ACTION	DESCRIPTION OF USAGE	EXAMPLES	REF. TO GRAMMARS
5. Present Perfect G., 1265-1266	A state of completion in pres. time (in indic. many times)	1. Extensive present perfect= a completed state		R., 895
		a. durative-punctiliar (or pf. of completed action)	John 19:30	B., #74
		b. punctiliar-durative (or pf. of existing state)	Matt. 4:7	B., #75
		2. Intensive (The punctiliar force is dropped and only the durative remains.)	Matt. 6:8 οἶδα Rev. 3:20 ἕστηκα John 1:18	R., 894; B., #77 R., 896
		*3. Pres. of broken continuity	John 5:24	R., 897
		*4. Gnomic	Jas. 5:2	R., 898
		*5. Futuristic (equals fut. perfect)		
		*6. Periphrastic	Mark 3:1	B., #84 D.M., 200-205
6. Past Perfect	State of completion in past time usually (used only in the indic.)	1. Extensive completed state in past time	John 6:17	R., 904; B., #89, 90
		2. Intensive	John 19:25	R., 904
		*3. Past Perfect of broken continuity	Luke 8:29	R., 905
		4. Periphrastic past perf.	John 19:11	R., 906; B., #91 D.M., 205-208
7. Future Perfect Very rare in N.T. G., 1268	State of completion in future time		Matt. 16:19 Matt. 18:18 (Luke 12:52)	B., #93, 94 R., 906 D.M., 206

New Testament Greek Syntax Chart - 8

C. THE MOODS (also spelled modes; See R., 320, 321)

General Statement: The moods, of which there are four in Greek, deal with the way the statement is made (the facts of the case have to be determined by the context). The moods, with a description of their character, are as follows:

a. Indicative - a definite assertion. When one states something as a fact or as that which he wishes to be thought of as true, he uses the indicative (D.M., 168-169).

b. Subjunctive - a doubtful assertion, with a good deal of probability that it may come to pass.

c. Optative - a doubtful assertion, with some possibility that it may come to pass (more doubtful than the subjunctive).

d. Imperative - a commanding assertion, with varying degrees of insistence.

The kinds of action expressed in the verbs of the dependent moods are:

a. The present tense carries linear or durative action.
b. The aorist tense carries punctiliar action.
c. The perfect tense expresses mainly a state of completion (called the extensive perfect; see page 197), although the linear action (called the intensive perfect) is sometimes expressed (see B., #101, 102). (On mood, see also D.M., 165-168.)

MOOD CHART

MOOD	USAGE	REMARKS CONCERNING USAGE	EXAMPLES	REFERENCE TO GRAMMARS
Subjunctive Cf. G., 1319, 1320; R., 924-934	1. Prohibition	Aorist subjunctive and μή; (the present imperative and μή also indicate prohibition)	Matt. 1:20	B., #162; R., 932
	2. Third class conditions	See CONDITIONS CHART (p. 203).	Gal. 1:8; John 14:15	R., 1012
	3. Hortatory	The first person plural of the subjunctive is used here.	Matt. 26:46	B., #160; R., 930
	4. Deliberative	In deliberative questions and rhetorical questions referring to the future.	Matt. 6:25; John 6:5	B., #168; G., #1367; R., 934
	5. Purpose (final clauses)	ἵνα (also ὅπως) and the sub-junctive	Matt. 1:22; Matt. 6:2	G., #1374
	6. Result (consecutive clauses)	ἵνα and the subjunctive	Rom. 11:11	B., #218; R., 997

New Testament Greek Syntax Chart - 9

MOOD	USAGE	REMARKS CONCERNING USAGE	EXAMPLES	REFERENCE TO GRAMMARS
Subjunctive (continued)	7. Object clause (also subject and appositional clauses)	a. ἵνα and the subjunctive b. μήποτε, and sometimes μή, or μή οὐ after verbs of fearing, striving, etc.	John 12:10 Matt. 5:29 John 17:3	R., 991 (cf. G., #1382) R., 987; B., #205, 206
	8. Temporal	ὡς (and sometimes ἄν) and the subjunctive	Rom. 15:24	R., 974
	9. As an emphatic future indicative (in the negative)	οὐ μή and the aorist subjunctive	John 18:11	B., 172; G., #1369; R., 1161 D.M., 170-172
Optative9 Cf. G., #1321, 1322 The negative is μή	1. Potential (or futuristic)	The optative is used "to express what would happen on the fulfillment of some supposed condition." ἄν is frequently used. "The presence of ἄν gives 'a contingent meaning' to the verb and makes one think of the unexpressed protasis of a fourth-class condition" (Robertson, op.cit., p. 937).	Acts 26:29 Acts 17:18	B., #178; R., 937, 938
	2. Deliberative	In an indirect question (sometimes ἄν)	Luke 6:11	R., 940
	3. Volitive (or optative of wishing)	Without ἄν	Philem. 20 Rom. 6:2	B., 175; R., 939
Imperative For practice: Hebrews 10:32-36; Rom. 12:1-2, 9-21; Hebrews 12:14-17	1. Commands and exhortations		Matt. 5:44 Matt. 6:6 Rev. 22:11	B., #180; R., 946, 947
	2. Prohibition	Present imperative and μή (or a few times third singular aorist imperative and μή)	Matt. 7:1 John 6:20	B., #184, 163; R., 947
	3. Entreaties and petitions	Tone of demand is softened to pleading.	Mark 9:22 John 17:11	B., #181; R., 947, 948
	4. Consent or permission		Matt. 8:32 Matt. 10:13 Matt. 26:45	B., #182; R., 948

9Only 67 optatives occur in the New Testament.

New Testament Greek Syntax Chart - 10

MOOD	USAGE	REMARKS CONCERNING USAGE	EXAMPLES	REF. TO GRAMMARS
Imperative cont...	5. Condition (a proposed hypothesis) (or concession)		John 2:19 Jas. 4:7	B., #182; R., 948 D.M., 174-176
Participle[10] Cf. G., #1560-1595 It is a verbal adjective. (B., #418; R. 1100ff.) The neg. is generally μή (cf. Robertson-Davis, Short Grammar, p. 385)	1. As an adjective	The adjectival aspect is prominent here, i.e., it stands between the article and the noun (no article sometimes).		R., 1104ff.
	a. As an attributive adj.		John 4:11	B., #420-433; R., 1105
	b. As a substantive	The article and partic. include the idea of the noun to be supplied (no article sometimes). ὁ φεύγων, the fleeing man, or the fleeing one.	Matt. 10:40 Luke 12:33	B., #456-463; R., 1108, 1109
	2. As a verb (or adverb)	The verbal aspect is prominent here.	Mark 14:72 (Cf. Mark 11:32)	B., 434
	a. As supplementary: 1) to the verb not in indir. discourse (periphrastic constr.)		Luke 11:14	R., 1119
For Practice: 1 Thess. 1:3-6 Eph. 1:15-22 Heb. 6:1-8 Eph. 4:17-24 Heb. 12:1-3 Heb. 10:19-25 Col. 1:3-12	2) in indirect discourse	This is after verbs of knowing, perceiving, showing, etc.	Matt. 16:28	R., 1122
	b. As circumstantial participle: 1) The general use	The general use is the participle without the article to indicate time, manner, means, cause, occasion, purpose, condition, concession, imperative.	John 16:8 Matt. 27:49 Luke 19:5	B., #434-451
	2) The special use-genitive absolute	The gen. absol. consists of a noun or pronoun along with a circumstantial partic., all in the genitive case.	Eph. 2:20	B., #458

[10]Although the participle and the infinitive are not strictly moods, they will be included here for convenience' sake.

New Testament Greek Syntax Chart – 11

MOOD	USAGE	REMARKS CONCERNING USAGE	EXAMPLES	REF. TO GRAMMARS
Participle cont...		The tense of the participle. Keep in mind that: 1) kind of action is important.		B., #115
		2) the tense of the partic. is relative to that of the main verb.	Heb. 11:21	R., 1111
		a. present tense: 1. simultaneous time with main verb (this is freq.) 2. antecedent time	John 9:8; Gal. 1:23	
		3. timeless (use as an adj. or noun)	Gal. 2:6 (Cf. Matt. 6:27)	B., #123
		b. aorist tense: 1. antecedent time (this is freq.) 2. simultaneous time	Matt. 4:2 John 5:15 Matt. 27:4	
		c. future tense-future with relation to the main verb	John 6:64 Matt. 27:49	B., #152
		d. perfect tense – a state of completion	John 17:23	R., 1116
				D.M., 220-233
Infinitive Cf. G., #1520-1559 B., #361; R., 1051 It is a verbal substantive. For Practice: 1 Thess.1:6-10 2 Thess.1:3-12	1. Subject of the verb	a. Plain infinitive b. τό and the infinitive c. τοῦ and the infinitive	Heb. 9:27 Rom. 7:18 Luke 17:1	B., #384; R., 1058 B., #393 B., #404
	2. Object	a. Of the verb: 1) Plain infinitive 2) τό and the infinitive 3) τοῦ and the infinitive	Phil. 4:11 Phil. 2:6 Matt. 21:32	B., #387; R., 1058 B., #394 B., #401, 404
		b. Of prepositions c. After nouns, adjectives: 1) plain infinitive (also after adverbs)	Heb. 2:15 Matt. 3:14 Luke 15:19 Acts 21:13	B., #406; R., 1068 R., 1075-1077 B., #376, 378
		2) τοῦ and the infinitive	Acts 23:15	B., #399, 400

New Testament Greek Syntax Chart – 12

MOOD	USAGE	REMARKS CONCERNING USAGE	EXAMPLES	REF. TO GRAMMARS
Infinitive cont....	3. Indirect discourse		Luke 24:23	B., #390; R., 1082
	4. Purpose	a. Plain Infinitive	Matt. 2:2	B., #366; R., 990
		b. τοῦ and the infinitive	Matt. 13:3	B., #397; R., 1087
		c. εἰς or πρός and the infinitive	Rom. 3:26;	R., 1071, 1075
		d. ὥστε and the infinitive	Matt. 13:30	
			Matt. 10:1	R., 990
	5. Result	a. Plain infinitive	Luke 10:40	B., #369; R., 1089
		b. ὥστε and the infinitive	Matt. 13:32	B., #371; R., 1000
		c. τοῦ and the infinitive	Rom. 6:6	B., #398; R., 990
	6. Time	a. "Before," πρίν, πρὶν ἤ or πρὸ τοῦ and the infinitive	Matt. 26:34; Matt. 1:18; Gal. 2:12	B., #380; R., 1074; R., 1091
		b. "While," ἐν τῷ and the infin.	Acts 9:3	R., 1072
		c. "After," μετὰ τό and the infin.	1 Cor. 11:25	R., 1074
	7. Cause	a. διὰ τό and the infinitive	Luke 11:8	R., 1070
		b. τῷ and the infinitive (once)	2 Cor. 2:13	B., #396; R., 1091
	8. Appositional and Epexegetical		Eph. 4:17; Rom. 1:28	R., 1078, 1086; D.M., 208
Negatives:				
Indicative	οὐ and μή		Matt. 25:42; Titus 1:11	R., 1157, 1168
Subjunctive	μή generally		Mark 12:14	R., 1160, 1169
Imperative			Luke 12:11	R., 1161, 1170
Infinitive			Mark 12:18	R., 1162, 1170
Participle	μή mostly (Matt. 12:30)	although sometimes οὐ (John 10:12)	1 Thess. 4:5	R., 1136, 1162, 1172
Optative	μή		Rom. 6:2	R., 1161, 1170
Question	1) οὐ	expects the answer, "Yes."	Luke 17:17	R., 1157, 1175;
	2) μή	expects the answer, "No."	John 21:5	D.M., 263-267

New Testament Greek Syntax Chart – 13

D. NEW TESTAMENT GREEK CONDITIONAL SENTENCES:

1. General Statement: In a condition the indicative mood makes a clear-cut assertion one way or another; the subjunctive and optative, a doubtful assertion (optative more doubtful than the subjunctive); and the imperative, a commanding assertion. Cf. R., 1004ff; B., #238ff; A. T. Robertson and W. H. Davis, A Short Grammar (New York: Harper and Brothers, 1933), p. 349.

2. Conditions Chart: Two types of conditions (Robt. 1004) --determined (1st and 2nd class) and undetermined (subjunctive and optative). The protasis is the conditional "if" clause; the apodosis is the conclusion.

CONDITIONS CHART

ELEMENTS

KIND	Protasis Particle	Protasis Verb	Apodosis Verb	Apodosis Particle	EXAMPLE
1st Class (a fact at least assumed as true)	εἰ (sometimes ἐάν)	any tense of the indic.	any tense of the indic. usually, or impv. or subj.		"If the world hates you, know that it has hated me first." (John 15:18; Matt. 4:3)
2nd Class (contrary to fact) a. Pres. time	εἰ	imperfect indic.	imperf. indic. or past tense of the indic.	ἄν	"If this one were the prophet, he would know." (Lk. 7:39)
b. Past time	εἰ	aorist indic. usually	aorist indic. usually	ἄν (when absent the context makes the condition clear)	"If these miracles had been done in Tyre and Sidon, they would have repented." (Matt. 11:21).
3rd Class	ἐάν, ἄν (sometimes εἰ)	aor. subj., pres. subj. or fut. ind.	variety of tenses (fut. ind.; pres. or aor. ind.; or impv.		John 13:17 (3rd and 1st here) "If this purpose shall be of men, it will be destroyed." (Acts 5:38)

New Testament Greek Syntax Chart -- 14

Conditions Chart cont...

ELEMENTS

KIND	Protasis		Apodosis		EXAMPLE
	Particle	Verb	Verb	Particle	
4th Class There is no com- plete 4th class condition in the New Testament. Examples: Protasis: 1 Pet. 3:14 Apodosis: Acts 8:31	εἰ	Optative	Optative	ἄν	Only fragments left; cf. Luke 1:62

Cf., R., 1004–1129; R.D., 162–163; D.M., 286–291.

New Testament Greek Syntax Chart - 15

E. TYPES OF SUBORDINATE CLAUSES AND PHRASES:

1. Infinitive Phrases

Introductory Words	Temporal	Causal	Purpose	Subject, Object Clauses	Result	Indirect Discourse	Reference to Grammars
a. ----			X	X	X	X	B., #366, 369, 390
b. διὰ τό		X					B., #406ff.
c. εἰς τό			X		X		B., #406ff.
d. ἐν τῷ	X						B., #406ff.
e. μετὰ τό	X						B., #406ff.
f. πρίν	X						B., #380
g. πρὸ τοῦ	X						B., #406ff.
h. πρὸς τό			X				B., #406ff.
i. τοῦ			X	X	X		B., #397, 398, 404
j. ὥστε		X	X		X		B., #371
							D.M., 214-220

New Testament Greek Syntax Chart - 16

2. Other Phrases and Clauses

Conj. or Introd. Word(s)	Mood (or Inf., Partic.)	Relative	Temporal	Causal	Purpose	Subj., obj., appos. clauses	Result	Local	Compar.	Dir., indir. disc.	Reference to Grammars
a. ----	Partic. (pres., fut.)				X						B., #442
b. διότι	Indic.			X							R., 964
c. ἐν ᾧ	Indic.		X	X							R.D., 325
d. ἐπεί	Indic.			X							R., 963
e. ἐπειδή	Indic.			X							R.D., 338
f. ἕως [11]	Indic. and Subj.		X								B., #321-330; B., 975-977; R.D., 325, 328
g. ἵνα	Subj. (sometimes fut., pres. indic.)				X	X	X				R.D., 340, 344, 346
h. καθότι	Indic.			X							R.D., 337, 335
i. μή (instead of ἵνα μή)	Subj. and fut. indic.					X			X		R.D., 345
j. μήποτε	Subj. and fut. indic.				X	X					R.D., 342, 345
k. ὅθεν	Indic.							X			R.D., 338, 332
l. ὅπου	Indic. (subj.)							X			R.D., 332
m. ὅπως	Subj.				X	X					R.D., 341, 344
n. ὅς, ὅστις	Subj. indic.	X									R., 953
o. ὅταν	Subj. (usually)		X								R.D., 326
p. ὅτε	Indic.		X								R.D., 326
q. ὅτι	Indic.			X						X	R.D., 337, 364
r. οὗ	Indic. (usually)							X			R.D., 332
s. ὡς	Indic. (usually)		X								R.D., 327
t. ὥστε	Inf. or indic.						X				D.M., 269-286, 291-295

11 ἄχρι, ἄχρι οὗ, ἄχρι ἧς ἡμέρας, μέχρι, μέχρι οὗ, πρὶν ἤ (ἄν) are similar.

F. PREPOSITIONS CHART:

This chart is based on usages given in Arndt, Gingrich and Danker's _Greek-English Lexicon of the New Testament_, and Thayer's _Greek-English Lexicon_. Compare also R., 571-636; R.D., 248-263; M., 98-107; D.M., 96-115. There are 17 regular prepositions, not counting ἀμφί which occurs only in composition (compounds).

THE CASES

PREPOSITION	Genitive	Dative	Accusative	SYNTACTICAL USAGE
ἀνά (denotes motion from a lower to a higher place)			up, upwards	1. As prep., with accusative 2. With μέσου and gen. of place, among, between, Matt. 13:25; with μέρος (in turn), 1 Cor. 14:27 3. Distributive use, ἀνὰ δύο, cf. Luke 10:1 4. Prefixed to verbs, it indicates up, to, back.
ἀντί (once it probably signified, over against, opposed to, before)	1. instead of [12] 2. for 3. in the place of 4. in behalf of			1. As prep. w. genitive, instead of, Luke 11:11; in the place of, 1 Cor. 11:15; in behalf of, Matt. 17:27 2. As conjunction, ἀνθ' ὧν (because, therefore), Luke 1:20; 12:3 3. Prefixed to nouns and verbs, it indicates, opposite, mutual efficiency of two, instead of, Jas. 4:15.

ἀπό (signifying separation, and origin)	1. Separation
	  a. from, Matt. 7:4
	2. Origin
	  a. from, down from Matt. 15:27
	  b. out of, from Mark 8:11
	3. Cause, means
	  a. because of, Luke 19:3
	  b. with the help of, Luke 15:16
				1. As prep. with genitive
				2. Quasi-adverbial force, Luke 14:18
				3. In composition it indicates, separation, cessation, departure, etc.

[12]Words underscored are meanings.

New Testament Greek Syntax Chart – 18

Prepositions Chart cont...

THE CASES

PREPOSITION	Genitive	Dative	Accusative	SYNTACTICAL USAGE

διά	1. Place
	  a. through, Acts 9:32
	  b. with, in, Rev. 21:24
	2. Time
	  a. throughout (during) Matt. 18:10
	3. Means, instrument
	  a. by means of, 2 John 12
			1. by reason of, because of, Rom. 8:3
			2. on acc. of, Matt. 6:25
			3. for the benefit of, for the sake of, Mark 2:27
				1. As prep. w. gen. and acc.
				2. As conjunction, διὰ τοῦτο, therefore
				3. In composition it indicates a passing through, completeness of action, distribution, separation, transfer, etc.

εἰς[13]
(denoting entrance into, or direction and limit)
			1. Place
			  a. into, John 18:1
			  b. to, in the vicinity of Mark 7:31
			  c. as far as, Luke 17:24
			2. Time
			  a. through, or for Matt. 21:19
			  b. for or on Matt. 6:34
			3. Direction
			  a. for benefit of Eph. 1:19
			  b. with respect or reference to Rom. 8:28
			  c. in order to (purpose) Luke 5:4 Matt. 26:28
				1. As prep. w. acc.
				2. Purpose phrases: εἰς τοῦτο – to this end, etc.
				3. Adverbial phrases: εἰς τὸ πάλιν – again, etc.
				4. In composition

[13]There is no fast rule concerning εἰς and ἐν in the N.T. Cf. R.D., 256.

New Testament Greek Syntax Chart - 19

Prepositions Chart cont...

THE CASES

PREPOSITION	Genitive	Dative	Accusative	SYNTACTICAL USAGE

ἐκ (ἐξ)	1. Place
	  a. from, John 6:31
	2. Origin, cause
	  a. From, John 8:41
	3. Time
	  a. from, Matt. 19:12
	  b. since, John 9:32
				1. As prep. w. genitive
				2. Equiv. to ἐν in some phrases (Mt. 24:17, etc.)
				3. Adverbial phrases
				4. In comp. it indicates egression, origin, completion.

ἐν		1. Place
		  a. in, Luke 7:37
		  b. at, among John 8:20; (in the presence of) 1 Cor. 2:6
		2. Instrument, cause, by means of, with, Rev. 17:16
		3. Time in, at, on, Matt. 27:40; during John 6:44
				1. As prep. w. dative
				2. In composition:
				  a. with adjs. it indicates lying in some place, possessed of, or noted for something.
				  b. With verbs it indicates remaining, motion into, on.

ἐπί (primary meaning upon)	1. Place
	  a. **upon** Mark 9:2
	  b. over Rom. 9:5
	  c. at, near Acts 5:23
	  d. before, in the presence of Matt. 28:14
	  e. on the basis of 1 Tim. 5:19
		1. Place
		  a. at, on, Rev. 4:9
		  b. on the ground of Matt. 4:4
		  c. for the purpose of, result, 2 Tim. 2:14
		2. Time
		  a. at, in, Heb. 9:15
		  b. while Eph. 4:26
			1. Place
			  a. on, Matt 15:35
			  b. near, up to, to, John 6:16
			  c. over Rom. 5:14
			  d. toward, on (goal), Acts 9:42
			  e. for (purpose) Matt. 3:7
			2. Time
			  a. during, (over a period), Luke 4:25
			  b. on, Luke 10:35
			3. Extent, measure, 2 Tim. 3:9
				1. As prep. w. gen., dat., acc.
				2. Adverbial phrases
				3. In composition it indicates rest, influence on, motion, imposition, increase, repetition, up, against.

Prepositions Chart cont....

THE CASES

PREPOSITION	Genitive	Dative	Accusative	SYNTACTICAL USAGE

κατά (indicating direction from a higher to a lower place)	1. against, Rev. 2:4
	 2. by (in swearing) Matt. 26:63
	 3. down, Matt. 8:32
	 4. throughout Acts 9:42
			1. Place
			  a. (down) through, Luke 8:39
			  b. toward, Phil. 3:14
			 2. Time
			  a. as on, about, Acts 12:1
			 3. Relations
			  a. in relation to, Rom. 1:3
			  b. in accordance with, just as, Gal. 4:28
			  c. because of, Rom. 8:28
				1. As prep. w. gen., acc.
				 2. Adverbial phrases. E.g., κατ' ἰδίαν – apart.
				 3. In composition it indicates down from, thoroughly, succession, under, dissolution, after, proportionately, against.

μετά (denoting association, union, sometimes less intimate than w. σύν)	1. Place
	  a. among, Mark 1:13
	 2. Accompaniment
	  a. with, Matt. 20:20
	 3. Attendant circumstance
	  a. of moods, feelings, Luke 14:9
	  b. of accompanying phenomena, Mark 10:30
			1. Place, Heb. 9:3
			 2. Time after, Matt. 17:1
				1. As prep. w. gen., acc.
				 2. In composition it indicates association, exchange, after.

παρά (denoting close proximity)	1. From the side of, Matt. 21:42; John 1:6	1. At or by (the side of)
		  a. near, beside John 19:25
		  b. before, in the sight of Rom. 2:13
			1. Space
			  a. by, along, Matt 4:18
			  b. to the side of, Mark 2:13
			  c. near, at, Luke 7:38
			  d. on, Mark 4:4
			 2. Comparison
			  a. more than, Rom. 14:5
			  b. instead of, Rom. 1:25
				1. As prep. w. gen., dat., acc.
				 2. In composition it indicates nearness, stealthiness, violation, neglect.

New Testament Greek Syntax Chart — 21

Prepositions Chart cont.

THE CASES

PREPOSITION	Genitive	Dative	Accusative	SYNTACTICAL USAGE
περί (denoting encompassing)	1. about, concerning 1 Cor. 7:1 2. With regard to, with respect to Acts 15:2 3. On account of, because of Luke 19:37		1. Around, about, Mark 4:10 2. Concerning, with regard to, 2 Tim. 2:18	1. As prep. w. gen., acc. 2. In composition it indicates round about, beyond.
πρό	1. Place before, in front of, Acts 12:6 2. Time before, Luke 11:38 3. Rank, above all, 1 Peter 4:8			1. As prep. w. genitive 2. In composition it indicates motion forward, before.
πρός	1. To the advantage of, Acts 27:34	1. At, near, (rarely used in the dative) John 18:16	1. Place, toward(s), to, Eph. 2:18 2. Time a. onward, Luke 24:29 b. for (a time), 1 Cor. 7:5 3. Goal: for, for the purpose of, Acts 3:10 4. Relationship, against, or with Acts 24:19 5. Connection a. with reference to; Mark 12:12 b. as far as, with regard to, Rom. 15:17 6. (in company) with Matt. 13:56	1. As prep. w. gen., dat., acc. 2. In composition it indicates motion to a goal, addition, vicinity, on, at.

New Testament Greek Syntax Chart - 22

Prepositions Chart cont....

THE CASES

PREPOSITION	Genitive	Dative	Accusative	SYNTACTICAL USAGE
σύν (denotes accompaniment and fellowship; sometimes more intimate than μετά)		1. with a. accompaniment and association, John 12:2 b. experience of something together, Acts 5:1 c. aid, 1 Cor. 15:10 d. combining persons and things, with, Rom. 8:32 e. New factor, besides, in addition, Luke 24:21		1. As prep. with dat. 2. In composition it indicates association, together, completely, with one's self.
ὑπέρ (denotes a state or motion over and beyond a place)	1. for (benefit of, sake of), Col. 1:7 2. in order to, Gal. 1:4; John 11:4 3. in the place of, on behalf of, Rom. 9:3 4. because of, Acts 5:41 5. concerning, John 1:30		1. over (above, more than, beyond), Eph. 1:22; Matt. 10:24	1. As prep. w. gen., acc. 2. In composition it indicates over, beyond, more than, for, in defense of.
ὑπό	1. by (agency) Matt. 1:22		1. under, below, subject to the power of, 1 Cor. 15:25; Luke 7:8 2. Time about, Acts 5:21	1. As prep. w. gen., acc. 2. In composition it indicates under, subjection, compliance, slightly.

New Testament Greek Syntax Chart – 23

G. CHART ON THE USE OF THE GREEK ARTICLE:

(Cf. G., #933–983; R., 754–796; R.D., 274ff; S., #1189–1199;[14] J.B. Mayor on the Epistle of James, clvi. ff. Cf. also D.M., 135–153.)

PRESENCE OR ABSENCE OF THE ARTICLE	USAGE	REMARKS	REFERENCE TO GRAMMARS
1. Presence Indicates	a. Definiteness: 1) with ordinary nouns	with the same ambiguity of definiteness or indefin. as in English. E.g., the man, the store.	G., #939; S., #1119
	2) with proper nouns sometimes		G., #941; R., 759
	3) with abstract terms sometimes	where the idea is definite in English without the article; e.g. ἡ ἀρετή (virtue), 1 Cor. 12:9–11	G., #942; S., #1131
	4) with nouns accompanied by pronouns and adjs. which are already definite in idea:		
	a. demonstrative pron.———	Usually; οὗτος ὁ ἄνθρωπος	G., #943
	b. possessive adj.———	Unless the adjective is predicate; John 17:10	G., #944a; R., 770
	c. the pronoun in the gen.		G., #944b
	b. Possessive pronoun force	E.g. ἀπενίψατο τὰς χεῖρας, he washed his hands, Matt. 27:24	G., #947; R., 769
	c. Generic force	a representative of a class; e.g. ὁ ἄνθρωπος, man, or mankind	G., #948; S., #1122, 1123
	d. Demonstrative force	ὁ δὲ εἶπεν, Matt. 14:18	R.D., 274; S., #1106–1107

[14]H.W. Smyth, Greek Grammar (Cambridge: Harvard University Press, 1959).

New Testament Greek Syntax Chart – 24

Chart on the Use of the Greek Article, continued.

PRESENCE OR ABSENCE OF THE ARTICLE	USAGE	REMARKS	REFERENCE TO GRAMMARS
2. Absence indicates	a. Indefiniteness	E.g., ἄνθρωπος, a man	R., 794; S., #1129
	b. Definiteness: 1) with noun to empha- size the quality	E.g., John 1:1	G., #954; R., 794; S., #1150, 1151
	2) with a predicate noun or adj. many times	E.g., πύλαι ᾄδου the gates of Hell, Matt. 16:18	R., 791; S., #1146, 1147
	3) with a definite depend- ent gen. sometimes	E.g., κύριος, θεός	R., 791; S., #1136, 1137
	4) with proper nouns sometimes	E.g., Gal. 5:20	R., 794; S., #1132, 1135
	5) with abstract terms	E.g., ἥλιος – Matt. 13:6 γῆ – Luke 2:14 νόμος – Rom. 2:12	R., 794; R.D., 282; S., #1141
	6) with definite unique objects or distinc- tive words	E.g., ἐν οἴκῳ – 1 Cor. 11:34 ἀπ οὐρανοῦ – Luke 17:29	R., 791; S., #1128
	7) with definite prep. phrases	E.g., ἀπὸ πρώτης ἡμέρας – Acts 20:18	R., 793; S., #1125
	8) with ordinal numbers usually		

New Testament Greek Syntax Chart - 25

H. CHART ON COORDINATING CONJUNCTIONS:[15]

CONJUNCTION	KIND	USAGE	REFERENCE TO GRAMMARS
ἀλλά	1. Adversative	a. It is used for: 1) opposition to concessions, "nevertheless, notwithstanding," John 16:7, 20. 2) an objection, John 7:27. 3) an exception, Rom. 4:2. 4) an ascensive gradation or transition (espec. with καί added), "nay rather, nay moreover," Luke 12:7. 5) in an apodosis after a condition or concessive protasis, with the meaning, "yet," Mark 14:29. b. It is used with other particles as ἀλλά γε, "yet at least, yea surely," I Cor. 9:2.	R.D., 316; Thayer, 27; A.G., 37-38
ἄρα		It has the idea of correspondence (R.D.). It differs from οὖν in giving a "subjective impression rather than a positive conclusion" (Liddell and Scott).[16]	R.D., 317; Thayer, 71; A.G., 103
γάρ	1. Inferential	It is composed of γε ἄρα and indicates affirmation and conclusion. For: a) Conclusion, "assuredly, verily, why", etc. (used in questions and answers including emotions). John 9:30	R.D., 317; Thayer, 109; A.G., 151

[15]Compare also D.M., 239-258; and A.G.D., (Arndt, Gingrich and Danker, A Greek-English Lexicon).

[16]Liddell and Scott, A Greek-English Lexicon, new ed. (Oxford: Clarendon Press, 1951).

New Testament Greek Syntax Chart — 26

Chart on Coordinating Conjunctions continued

CONJUNCTION	KIND	USAGE	REFERENCE TO GRAMMARS
(γάρ continued)		b. Cause or Reason (for a preceding statement). Where several γάρ appear in a series, each γάρ can reinforce the same gen. idea expressed in each clause, or each succeeding γάρ can give the reason for the immediate preceding clause. c. Explanation, illustration of a preceding thought, an exposition of the thing just announced; "for," e.g., "that is, namely." Matt. 19:12	
δέ	1. Adversative "but, moreover"	a. "but" b. After negative sentences, "but rather", Matt. 6:19, 20 c. "I say," "and that," "so then" (the English trans. for a suppressed negative clause), when joined to terms repeated with additional modifiers for more exact definition. Rom. 3:21, 22 (δικαιοσύνη repeated).	R.D., 316; Thayer, 125; A.G., 170
	2. Copulative	It makes a transition to something new, "now" or "and." Matt. 1:2-20	
εἴτε	1. Disjunctive (tending to disjoin)	εἴτε...εἴτε, "whether...or."	R.D., 317; Thayer, 172; A.G., 219, 233
ἤ	1. Disjunctive	a. to distinguish things, "or" b. in a disjunctive question John 7:17 (whether...or) c. with other particles, as ἀλλά, γάρ etc. d. as a comparative conj., "than"	R.D., 317; Thayer, 275; A.G., 342, 343

New Testament Greek Syntax Chart - 27

Chart on Coordinating Conjunctions continued

CONJUNCTION	KIND	USAGE	REFERENCE TO GRAMMARS
καί	1. Copulative	Used to connect words and sentences: a. generally (clauses also) b. epexegetically (i.e., with an additional explanation), "and indeed, namely," Acts 23:6. c. with καί...καί, "both..and" "as well..as."	R.D., 316; Thayer, 315; A.G., 392-394
	2. Adverbial	Used: a. Alone: 1) "also, likewise," Matt. 5:39. 2) "even." b. Joined to pronouns and particles, "also."	
	3. Adversative	"and yet, but," Luke 12:24	
μηδέ	1. Disjunctive	It continues a negation or prohibition, "but not, and not, neither," Matt. 22:29.	R.D., 317; Thayer, 411; A.G., 519
μήτε	1. Disjunctive	"neither...nor."	R.D., 317; Thayer, 413; A.G., 521
οὐδέ	1. Disjunctive	a. Continues a negation: 1) "and not." It considers things that are equal and mutually exclusive (cf. οὔτε). "nor..nor." 2) "also not, neither," Matt. 6:15. b. Just makes a negation, "not even," Mark 6:31.	R.D., 317; Thayer, 461; A.G., 595, 596
οὖν	1. Inferential	It indicates that something necessarily follows from another: a. in exhortations, "wherefore," Rom. 6:12.	R.D., 317; Thayer, 463; A.G., 597

New Testament Greek Syntax Chart - 28

Chart on Coordinating Conjunctions continued

CONJUNCTION	KIND	USAGE	REFERENCE TO GRAMMARS
(οὖν continued)		b. in questions, "then, therefore," Rom. 6:1. c. in epanalepsis (resumption after an interruption), Luke 3:7. d. in summation. e. in transition (in hist. discourse), John 1:22. f. with other conjs. (εἰ οὖν "if then", etc.).	
οὔτε	1. Disjunctive	It connects parts of the same thing (cf. οὐδέ): a. singly, "and not." b. οὔτε...οὔτε, "neither...nor"	R.D., 317; Thayer, 466; A.G., 600
πλήν	1. Adversative	At the beginning of a sentence to restrict or unfold the preceding; "moreover, besides, but nevertheless"	R.D., 317; Thayer, 517; A.G., 675
τέ	1. Copulative	a. Standing alone it joins: 1) parts of the same sentence, Matt. 28:12. 2) complete sentences, John 4:42. b. τέ...καί, "not only...but also." c. τέ...τέ, "as...so" (these present as parallels the sentences or phrases which they connect), Acts 2:46. d. τε γάρ "for indeed" (τέ connects, γάρ gives the reason), Rom. 1:26.	R.D., 316; Thayer, 616; A.G., 815

New Testament Greek Syntax Chart - 29

I. CHART ON INTENSIVE PARTICLES:17

PARTICLE	USAGE	REMARKS	REFERENCE TO GRAMMARS

γέ	1. To minify
	
	2. To magnify
	3. To strengthen the force of other particles:
		I.e., to make less, "indeed, truly, at least," Luke 11:8; "even," Rom. 8:32.
		
		a. ἀλλά γε, "yet at least"
		b. ἄρα γε, "surely then, so then"
		c. εἰ γε followed by the indic., "if indeed, seeing that"
		d. εἰ δὲ μή γε:
		  1) after affirmative sentences, "but unless perchance; but if not," Matt. 6:1
		  2) after neg. sentences, "otherwise, else," Matt. 9:17
		e. καί γε, "and truly," Acts 2:18
		f. μεν οὖν γε, "nay surely; nay rather," Rom. 9:20
			R.D., 394; Thayer, 110; A.G., 152

δή	1. Joined to a rel. pronoun (once), Matt. 13:23, "who then." 2. Joined to impvs. and hortatory subjunctives	It indicates that "what it introduces can be taken as something settled, laid down in deed and in truth" (Klotz; quoted in Thayer). It indicates urgency; "at once, now only," Luke 2:15.	R.D., 395; Thayer, 131; A.G., 177
μέν	1. Followed further on in the sentence by an adversative particle:	It is an affirmative particle, "indeed." a. μέν concessive, and δέ or ἀλλά) restrictive, corrective, or amplificatory; "indeed... but, yet, on the other hand," Matt. 3:11. b. μέν not concessive, but still adversative, Luke 11:48.	R.D., 396; Thayer, 387; A.G., 503, 504

17Compare D.M., 258-267.

New Testament Greek Syntax Chart – 30

Chart on Intensive Particles continued

PARTICLE	USAGE	REMARKS	REFERENCE TO GRAMMARS
(μέν continued)	2. Not followed by δέ nor any other adversative particle when:	c. μὲν...δέ meaning "both ... and; as well...as; not only... but also." John 16:9-11, οὐ μὲν ...οὐ δέ some, others. a. the antithesis is evident from the context, Col. 2:23. b. the antithesis is brought out by another type of construction. Acts 19:4; Rom. 7:12. c. the writer had a δέ in mind but became involved in an explanation of details relating to the first member (with the μέν), 2 Cor. 12:12. d. the combination is μὲν οὖν "so, then; now, therefore"; Acts 1:18.	
μέν τοι	1. A particle of affirmation and of opposition	It means "but yet; nevertheless" John 4:27.	R.D., 396; Thayer, 399; A.G., 504
ναί	1. An affirmative and confirmative particle	It means "yea, verily, truly, assuredly, even so" (a repeated ναί, "most assuredly"); Matt. 11:26.	Thayer, 422; A.G., 534
πέρ	1. Used with ὅς. 2. Used with other particles (as διό περ) with idea of "thoroughly."	It is related to περί; has the idea of "thoroughly."	R.D., 396; Thayer, 500; A.G., 649
τοί	1. Always used with other particles in N.T. as: ἤτοι, καί τοι.	It is equivalent to the idea "on this account" (or "you then").	R.D., 396; A.G., 828

PRONUNCIATION OF THE ALPHABET IN MODERN GREEK

Form	Name		Represented in Phonetic Pronunciation by	Pronounced as
A α	ἄλφα	(ál´fa)	a	a in father
B β	βῆτα	(vĭ´tä)	v	v in victory
Γ γ	γάμα	(yå´mä)	y	y in yes or year
Δ δ	δέλτα	(thĕl´ta)	th	th in they
E ε	ἔψιλον	(ĕpsĭlŏn´)	e	e in red
Z ζ	ζῆτα	(zĭ´tä)	z	z in zero
H η	ἦτα	(ĭ´ta)	í, ĭ	i in ill or machine
θ ϑ	θῆτα	(thĭ´tä)	th	th in thin
I ι	ἰῶτα	(ĭ ō´tä)	í, ĭ	i in ill or machine
K κ	κάππα	(kå´på)	k	k in king
Λ λ	λάμβδα	(låm´vthå)	l	l in lot
M μ	μῦ	(mĭ)	m	m in mother
N ν	νῦ	(nĭ)	n	n in now
Ξ ξ	ξῦ	(ksĭ)	x, ks	x in extra
O o	ὁ μικρόν	(ŏ mĭkron´)	o	o in corporal
Π π	πῦ	(pĭ)	p	p in paper
P ρ	ῥῶ	(rŏ)	r	r in red
Σ σ,ς	σίγμα	(sĭy´må)	s	s in sister
T τ	ταῦ	(tåf)	t	t in tin
Y υ	ὖψιλόν	(ĭ psĭlŏn´)	í, ĭ	i in ill or machine
Φ φ	φῦ	(fĭ)	f	f in fat
X χ	χῦ	(hï)	h	h in hill, but heavily aspirated
Ψ ψ	ψῦ	(psĭ)	ps	ps in lips
Ω ω	ὦ μέγα	(ŏ mĕ´yå)	o	o in corporal

SOME COMMON EXPRESSIONS IN MODERN GREEK

Εἶμαι καλός· δὲν εἶμαι κακός.	I am good; I am not bad.
Πῶς εἶσαι; Εἶσαι καλά;	How are you? Are you well?
Ναί. Εἶμαι πολὺ καλά. Εὐχαριστῶ.	Yes; I am very well. Thank you.
Εἶσθε καλά;	Are you well?
Ἡμεῖς εἶμεθα πολὺ καλά.	We are very well.
Ἡμεῖς πῶς εἶσθε;	How are you?
Ἐγὼ εἶμαι ἐδῶ.	I am here.
Εἶναι καλὰ βιβλία;	Are they good books?
Εἶναι πολὺ καλὰ βιβλία.	They are very good books.
Ποῦ εἶναι ὁ φίλος σου;	Where is your friend?
Εἶναι σ' ἐκεῖνο τὸ δωμάτιον.	He is in that room.
Τί θέλετε τώρα, κύριε;	What do you want now, sir?
Κύτταξε ἐκεῖ, Γιάννη.	Look there, John.
Τί εἶναι τοῦτο;	What is this?
Τί εἶναι τοῦτο τὸ πρᾶγμα;	What is this thing?
Εἶναι μολύβι.	It is a pencil.
Εὐχαριστῶ πολύ.	I thank you very much.
Παρακαλῶ, κύριε.	Please don't mention it, sir.
Αὐτὸ εἶναι καλλίτερο.	This is better.
Πήγαινε νὰ τὸ φέρῃς, παρακαλῶ.	Go and bring it, please.
Τί θέλετε νὰ πιῆτε; Τσάι, καφέ, ἢ γάλα;	What do you want to drink? Tea, coffee, or milk?
Ὄχι, εὐχαριστῶ.	No, thank you.
Σᾶς παρακαλῶ.	Please.
Καλημέρα, Γεώργο. Τί κάνεις;	Good morning, George. How do you do?
Πολὺ καλά, Γιάννη. Πῶς εἶσθε σεῖς;	Very well, John. How are you?
Δὲν εἶμαι τόσον καλὰ σήμερα. Εἶμαι ἄρρωστος.	I am not so well today. I am sick.

Εἶσαι ἄρρωστος; Τί ἔχεις;	Are you sick? What is the matter with you?
Δὲν εἰξεύρω.	I do not know.
Ἔχω κάτι διὰ σέ.	I have something for you.
Τί εἶναι;	What is it?
Σᾶς εὐχαριστῶ πολύ, κύριε. Εἶσθε πολὺ καλός.	I thank you very much, sir. You are very kind.
Μάλιστα, κύριε.	Yes, sir.
Ποῦ πηγαίνετε τώρα;	Where are you going now?
Πηγαίνω σπῆτι.	I am going home.
Χαίρετε.	Good-bye.
Εἶνε πολὺ ἀκριβά.	They are very expensive.
Ἔχετε δίκαιον, φίλε μου.	You are right, my friend.
Ἔβρεχε ὅλην τὴν ἡμέραν.	It rained (was raining) all day.
Δυποῦμαι πολὺ ποῦ τὸ ἀκούω.	I am very sorry to hear it.
Χαίρω νὰ τὸ ἀκούω.	I am glad to hear it.
Ἦσο ἄρρωστος προχθές;	Were you ill day before yesterday?
Ναί. Ἤμουν ἄρρωστος.	Yes. I was ill.
Τί εἶχες;	What was the matter with you? (What had you?)
Τώρα εἶμαι ἐντελῶς καλά.	Now I am perfectly well.
Δὲν ἔχομεν καιρόν.	We have no time.
Τί ἔπαθες;	What is the matter with you?
Ἡμεῖς εἴμεθα ἐντελῶς ἕτοιμοι νὰ φύγωμεν.	We are quite ready to leave.
Τώρα εἴμεθα ὅλοι ἕτοιμοι.	Now we are all ready.
Εἶνε πολὺ ζέστη ἐδῶ.	It is very warm here.
Ἄς πᾶμε εἰς τὴν στέγην νὰ πάρωμεν ὀλίγον ἀέρα.	Let us go on the roof to get a little air.

Δὲν ἔχομεν καιρὸν νὰ χάσωμεν.	We have no time to lose.
Μπορεῖτε νὰ πᾶτε ἐκεῖ τὸ ἀπόγευμα.	You can go there in the afternoon.
Δὲν εἶνε τόσον ἀργὰ ἀκόμη.	It is not so late yet.
Εἶνε ἀρκετὰ ἀργά.	It is late enough.
Πρέπει νὰ πηγαίνωμεν.	We must be going.
Χαίρετε, Κύριε Παῦλε.	Good-bye, Mr. Paul.
Θὰ ἔλθετε μαζύ μου;	Will you come with me?
Ναί, θὰ ἔλθω.	Yes, I will come.
Νομίζω πῶς θὰ βρέξῃ αὔριον.	I think (that) it will rain tomorrow.
Ποῖον εἶνε τὸ ὄνομά σου;	What is your name?
Ὀνομάζομαι Γεώργιος Μῆτρος.	My name is George Metros.
Πόσων ἐτῶν εἶσαι;	How old are you?
Εἶμαι εἴκοσι ἒξ ἐτῶν.	I am twenty-six years old.
Τί ἐργασίαν εἰμπορεῖς νὰ κάμῃς;	What work can you do?
Ποιὰ εἶνε ἡ δουλειά σου;	What is your business?
Τί ὥρα εἶναι;	What time is it?
Εἰμπορεῖτε νὰ μοῦ πῆτε τὴν ὥραν, παρακαλῶ;	Can you tell me the time, please?
Μάλιστα, κύριε. Εἶνε περίπου δέκα.	Yes, sir. It is about ten (o'clock).
Ὄχι, ἔχω λάθος. Εἶνε μόνον ἐννέα καὶ μισή.	No, I am mistaken. It is only half past nine.
Δὲν εἶνε ἐννέα καὶ μισή. Εἶνε δέκα παρὰ εἴκοσι.	It is not half past nine. It is twenty (minutes) to ten.
Σᾶς παρακαλῶ νὰ μὲ περιμένετε ἐδῶ.	I beg you to wait for me here.
Εἶναι πολὺ καλὸν μέρος.	It is a very good place.
Νά, ἐδῶ εἴμεθα.	Here we are.
Συγγνώμην, κύριε.	Pardon me, sir.

Σᾶς ζητῶ συγγνώμην, κύριε.

I beg your pardon, sir.

Σήμερον εἶνε ζεστά, ἀλλὰ ἦτο ζεστότερα χθές.

Today it is warm, but it was warmer yesterday.

Ἡ ἐργασία σου εἶνε εὔκολος.

Your work is easy.

Βλέπω ἔχεις πολλὰ χρήματα.

I see you have much money.

Κύτταξε!

Look!

Νομίζω εἶνε ἀρκετὰ εὔθηνά.

I think it is cheap enough.

Δὲν εἰμπορῶ νὰ ἐξοδεύω πολλά, ὅπως γνωρίζεις.

I can't spend much, (as) you know.

ἀγαθός, ή, όν — good

ἀγαπάω — I love

ἀγάπη — love

ἀγαπητός, ή, όν — beloved

ἄγγελος — messenger, angel

ἅγιος, α, ον — holy; plural, as a noun, saints

ἀγοράζω — I buy (cf. agora, marketplace)

ἀγρός, οῦ, ὁ — field (agrarian)

ἄγω — I lead

ἀδελφός, οῦ, ὁ — brother (Philadelphia, brotherly love)

αἷμα, ατος, τό — blood (anemia)

αἴρω — I take up, take away

αἰτέω — I ask

αἰών, ῶνος, ὁ — age, eternity

αἰώνιος, ον — eternal (aeonian)

ἀκάθαρτος, ον — unclean

ἀκολουθέω — I follow (takes the dative) (cf. acolyte, the assistant who carries the wine and the water and the lights at Mass; he follows the priest)

ἀκούω — I hear (acoustics)

ἀλήθεια, ας, ἡ — truth

ἀληθινός, ή, όν — true

ἀλλά — but, except (conjunction)

ἀλλήλων — of one another (parallel, alongside one another)

ἄλλος, η, ο — other, another (allegory, description of one thing under the image of another)

ἁμαρτάνω — I sin (cf. hamartiology)

ἁμαρτία, ας, ἡ — sin (ἁμαρτωλός, όν, sinful, sinner)

ἀμήν — verily, truly (amen)

ἄν — an untranslatable word, which causes a statement otherwise definite to be contingent

ἀναβαίνω — I go up

ἀναγινώσκω — I read, read in public worship

ἀνάστασις, εως, ἡ — resurrection (Anastasia, a girl's name)

ἄνεμος, ου, ὁ — wind (anemometer)

ἀνήρ, ἀνδρός, ὁ — man (polyandry, having many husbands)

ἄνθρωπος, ου, ὁ — man, human being

ἀνίστημι — I rise, stand up, raise

ἀνοίγω — I open

ἄξιος, α, ον — worthy (axiom; in philosophy and psychology, axiological, pertaining to the science of value)

ἀπαγγέλλω — I announce

ἅπας, ασα, αν — all (alternate form of πᾶς)

ἀπέρχομαι — I depart

ἀπό — with the genitive, from (apostasy, a standing off from)

ἀποδίδωμι — I give back, pay; middle, I sell

ἀποθνῄσκω — I die

ἀποκρίνομαι — I answer

ἀποκτείνω — I kill

ἀπόλλυμι — I destroy; middle, I perish (Apollyon, the angel of the bottomless pit, Rev. 9:11)

ἀπολύω — I release, dismiss

ἀποστέλλω — I send (with a commission) (cf. Apostle)

ἅπτομαι — I touch

ἄρα — then, therefore

ἀρνέομαι — I deny

ἀρνίον, ου, τό — lamb

ἄρτι — now, just now

ἄρτος, ου, ὁ — bread, loaf

ἀρχή, ῆς, ἡ — beginning (archaic)

ἀρχιερεύς, έως, ὁ — chief priest, high priest

ἄρχομαι — (middle use) I begin

ἄρχω — I rule

ἄρχων, οντος, ὁ — ruler (monarch)

ἀσθενέω — I am weak, am sick

ἀσπάζομαι — I greet, salute

αὐτός, αὐτή, αὐτό — he, she, it, same, self

ἀφίημι — I let go, permit, forgive (aphesis, the gradual loss of a short unaccented initial vowel, as "squire" for "esquire")

ἄχρι, ἄχρις — with the gen., as far as, up to; as a conjunction, until

βάλλω — I throw, put (ballistics, science of the motion of projectiles)

βαπτίζω — I baptize

βασιλεία — kingdom

βασιλεύς, έως, ὁ — a king (Basil)

βιβλίον, ου, τό — a book (Bible)

βλασφημέω — I revile, blaspheme

βλέπω — I see

βούλομαι — I wish, determine

γαμέω — I marry (monogamous)

γάρ — for

γέ — indeed, even, really, at least

γενεά, ᾶς, ἡ — generation (genealogy)

γεννάω — I beget (cf. hydrogen, so-called as being the generator of water)

γῆ, γῆς, ἡ — earth (geopolitics)

γίνομαι — I become, am

γινώσκω — I come to know, learn

γλῶσσα, ης, ἡ — tongue, language (glossolalia, the gift of speaking in tongues)

γνῶσις, εως, ἡ — wisdom (Gnostic)

γραμματεύς, έως, ὁ — scribe (grammatical)

γραφή, ῆς, ἡ — writing, Scripture (Hagiographa, the holy writings; the section of the O.T. other than the Law and the Prophets)

γράφω	I write	δικαιόω	I justify, pronounce righteous
γυνή, γυναικός, ἡ	woman, wife (misogynist, a woman hater)	διό	wherefore
		διώκω	I pursue, persecute
δαιμόνιον, ου, τό	demon	δοκέω	I think, seem (docetism, the early heresy that Christ's body was phantasmal or of celestial substance which merely seemed human)
δέ	but, and		
δεῖ	(impersonal verb) it is necessary		
δεικνύω, δείκνυμι	I show (in logic, apodeictic, of clear demonstration)	δόξα, ης, ἡ	glory (doxology)
		δοξάζω	I glorify
δεξιός, ά, όν	right	δοῦλος, ου, ὁ	slave, servant
δεύτερος, α, ον	second (Deuteronomy)	δύναμαι	I am powerful, able
δέχομαι	I receive	δύναμις, εως, ἡ	power (dynamite)
δέω	I bind (diadem, literally, something bound around or across)	δυνατός, ή, όν	powerful, possible
		δύο	two (dyad)
διά	with gen., through; with accus., on account of	δώδεκα	twelve (dodecagon)
		δῶρον, ου, τό	gift
διάβολος, ου, ὁ	slanderous; as a noun, accuser, the devil	ἐάν	if (with subjunctive)
διαθήκη, ης, ἡ	a covenant	ἑαυτοῦ, ῆς, οῦ	of himself, herself, itself
διακονέω	I wait upon, serve (deacon)	ἐγγίζω	I come near
		ἐγγύς	near
διακονία, ας, ἡ	waiting at table, service, ministry	ἐγείρω	I raise up
		ἐγώ	I (ego)
διάκονος, ου, ὁ	servant, deacon	ἔθνος, ους, τό	nation; plural, Gentiles (ethnology)
διδάσκαλος, ου, ὁ	teacher (didactic)		
διδάσκω	I teach	εἰ	if
διδαχή, ῆς, ἡ	teaching	εἶδον	I saw (idea)
δίδωμι	I give (antidote)	εἰμί	I am
διέρχομαι	I pass through	εἶπον	I said (epic)
δίκαιος, α, ον	right, just, righteous	εἰρήνη, ης, ἡ	peace (Irene)
δικαιοσύνη, ης, ἡ	righteousness		

Greek	English
εἰς	toward, unto, into (with the accusative)
εἷς, μία, ἕν	one
εἰσέρχομαι	I go in, into; enter
ἐκ, ἐξ	from, out from, by (with the genitive)
ἕκαστος, η, ον	each, every
ἐκβάλλω	I cast out, exclude
ἐκεῖ	there, in that place (adverb)
ἐκεῖνος, η, ο	that, he, she, it (demonstrative pronoun)
ἐκκλησία, ας, ἡ	church, congregation, assembly
ἐκπορεύομαι	I go, or, come out
ἐλεάω, ἐλεέω	I am merciful, show kindness
ἐλπίζω	I hope, hope for
ἐλπίς, ίδος, ἡ	hope
ἐμαυτοῦ, ῆς	of myself (reflexive pronoun)
ἐμός, ή, όν	my, mine
ἔμπροσθεν	before, in front of (with the genitive); in front (adverb)
ἐν	in, on, by, among (with the dative)
ἐνδύω	I put on, clothe
ἐντολή, ῆς, ἡ	commandment, order
ἐνώπιον	before (with the genitive)
ἐξέρχομαι	I go out
ἔξεστι	It is lawful
ἐξουσία, ας, ἡ	authority
ἔξω	without; outside
ἐπαγγελία, ας, ἡ	promise
ἐπεί	when, since (conjunction)
ἐπερωτάω	I ask, question, ask for
ἐπί	on, upon (with the genitive); on, at, with (with the dative); against, for (with the accusative)
ἐπιγινώσκω	I know, come to know, know fully, understand
ἐπιθυμία	eager desire, passion
ἐπικαλέω	I call; call upon (middle)
ἐπιστρέφω	I turn to, return
ἐπιτίθημι	I lay on, put, place
ἐπιτιμάω	I order, rebuke, warn
ἑπτά	seven (heptagon)
ἐργάζομαι	I work, perform (energy)
ἔργον, ου, τό	work, deed
ἔρημος, ου, ἡ	desert, deserted place; lonely, deserted (adjective)
ἔρχομαι	I come, go (deponent)
ἐρῶ	I will say (future of λέγω)
ἐρωτάω	I ask, request, entreat
ἐσθίω	I eat, consume (anthropophagous, man-eating)
ἔσχατος, η, ον	last (eschatology)
ἕτερος, α, ον	other, another, different (heterodox)
ἔτι	still, yet, even (adverb)
ἑτοιμάζω	I prepare, make ready
ἕτοιμος, η, ον	ready, prepared
ἔτος, ους, τό	year (The Etesian winds in the Mediterranean blow annually)
εὐαγγελίζω	I bring good news, preach good news
εὐαγγέλιον, ου, τό	good news, Gospel

εὐθέως (εὐθύς) — immediately, at once

εὐλογέω — I bless (eulogize)

εὑρίσκω — I find (Eureka, I have found it)

εὐχαριστέω — I give thanks (Eucharist)

ἐχθρός, ά, όν — enemy, hated

ἔχω — I have, hold

ἕως — until; with the genitive, until, as far as

ζάω — I live, am alive

ζητέω — I seek, attempt

ζωή, ῆς, ἡ — life

ἤ — or (ἤ....ἤ, either.... or)

ἡγέομαι — I consider, regard, think, rule

ἤδη — now, already (adverb)

ἥλιος, ου, ὁ — sun (helium)

ἡμέρα, ας, ἡ — day (ephemeral, for a day)

θάλασσα, ης, ἡ — sea, lake (thalassocracy)

θάνατος, ου, ὁ — death (thanatopsis, a view of, or meditation on death)

θαυμάζω — I marvel, wonder, am amazed

θέλημα, ατος, τό — will, wish, desire (Monothelite, one holding that Christ had but one, a divine, will; condemned by the Sixth Council, A.D. 680)

θέλω — I will, wish, desire

θεός, οῦ, ὁ — God (theology)

θεραπεύω — I heal (therapeutic); serve (Acts 17:25)

θεωρέω — I look at, behold (theorem, theory)

θηρίον, ου, τό — wild animal, beast

θλίψις, εως, ἡ — tribulation, distress

θρόνος, ου, ὁ — throne

θύρα, ας, ἡ — gate, door, entrance

θυσία, ας, ἡ — sacrifice, offering

ἴδιος, α, ον — one's own, personal

ἱερεύς, έως, ὁ — priest (hierarchy)

ἱερόν, οῦ, τό — temple, temple courts

ἱκανός, ή, όν — worthy, fit, sufficient, able

ἱμάτιον — garment, clothing (of outer garments)

ἵνα — in order that, so that, that

ἵστημι — I cause to stand, stand

ἰσχυρός, ά, όν — strong, powerful

καθαρίζω — I cleanse (catharsis)

κάθημαι — I sit (deponent)

καθίζω — I seat, sit (cf. cathedral, the church which contains the bishop's seat)

καθώς — as, just as, because, in so far as (adverb)

καί — and, even, also (καί.... καί, both....and), namely (conjunction)

καινός, ή, όν	new	λαός, οῦ, ὁ	people, crowd (laity)
καιρός, οῦ, ὁ	fitting season, opportunity, time	λέγω	I say, speak (Compare words in -logy, -logue)
κακός, ή, όν	evil, bad, wrong (cacophony, discord)	λίθος, ου, ὁ	stone
καλέω	I call, name, invite	λογίζομαι	I account, reckon
καλός, ή, όν	good, beautiful, right	λόγος, ου, ὁ	word, account, reason
καλῶς	well (adverb)	λοιπός, ή, όν	remaining, rest, other (adjective); henceforth (adverb)
καρδία, ας, ἡ	heart, mind, will, desire	λύω	I loose, untie, release
καρπός, οῦ, ὁ	fruit, harvest, result	μαθητής, οῦ, ὁ	disciple, pupil
κατά	down from, against (with the genitive); according to (with the accusative)	μακάριος, α, ον	blessed, happy
		μᾶλλον	more (adverb)
		μαρτυρέω	I bear witness, testify, affirm, confirm, speak well of
καταβαίνω	I go down, come down		
κατοικέω	I live, settle (intransitive); inhabit, dwell in (transitive)	μαρτυρία, ας, ἡ	testimony, witness, evidence
καυχάομαι	I boast, rejoice	μάρτυς, υρος, ὁ	witness (martyr)
κεφαλή, ῆς, ἡ	head (encephalitis)	μάχαιρα, ης, ἡ	sword
κηρύσσω	I proclaim, preach	μέγας, μεγάλη, μέγα	large, great (of a loud sound; strong wind; high fever) (megaphone)
κλαίω	I weep, cry		
κόσμος, ου, ὁ	world, world order, universe	μέλλω	I am about to, am going to, intend, must
κράζω	I cry out, call out		
κρατέω	I grasp, take hold of	μέλος, ους, τό	member
κρίμα, ατος, τό	judgment, decision	μέν	on the one hand, indeed (postpositive particle, on the one hand; often used with δέ)
κρίνω	I judge, decide		
κρίσις, εως, ἡ	judgment, judging	μένω	I remain, stay
κύριος, ου, ὁ	Lord		
		μέρος, ους, τό	part (pentamerous, of five parts)
λαλέω	I speak		
λαμβάνω	I take, receive	μέσος, η, ον	middle, in the middle

μετά	with (with genitive), after (with accusative)	οἶνος, ου, ὁ	wine
μετανοέω	I repent	ὀλίγος, η, ον	little, few (oligarchy)
μή	not, lest	ὅλος, η, ον	whole, all, complete
μηδέ	nor, and not, not even	ὅμοιος, α, ον	like (Homoiousian, one holding that Father and Son in the Godhead are of like, but not the same, substance; a semi-Arian)
μηδείς, μηδεμία, μηδέν	no one, nothing		
μήτε	and not, neither, nor	ὁμοίως	likewise, so (adverb)
μήτηρ, μητρός, ἡ	mother (maternal)	ὄνομα, ατος, τό	name
μικρός, ά, όν	small, little (adjective) (microscope; omicron, little o)	ὀπίσω	behind, after (with genitive); back, behind (adverb) (opisthograph, a manuscript written on both the front and back, Rev. 5:1)
μισέω	I hate (misogynist, a woman hater)		
μισθός, οῦ, ὁ	wages, reward		
μνημεῖον, ου, τό	tomb, monument	ὅπου	where, whither
μόνος, η, ον	alone, only (monologue)	ὅπως	that, in order that (with the subjunctive; compare ἵνα)
μυστήριον, ου, τό	mystery		
		ὁράω	I see, perceive
ναί	yes, certainly	ὀργή, ῆς, ἡ	anger, wrath
ναός, οῦ, ὁ	temple (inner part of the Jewish temple)	ὄρος, ὄρους, τό	mountain (orology, the study of mountains)
νεκρός, ά, όν	dead (necropolis)	ὅς, ἥ, ὅ	who, which
νόμος, ου, ὁ	law (Deuteronomy)	ὅσος, η, ον	as great as, as many as
νῦν	now (adverb)		
νύξ, νυκτός, ἡ	night	ὅστις, ἥτις, ὅ τι	whoever, whichever
ὁ, ἡ, τό	the (article, masculine, feminine, neuter)	ὅταν	whenever (ὅτε+ἄν, with the subjunctive)
ὁδός, οῦ, ἡ	way, road, journey (anode, cathode, electrical terminals)	ὅτε	when, while (conjunction)
		ὅτι	that, because
οἶδα	I know (second perfect with present meaning)	οὐ, οὐκ, οὐχ	not (adverb)
οἰκία, ας, ἡ	house	οὐά	aha! (interjection)
οἰκοδομέω	I build, edify	οὐαί	woe! alas!
οἶκος, ου, ὁ	house (economy)	οὐδέ	and not, not even, neither, nor

οὐδείς, οὐδεμία, no one, nothing, none
  οὐδέν

οὐκέτι   no longer (adverb)

οὖν   therefore, then

οὔπω   not yet (adverb)

οὐρανός, οῦ, ὁ heaven

οὖς, ὠτός, τό   ear (otology)

οὔτε   nor, neither...
               nor

οὗτος, αὕτη,   this, he, she, it
  τοῦτο

οὕτως   thus, in this way

οὐχί   not (emphatic form
               of οὐ)

ὀφειλέτης, ου, ὁ debtor

ὀφείλω   I owe, ought

ὀφθαλμός, οῦ, ὁ eye (ophthalmology)

ὄχλος, ου, ὁ   crowd, multitude (och-
               locracy, mob rule)

παιδίον, ου, τό child, infant

πάλιν   again, once more
               (adverb) (palimpsest,
               a manuscript used again,
               the earlier writing
               having been eradicated)

πάντοτε   always (adverb)

παρά   from (with the geni-
               tive); beside, in the
               presence of (with the
               dative); alongside of
               (with the accusative)

παραβολή, ῆς, ἡ parable

παραγγέλλω   I command, order

παραγίνομαι   I come, arrive,
               appear

παρακαλέω   I exhort, encourage

παράκλησις, εως, ἡ exhortation, conso-
               lation (Paraclete)

παραλαμβάνω   I receive, take along

παρέρχομαι   I pass by, arrive

παρίστημι   I am present, stand by

παρρησία, ας, ἡ boldness, confidence

πᾶς, πᾶσα, πᾶν all, every, each

πάσχα, τό   Passover (paschal)
               (indeclinable)

πάσχω   I suffer, endure

πατήρ, πατρός, ὁ father (paternal)

πείθω   I persuade, convince

πειράζω   I test, tempt

πέμπω   I send

πέντε   five

περί   concerning, about
               (with the genitive);
               around (with the
               accusative)

περιπατέω   I walk, conduct oneself

περισσεύω   I abound, have plenty

περιτομή, ῆς, ἡ circumcision

πίνω   I drink

πίπτω   I fall

πιστεύω   I believe (in), have
               faith (in)

πίστις, εως, ἡ faith, belief, trust

πιστός, ή, όν   faithful, believing

πλανάω   I lead astray (planet,
               to the ancients an
               apparently wandering
               celestial body)

πλείων, πλεῖον, more, larger, a larger
  or πλέον, ονος number

πλῆθος, ους, τό	multitude (cf. plethora)	προσκαλέομαι	I summon
πλήν	however, only; with genitive, except	προσκυνέω	I worship
πλοῖον, ου, τό	boat	προσφέρω	I bring to, offer
πλούσιος, α, ον	rich (plutocrat)	πρόσωπον, ου, τό	face (prosopography, description of personal appearance)
πνεῦμα, ατος, τό	spirit	προφητεύω	I prophesy
πόθεν	whence?	προφήτης	prophet
ποιέω	I make, do (poem)	πρῶτος, η, ον	first (protozoa)
ποῖος, α, ον	what sort of? what?	πτωχός, ή, όν	poor; poor man
πόλις, πόλεως, ἡ	city (Neapolis, new city, Acts 16:11)	πῦρ, πυρός, τό	fire (pyre)
πολύς, πολλή, πολύ	much; plural, many (polytheism)	πῶς	how?
πονηρός, ά, όν	evil	ῥῆμα, ατος, τό	a word (rhetoric)
πορεύομαι	I go, proceed		
ποτέ	at some time, once, ever	σάββατον, ου, τό	Sabbath
ποτήριον, ου, τό	cup	σεαυτοῦ	of yourself
ποῦ	where? whither?	σημεῖον, ου, τό	sign (semaphore, bearing a sign)
πούς, ποδός, ὁ	foot (podium)	σήμερον	today
πράσσω	I do, perform (praxis, practice)	σκανδαλίζω	I cause to stumble, offend (scandalize)
πρεσβύτερος, ου, ὁ	elder (presbyter)	σκοτία, ας, ἡ; σκότος, ου, ὁ	darkness (scotoscope, a field glass for seeing at night)
πρό	with the genitive, before (prologue)	σοφία, ας, ἡ σοφός, ή, όν	wisdom (philosophy) wise
πρόβατον, ου, τό	a sheep	σπείρω σπέρμα, ατος, τό	I sow seed (sperm)
πρός	with the accusative, to, toward, with	σταυρόω	I crucify
προσέρχομαι	(deponent) I come to	στόμα, ατος, τό	mouth (stomach)
προσευχή, ῆς, ἡ	prayer	σύ	you
προσεύχομαι	(deponent) I pray	σύν	with the dative, with (syntax)

συνάγω	I gather together (synagogue)	τρεῖς, τρία	three (triad)
συναγωγή, ῆς, ἡ	synagogue	τρίτος, η, ον	third
συνείδησις, εως, ἡ	conscience	τυφλός, ή, όν	blind (typhlosis, medical blindness)
συνέρχομαι	I come together	ὕδωρ, ὕδατος, τό	water (hydroplane)
σῴζω	I save (sozin, any defensive protein in an animal body; soteriology)	υἱός, οῦ, ὁ	son
		ὑπάγω	I go, depart
σῶμα, ατος, τό	body (somatic)	ὑπάρχω	I am, exist (τὰ ὑπάρχοντα, possessions)
σωτηρία, ας, ἡ	salvation (soteriology)		
τέ	and (an enclitic connective particle, weaker in force than καί)	ὑπέρ	with the genitive, in behalf of; with the accusative, above (hypercritical)
τέκνον, ου, τό	child	ὑπό	with the genitive, by; with the accusative, under (hypodermic)
τελέω	I finish, fulfill (teleology)		
τέλος, ους, τό	end	ὑπομονή, ῆς, ἡ	steadfastness, endurance
		ὑποστρέφω	I return
τέσσαρες, ων	four (Diatessaron of Tatian, A.D. 170, harmony of the Gospels; literally, through the four)	ὑποτάσσω	I subject, put in subjection (hypotaxis, subordination of clauses)
τηρέω	I keep	φαίνω	I shine, appear (phenomenon, phantom)
τίθημι	I place, put	φανερόω	I make manifest
τιμή, ῆς, ἡ	honor, price (cf. Timothy, honoring God)	φέρω	I bear, carry
τις, τι	someone, something, anyone, a certain one	φεύγω	I flee
		φημί	I say
τίς, τί	who? what? which? why?	φίλος, ου, ὁ	friend (bibliophile)
τοιοῦτος, αυτη, οὗτον, οὗτο	of such a quality as, such (qualitative adjective)	φοβέομαι	I fear, be afraid (deponent) (phobia)
τόπος, ου, ὁ	place (topography)	φόβος, ου, ὁ	fear, terror
τότε	then, at that time (adverb)	φυλακή, ῆς, ἡ	prison, jail, watch, guard

φυλάσσω — I guard, keep

φυλή, ῆς, ἡ — tribe, nation, people (In zoology a phylum is one of the large, basic divisions of the animal kingdom.)

φωνέω — I call, summon (phonetic)

φωνή, ῆς, ἡ — sound, voice, language

φῶς, φωτός, τό — light (phosphorous, photography)

χαίρω — I rejoice, am glad

χαρά, ᾶς, ἡ — joy, gladness, happiness

χάρις, ιτος, ἡ — grace, kindness, mercy, goodwill, a favor, gift, thanks, gratitude (charismatic)

χείρ, χειρός, ἡ — hand (βάλλω χ. ἐπί, arrest, seize), power, authority (chirography)

χρεία — need, necessity

χρόνος, ου, ὁ — time (chronometer)

χωρίς — without, apart from (with the genitive)

ψυχή, ῆς, ἡ — soul, self, inner life, person, human being (psycho-)

ὧδε — here, in this place (adverb)

ὥρα, ας, ἡ — hour, moment, instant (horoscope, prediction based on the hour of a person's birth)

ὡς — as, like (comparison); how, that (introducing discourse); as (sense of "to be"); as, when, after (temporal and consequential)

ὥσπερ — as, just as, even as

ὥστε — that, so that (often followed by the accusative and the infinitive)

VOCABULARY

ENGLISH - GREEK

able	ἱκανός, ή, όν	(I) announce	ἀπαγγέλλω
(I) abound	περισσεύω	another	ἕτερος, α, ον
about	ὡς; περί (with the genitive)	(I) answer	ἀποκρίνομαι
above	ὑπέρ (with the accusative)	anyone	τις, τι
according to	κατά	(I) appeal to	ἐπικαλέω
(I) account	λογίζομαι	(I) appear	φαίνω
accuser	διάβολος, ου, ὁ	(I) arise	ἀνίστημι
a certain one	τις, τι	around	περί (with the accusative)
after	μετά (with the accusative)	(I) arrive	παραγίνομαι; παρέρχομαι
again	πάλιν	as	καθώς, ὡς
against	κατά (with the genitive)	as far as	ἄχρι, ἄχρις; ἕως (with the genitive)
(an) age	αἰών, ῶνος, ὁ	as great as	ὅσος, η, ον
alas!	οὐαί	(I) ask	αἰτέω; ἐπερωτάω, ἐρωτάω
all	πᾶς, πᾶσα, πᾶν; ἅπας, ασα, αν	as many as	ὅσος, η, ον
alone	μόνος, η, ον	at least	γέ
alongside of	παρά (with the accusative)	at some time	ποτέ
already	ἤδη	at that time	τότε
also	καί	authority	ἐξουσία, ας, ἡ
always	πάντοτε		
(I) am	εἰμί; ὑπάρχω; γίνομαι		
(I) am about to	μέλλω		
among	ἐν	bad	κακός, ή, όν
and	καί; δέ; τέ	(I) baptize	βαπτίζω
and not	οὐδέ	(I) bear	φέρω
angel	ἄγγελος, ου, ὁ	(I) bear witness	μαρτυρέω
anger	ὀργή, ῆς, ἡ	beautiful	καλός, ή, όν

because	ὅτι	but	ἀλλά; δέ
(I) become	γίνομαι	but not	μηδέ
before	ἔμπροσθεν; ἐνώπιον (with the genitive)	(I) buy	ἀγοράζω
(I) beget	γεννάω	by	ἐν (with the dative); ὑπό (with the genitive)
(I) begin	ἄρχομαι (middle)		
beginning	ἀρχή, ῆς, ἡ		
behind	ὀπίσω	(I) call	καλέω, ἐπικαλέω, φωνέω
(I) behold	θεωρέω	(I) carry	φέρω
belief	πίστις, εως, ἡ	(I) cast out	ἐκβάλλω
believing	πιστός, ή, όν	(I) cause to rise	ἀνίστημι
beloved	ἀγαπητός, ή, όν	(I) cause to stand	ἵστημι
beside	παρά (with dat.)	(I) cause to stumble	σκανδαλίζω
(I) bind	δέω	(I) charge	παραγγέλλω
blaspheme	βλασφημέω	(I) am chief	ἡγέομαι
(I) bless	εὐλογέω	chief priest	ἀρχιερεύς, έως, ὁ
blessed	μακάριος, α, ον	child	παιδίον, ου, τό; τέκνον, ου, τό
blind	τυφλός, ή, όν	church	ἐκκλησία, ας, ἡ
blood	αἷμα, αἵματος, τό	circumcision	περιτομή, ῆς, ἡ
(I) boast	καυχάομαι	city	πόλις, πόλεως, ἡ
boat	πλοῖον, ου, τό	(I) cleanse	καθαρίζω
body	σῶμα, ατος, τό	(I) clothe	ἐνδύω
boldness	παρρησία, ας, ἡ	(I) come	ἔρχομαι; παραγίνομαι
book	βιβλίον, ου, τό	(I) come near	ἐγγίζω
bread	ἄρτος, ου, ὁ	(I) come to	προσέρχομαι
(I) bring good news	εὐαγγελίζω	(I) come to know	γινώσκω; ἐπιγινώσκω
brother	ἀδελφός, οῦ, ὁ	(I) come together	συνέρχομαι
(I) build	οἰκοδομέω	(I) command	παραγγέλλω
		commandment	ἐντολή, ῆς, ἡ

community, church	ἐκκλησία, ας, ἡ	(I) die	ἀποθνήσκω
concerning	περί (with gen.)	different	ἕτερος, α, ον
confidence	παρρησία, ας, ἡ	disciple	μαθητής, οῦ, ὁ
congregation	ἐκκλησία, ας, ἡ	(I) dismiss	ἀπολύω
conscience	συνείδησις, εως, ἡ	(I) do	ποιέω; πράσσω
considerable	ἱκανός, ή, όν	door	θύρα, ας, ἡ
consolation	παράκλησις, εως, ἡ	down from	κατά (with genitive)
(a) covenant	διαθήκη, ης, ἡ	(I) drink	πίνω
crowd	ὄχλος, ου, ὁ	during	διά (with genitive)
(I) crucify	σταυρόω		
(I) cry out	κράζω	each	ἕκαστος, η, ον
cup	ποτήριον, ου, τό	eager desire	ἐπιθυμία, ας, ἡ
		ear	οὖς, ὠτός, τό
darkness	σκότος, ους, τό	earth	γῆ, γῆς, ἡ
(a) day	ἡμέρα, ας, ἡ	(I) eat	ἐσθίω
deacon	διάκονος, ου, ὁ	(I) edify	οἰκοδομέω
dead	νεκρός, ά, όν	elder	πρεσβύτερος, ου, ὁ
death	θάνατος, ου, ὁ	end	τέλος, ους, τό
delight, joy	χαρά, ᾶς, ἡ	endurance	ὑπομονή, ῆς, ἡ
demon	δαιμόνιον, ου, τό	(I) enter	εἰσέρχομαι
(I) deny	ἀρνέομαι	(I) entreat	ἐρωτάω
(I) depart	ἀπέρχομαι; ὑπάγω	eternal	αἰώνιος, ον
(the) desert	ἔρημος, ου, ἡ	even	καί
deserted	ἔρημος, ον	even as	καθώς; ὥσπερ
(I) desire	θέλω; ἐπιθυμέω	ever	ποτέ
(I) destroy	ἀπόλλυμι	every	πᾶς, πᾶσα, πᾶν ἕκαστος, η, ον
(I) determine, plan	βούλομαι	evidence	μαρτυρία, ας, ἡ
devil	διάβολος, ου, ὁ	evil	κακός, ή, όν; πονηρός, ά, όν

except	ἀλλ' ἤ; πλήν (with the genitive)	from	ἐκ, ἐξ; ἀπό; παρά (all with the genitive)
(I) exhort	παρακαλέω	fruit	καρπός, οῦ, ὁ
exhortation	παράκλησις, εως, ἡ	(I) fulfill	πληρόω; τελέω
(I) exist	εἰμί; ὑπάρχω	garment	ἱμάτιον, ου, τό
face	πρόσωπον, ου, τό	(I) gather together	συνάγω
faith	πίστις, εως, ἡ	generation	γενεά, ᾶς, ἡ
(I have) faith in	πιστεύω	Gentiles	ἔθνος, ους, τό
faithful	πιστός, ή, όν	(I) give; gift	δίδωμι; δῶρον, ου, τό
father	πατήρ, πατρός, ὁ	(I) give back	ἀποδίδωμι
fear	φόβος, ου, ὁ	(I) give thanks	εὐχαριστέω
few	ὀλίγος, η, ον	(I) glorify	δοξάζω
field	ἀγρός, οῦ, ὁ	glory	δόξα, ης, ἡ
(I) find	εὑρίσκω	(I) go	ἔρχομαι; πορευομαι; ὑπάγω
(I) finish	τελέω	God	θεός, οῦ, ὁ
fire	πῦρ, πυρός, τό	(I) go down	καταβαίνω
first	πρῶτος, η, ον	(I) go in (into)	εἰσέρχομαι
fitting season	καιρός, οῦ, ὁ	good	ἀγαθός, ή, όν; καλός, ή, όν
five	πέντε	(I) go out	ἐξέρχομαι; ἐκπορεύομαι
(I) flee	φεύγω	(I) go up	ἀναβαίνω; ἀνέρχομαι
(I) follow	ἀκολουθέω	grace	χάρις, ιτος, ἡ
foot	πούς, ποδός, ὁ	(I) grasp	κρατέω
for	γάρ	great	μέγας, μεγάλη, μέγα
(I) forgive	ἀφίημι	(I) greet	ἀσπάζομαι
for the rest	λοιπός, ή, όν	guard, guard post	φυλακή, ῆς, ἡ
four	τέσσαρες, neuter, τέσσαρα; genitive, τεσσάρων	(I) guard	φυλάσσω; φρουρέω

English-Greek Vocabulary

hand	χείρ, χειρός, ἡ	just as	ὥσπερ
happy	μακάριος, α, ον	just now	ἄρτι
(I) hate	μισέω	(I) justify	δικαιόω
hated	ἐχθρός, ά, όν		
(I) have	ἔχω		
(I) have mercy	ἐλεέω	lake	θάλασσα, ης, ἡ
he	αὐτός, οὗτος	lamb	ἀρνίον, ου, τό
head	κεφαλή, ῆς, ἡ	language	γλῶσσα, ης, ἡ
(I) heal	θεραπεύω	large	μέγας, μεγάλη, μέγα
(I) hear	ἀκούω	larger	πλείων, πλεῖον or πλέον, gen., ονος
heart	καρδία, ας, ἡ	last	ἔσχατος, η, ον
heaven	οὐρανός, οῦ, ὁ	law	νόμος, ου, ὁ
henceforth	λοιπόν (τό), τοῦ λοιποῦ	(I) lay upon	ἐπιτίθημι
here	ὧδε	(I) lead	ἄγω
high priest	ἀρχιερεύς, έως, ὁ	(I) lead astray	πλανάω
hither	ὧδε	(I) learn	γινώσκω
holy	ἅγιος, α, ον	lest	μή
honor	τιμή, ῆς, ἡ	(I) let go	ἀφίημι
hope	ἐλπίς, ίδος, ἡ	life	ζωή, ῆς, ἡ; ψυχή, ῆς, ἡ
(I) hope	ἐλπίζω	light	φῶς, φωτός, τό
hour	ὥρα, ας, ἡ	like	ὅμοιος, α, ον
house	οἰκία, ας, ἡ; οἶκος, ου, ὁ	likewise	ὁμοίως
if	εἰ; ἐάν	little	μικρός, ά, όν; ὀλίγος, η, ον
journey	ὁδός, οῦ, ἡ	(I) live	ζάω
joy	χαρά, ᾶς, ἡ	loaf	ἄρτος, ου, ὁ
(I) judge	κρίνω	(I) look at	θεωρέω
judgment	κρίμα, ατος, τό; κρίσις, εως, ἡ	(I) loose	λύω
just	δίκαιος, α, ον	Lord	κύριος, ου, ὁ

love	ἀγάπη, ης, ἡ	near	ἐγγύς
(I) love	ἀγαπάω	(a) need	χρεία, ας, ἡ
loving	φίλος, η, ον	neither	οὐδέ, μηδέ; οὔτε, μήτε
		new	καινός, ή, όν
		night	νύξ, νυκτός, ἡ
(I) make	ποιέω	no longer	οὐκέτι
man	ἀνήρ, ἀνδρός, ὁ; ἄνθρωπος, ου, ὁ	no one	οὐδείς, οὐδεμία, οὐδέν; μηδείς, μηδεμία, μηδέν
many	πολύς, πολλή, πολύ	nor	οὐδέ, μηδέ; οὔτε, μήτε
(I) marry	γαμέω	not	οὐ, οὐκ, οὐχ (οὐχί, emphatic form); μή
(I) marvel	θαυμάζω	not even	οὐδέ; μηδέ
member	μέλος, ους, τό	now	ἄρτι; ἤδη; νῦν
messenger	ἄγγελος, ου, ὁ		
middle	μέσος, η, ον		
mine	ἐμός, ἐμή, ἐμόν	(I) offend	σκανδαλίζω
ministry	διακονία, ας, ἡ	(I) offer	προσφέρω
more	μᾶλλον	of myself	ἐμαυτοῦ
mother	μήτηρ, μητρός, ἡ	of one another	ἀλλήλων
mountain	ὄρος, ὄρους, τό	of such a quality, as	τοιοῦτος, -αύτη, -οῦτον, or -οῦτο
mouth	στόμα, ατος, τό	of yourself	σεαυτοῦ
much	πολύς, πολλή, πολύ	on	ἐν (with dat.); ἐπί (with gen., dat. and acc.); παρά (with acc.)
multitude	ὄχλος, ου, ὁ; πλῆθος, ους, τό	on account of	διά (with acc.); ἐπί (with gen. and acc.)
my	ἐμός, ἐμή, ἐμόν	once	ποτέ
mystery	μυστήριον, ου, τό	one	εἷς, μία, ἕν
		one's belongings	τὰ ἴδια; τὰ ὑπάρχοντα
		one's own	ἴδιος, α, ον
(I) name	καλέω, ἐπικαλέω	only	μόνος, η, ον; πλήν
(a) name	ὄνομα, ατος, τό	on the one hand	μέν (on the other hand, δέ)
nation	ἔθνος, ους, τό		

English—Greek Vocabulary

(I) open	ἀνοίγω	plural	πολύς, πολλή, πολύ
opportunity	καιρός, οῦ, ὁ	poor	πτωχός, ή, όν
or	ἤ	poor man	πτωχός, οῦ, ὁ
other	ἄλλος, η, ο; ἕτερος, α, ον	possible	δυνατός, ή, όν
(I) ought	ὀφείλω	powerful	δυνατός, ή, όν
out of	ἐκ, ἐξ (with the genitive)	(I) pray	προσεύχομαι (depon.)
outside	ἔξω	prayer	προσευχή, ῆς, ἡ
(I) owe	ὀφείλω	(I) prepare	ἑτοιμάζω
		(I am) present	παρίστημι
		price	τιμή, ῆς, ἡ
parable	παραβολή, ῆς, ἡ	priest	ἱερεύς, έως, ὁ
part	μέρος, ους, τό	prison	φυλακή, ῆς, ἡ
pass away	παρέρχομαι	(I) proceed	πορεύομαι
pass by	παρέρχομαι	(I) proclaim	κηρύσσω
pass through	διέρχομαι	promise	ἐπαγγελία, ας, ἡ
passion	ἐπιθυμία, ας, ἡ	(I) pronounce righteous	δικαιόω
passover	πάσχα, τό	(I) prophesy	προφητεύω
(I) pay	ἀποδίδωμι	prophet	προφήτης, ου, ὁ
peace	εἰρήνη, ης, ἡ	(I) pursue	διώκω
people	λαός, οῦ, ὁ	(I) put	τίθημι; βάλλω
(I) perform	πράσσω	(I) put on	ἐνδύω
(I) perish	ἀπόλλυμι (middle)·		
(I) permit	ἀφίημι		
(I) persecute	διώκω	(I) question	ἐπερωτάω
person	ψυχή, ῆς, ἡ		
persuade	πείθω		
place	τόπος, ου, ὁ	(I) read	ἀναγινώσκω
(I) place	τίθημι	(I) realize	γινώσκω

really	γέ		sabbath	σάββατον, ου, τό
reason	λόγος, ου, ὁ		sacrifice	θυσία, ας, ἡ
(I) rebuke	ἐπιτιμάω		said	εἶπον
(I) receive	λαμβάνω; δέχομαι; παρα-λαμβάνω		(I) salute	ἀσπάζομαι
(I) reckon	λογίζομαι		salvation	σωτηρία, ας, ἡ
(I) recognize	ἐπιγινώσκω		same	αὐτός, αὐτή, αὐτό
(I) regard	ἡγέομαι		(I) save	σῴζω
(I) rejoice	χαίρω		(I) saw	εἶδον
(I) release	ἀπολύω		(I) say	λέγω; φημί
(I) remain	μένω		(I) shall say	ἐρῶ
remaining	λοιπός, ή, όν		scribe	γραμματεύς, έως, ὁ
(I) repent	μετανοέω		scripture	γραφή, ῆς, ἡ
(the) rest	λοιπός, ή, όν		sea	θάλασσα, ης, ἡ
resurrection	ἀνάστασις, εως, ἡ		second	δεύτερος, α, ον
(I) return	ἐπιστρέφω; ὑποστρέφω		(I) see	βλέπω; ὁράω
(I) revile	βλασφημέω		seed	σπέρμα, ατος, τό
reward	μισθός, οῦ, ὁ		(I) seek	ζητέω
rich	πλούσιος, α, ον		(I) seem	δοκέω
right	δίκαιος, α, ον		(I) sell	ἀποδίδωμι (middle)
righteous	δίκαιος, α, ον		(I) send	ἀποστέλλω; πέμπω
righteousness	δικαιοσύνη, ης, ἡ		servant	δοῦλος, ου, ὁ
road	ὁδός, οῦ, ἡ		(I) serve	διακονέω
(I) rule	ἄρχω		service	διακονία, ας, ἡ
ruler	ἄρχων, οντος, ὁ		seven	ἑπτά
			she	αὕτη; αὐτή
			sheep	πρόβατον, ου, τό
			(I) shine	φαίνω

English-Greek Vocabulary

(I) show	δεικνύω, δείκνυμι
(I am) sick	ἀσθενέω
(a) sign	σημεῖον, ου, τό
sin	ἀμαρτία, ας, ἡ
(I) sin	ἀμαρτάνω
since	ἐπεί
sinful	ἀμαρτωλός, όν
(I) sit	καθίζω
slanderous	διάβολος, ου, ὁ
slave	δοῦλος, ου, ὁ
small	μικρός, ά, όν
solitary	ἔρημος, ον
someone	τις
something	τι
son	υἱός, οῦ, ὁ
so that	ὥστε
soul	ψυχή, ῆς, ἡ
sound	φωνή, ῆς, ἡ
(I) sow	σπείρω
(I) speak	λαλέω; λέγω
spirit	πνεῦμα, ατος, τό
(I) stand	ἵστημι
(I) stand by	παρίστημι
steadfastness	ὑπομονή, ῆς, ἡ
still	ἔτι
stone	λίθος, ου, ὁ
straightway	εὐθέως, εὐθύς
strong	ἰσχυρός, ά, όν

(I) subject	ὑποτάσσω
such, of such a quality	τοιοῦτος, -αύτη, -οῦτον or -οῦτο
sufficient	ἱκανός, ή, όν
(I) summon	προσκαλέομαι
sun	ἥλιος, ου, ὁ
(a) sword	μάχαιρα, ης, ἡ
synagogue	συναγωγή, ῆς, ἡ
(I) take	λαμβάνω
(I) take along	παραλαμβάνω
(I) take away	αἴρω
(I) take up	αἴρω
(I) teach	διδάσκω
teacher	διδάσκαλος, ου, ὁ
temple (area)	ἱερόν, οῦ, τό
temple (building)	ναός, οῦ, ὁ
tempt	πειράζω
terror	φόβος, ου, ὁ
test, tempt	πειράζω
testify	μαρτυρέω
testimony	μαρτυρία, ας, ἡ
that	ἵνα; ὅπως; ὡς
that time	τότε
the	ὁ, ἡ, τό
then	ἄρα; τότε
there	ἐκεῖ
therefore	ἄρα
(I) think	δοκέω; ἡγέομαι

third	τρίτος, η, ον	until	ἕως
this	οὗτος, αὕτη, τοῦτο	unto	εἰς
three	τρεῖς, τρία	upon	ἐπί (with genitive; with accusative)
throne	θρόνος, ου, ὁ		
through	διά (w. genitive)	up to	ἄχρι, ἄχρις
throughout	κατά (w. accusative)		
(I) throw	βάλλω	verily	ἀμήν
thus	οὕτως	voice	φωνή, ῆς, ἡ
time	καιρός, οῦ, ὁ; χρόνος, ου, ὁ		
to	πρός; εἰς		
today	σήμερον	wages	μισθός, οῦ, ὁ
tomb	μνημεῖον, ου, τό	(I) wait upon	διακονέω
tongue	γλῶσσα, ης, ἡ	waiting on table	διακονία, ας, ἡ
(I) touch	ἅπτομαι	(I) walk	περιπατέω
toward	εἰς	(I) warn	ἐπιτιμάω
towards	πρός (w. accusative)	watch	φυλακή, ῆς, ἡ
tribe	φυλή, ῆς, ἡ	way	ὁδός, οῦ, ἡ
tribulation	θλίψις, εως, ἡ	(I am) weak	ἀσθενέω
truly	ἀμήν; ναί	(I) weep	κλαίω
trust	πίστις, εως, ἡ	well	καλῶς
truth	ἀλήθεια, ας, ἡ	what	ποῖος, α, ον
(I) turn to	ἐπιστρέφω	what sort of	τίς, τί
twelve	δώδεκα	when	ὅτε; ἐπεί
two	δύο	whence	πόθεν
		whenever	ὅταν
		where	ποῦ
		wherefore	διό
unclean	ἀκάθαρτος, ον	which	τί; ὅ
under	ὑπό (with accusative)		

whichever	ὃ ἄν, ὃ ἐάν; ὅ,τι	(I) work	ἐργάζομαι
whither	ποῦ	world	κόσμος, ου, ὁ
who	ὅς, ἥ; τίς	(I) worship	προσκυνέω
whoever	ὃς ἄν, ἣ ἄν, or ὃς ἐάν, ἣ ἐάν, or ὅστις, ἥτις	worthy	ἄξιος, α, ον
		(I) write	γράφω
whole	ὅλος, η, ον	writing	γραφή, ῆς, ἡ
why	τί	year	ἔτος, ους, τό
wife	γυνή, γυναικός, ἡ	yes	ναί
(a) wild beast	θηρίον, ου, τό	yet	ἔτι
wilderness	ἔρημος, ου, ἡ	you	σύ
will	θέλημα, ατος, τό		
(I) will	θέλω		
wind	ἄνεμος, ου, ὁ		
wine	οἶνος, ου, ὁ		
wisdom	γνῶσις, εως, ἡ; σοφία, ας, ἡ		
wise	σοφός, ή, όν		
(I) wish	βούλομαι; θέλω		
with	μετά (gen.); πρός (accus.); σύν (dat.)		
without	χωρίς (gen.); ἔξω (adv.)		
witness	μάρτυς, υρος, ὁ		
woe!	οὐαί		
woman	γυνή, γυναικός, ἡ		
word	λόγος, ου, ὁ; ῥῆμα, ατος, τό		
work	ἔργον, ου, τό		

Paradigms of the Omega Verb λύω
Active Voice

	Present	Imperfect	Future	1 Aorist	1 Perfect	1 Pluperfect
Ind.	λύω	ἔλυον	λύσω	ἔλυσα	λέλυκα	ἐλελύκειν
	λύεις	ἔλυες	λύσεις	ἔλυσας	λέλυκας	ἐλελύκεις
	λύει	ἔλυε(ν)	λύσει	ἔλυσε(ν)	λέλυκε	ἐλελύκει
	λύομεν	ἐλύομεν	λύσομεν	ἐλύσαμεν	λελύκαμεν	ἐλελύκειμεν
	λύετε	ἐλύετε	λύσετε	ἐλύσατε	λελύκατε	ἐλελύκειτε
	λύουσι(ν)	ἔλυον	λύσουσι(ν)	ἔλυσαν	λέλυκαν -κασι(ν)	ἐλελύκεισαν
Subj.	λύω			λύσω	λελύκω	
	λύῃς			λύσῃς	λελύκῃς	
	λύῃ			λύσῃ	λελύκῃ	
	λύωμεν			λύσωμεν	λελύκωμεν	
	λύητε			λύσητε	λελύκητε	
	λύωσι(ν)			λύσωσι(ν)	λελύκωσι(ν)	
Opt.	λύοιμι		λύσοιμι	λύσαιμι	λελύκοιμι	
	λύοις		λύσοις	λύσαις	λελύκοις	
	λύοι		λύσοι	λύσαι	λελύκοι	
	λύοιμεν		λύσοιμεν	λύσαιμεν	λελύκοιμεν	
	λύοιτε		λύσοιτε	λύσαιτε	λελύκοιτε	
	λύοιεν		λύσοιεν	λύσαιεν	λελύκοιεν	
Impv.	λῦε			λῦσον		
	λυέτω			λυσάτω		
	λύετε			λύσατε		
	λυέτωσαν			λυσάτωσαν		
	-όντων			-άντων		
Inf.	λύειν		λύσειν	λῦσαι	λελυκέναι	
Part.	λύων		λύσων	λύσας	λελυκώς	
	λύουσα		λύσουσα	λύσασα	λελυκυῖα	
	λῦον		λῦσον	λῦσαν	λελυκός	

Middle—Passive

	Present	Imperfect	Perfect	Pluperfect
Ind.	λύομαι	ἐλυόμην	λέλυμαι	ἐλελύμην
	λύῃ	ἐλύου	λέλυσαι	ἐλέλυσο
	λύεται	ἐλύετο	λέλυται	ἐλέλυτο
	λυόμεθα	ἐλυόμεθα	λελύμεθα	ἐλελύμεθα
	λύεσθε	ἐλύεσθε	λέλυσθε	ἐλέλυσθε
	λύονται	ἐλύοντο	λέλυνται	ἐλέλυντο

Middle–Passive
(continued)

	Present	Imperfect	Perfect	Pluperfect
Subj.	λύωμαι		λελυμένος ὦ	
	λύῃ		λελυμένος ᾖς	
	λύηται		λελυμένος ᾖ	
	λυώμεθα		λελυμένοι ὦμεν	
	λύησθε		λελυμένοι ἦτε	
	λύωνται		λελυμένοι ὦσι(ν)	
Opt.	λυοίμην		λελυμένος εἴην	
	λύοιο		λελυμένος εἴης	
	λύοιτο		λελυμένος εἴη	
	λυοίμεθα		λελυμένοι εἴημεν	
	λύοισθε		λελυμένοι εἴητε	
	λύοιντο		λελυμένοι εἴησαν	
Impv.	λύου		λέλυσο	
	λυέσθω		λελύσθω	
	λύεσθε		λέλυσθε	
	λυέσθωσαν		λελύσθων	
	-σθων			
Inf.	λύεσθαι		λελύσθαι	
Part.	λυόμενος		λελυμένος	
	λυομένη		λελυμένη	
	λυόμενον		λελυμένον	

Middle

	Future	Aorist
Ind.	λύσομαι	ἐλυσάμην
	λύσῃ	ἐλύσω
	λύσεται	ἐλύσατο
	λυσόμεθα	ἐλυσάμεθα
	λύσεσθε	ἐλύσασθε
	λύσονται	ἐλύσαντο
Subj.		λύσωμαι
		λύσῃ
		λύσηται
		λυσώμεθα
		λύσησθε
		λύσωνται

Middle
(continued)

	<u>Future</u>	<u>Aorist</u>
Opt.	λυσοίμην	λυσαίμην
	λύσοιο	λύσαιο
	λύσοιτο	λύσαιτο
	λυσοίμεθα	λυσαίμεθα
	λύσοισθε	λύσαισθε
	λύσοιντο	λύσαιντο
Impv.		λῦσαι
		λυσάσθω
		λύσασθε
		λυσάσθωσαν
		-άσθων
Inf.	λύσεσθαι	λύσασθαι
Part.	λυσόμενος	λυσάμενος
	λυσομένη	λυσαμένη
	λυσόμενον	λυσάμενον

Passive

	<u>Future</u>	<u>Aorist</u>
Ind.	λυθήσομαι	ἐλύθην
	λυθήσῃ	ἐλύθης
	λυθήσεται	ἐλύθη
	λυθησόμεθα	ἐλύθημεν
	λυθήσεσθε	ἐλύθητε
	λυθήσονται	ἐλύθησαν
Subj.		λυθῶ
		λυθῇς
		λυθῇ
		λυθῶμεν
		λυθῆτε
		λυθῶσι(ν)
Opt.	λυθησοίμην	λυθείην
	λυθήσοιο	λυθείης
	λυθήσοιτο	λυθείη
	λυθησοίμεθα	λυθείημεν
	λυθήσοισθε	λυθείητε
	λυθήσοιντο	λυθείησαν

Passive
(continued)

	Future	Aorist
Impv.		λύθητι λυθήτω
		λύθητε λυθήτωσαν -θέντων
Inf.	λυθήσεσθαι	λυθῆναι
Part.	λυθησόμενος λυθησομένη λυθησόμενον	λυθείς λυθεῖσα λυθέν

Future Perfect

Ind.	λελύσομαι λελύσῃ λελύσεται
	λελυσόμεθα λελύσεσθε λελύσονται
Subj.	----------
Opt.	λελυσοίμην λελύσοιο λελύσοιτο
	λελυσοίμεθα λελύσοισθε λελύσοιντο
Impv.	----------
Inf.	λελύσεσθαι
Part.	λελυσόμενος λελυσομένη λελυσόμενον

Accents, 3, 4.
  Acute
  Circumflex
  Grave
Adjectives, 18, 98-100.
Adverbs, 99.
Alphabet, 1.
Article, The, 11, 19, 20;
  The chart, 213, 214.

Cases, 9;
  The Chart, 191-194.
Clauses, coordinating and
  subordinating, 101, 102.
Conditional sentences, 95, 203, 204.
Conjugation of the regular indicative
  verb, luo, 5, 6, 12, 13, 14, 27,
  28, 30-33.
Conjugation of the contract verb,
  72-77.
Conjugation of the mi verb, 80-87.
Comparatives, superlatives, 98, 99.
Consonants and vowels, 2.
Contract verbs, 72-77.

Declensions, 8, 11, 17, 18, 37-40, 43,
  44;
  The charts, 171-174.
Demonstrative Pronouns, 23, 24.
Diagramming Greek Sentences, 185-190.
Diphthongs, 2.

Enclitics, proclitics, 3.
English to Greek Supplementary
  Sentences, 105-109.

First declension, 11, 17, 18, 171.

Greek Moods explained, 41, 42, 61, 69,
  198.
Greek Reader Notes for John 1-5
  Simplified, 123-159.
Greek Reader Text on John 1-5
  Simplified, 110-122.

Imperative, 69;
  The chart, 198-200.
Indicative, 5, 61, 198.
Infinitive, 67, 68;
  The chart, 201, 202.

Kind of Action, 5, 12-14, 26-28, 30-33,
  45, 48, 57, 198.

Lesson Plans, 160-167.
  For Intermediate Greek, 160-161.
  For Advanced Greek, 162-167.
Liquid Verbs, 77.

Mi verbs, 80-87.
Moods explained, 41, 42, 61, 69, 198.
Movable nu, 5, footnote 3.

Negatives, 33, 202.
Numbers, 101.

Optative, 95-97, 178, 198, 199.

Paradigms of the Omega Verb luo,
  248-251.
Parsing Number System, 6, 7, 170.
Parsing verb forms, 6, 7, 93, 96, 103,
  104, 170.
Participles, 45, 46, 50-56, 200, 201.
Particles chart, 219, 220.
Perfect tense, formation of, 177.
Prepositions, 25;
  The chart, 207-212.
Principal parts of verbs, 45, 48, 52,
  57, 61, 66, 71, 79, 88.
Principles of the New Testament Greek
  Verb, 175-178.
Proclitics, enclitics, 3.
Pronouns -
  Personal, 21, 22.
  Demonstrative, 23, 24.
  Interrogative, indefinite, 44.
  Relative, 24.
Pronunciation of The Alphabet, and
  Expressions, in Modern Greek,
  221-225.
Punctuation, 3.
Purpose clauses, 95.

Questions, negatives, 33.

Relative pronouns, 24, 89.

Second aorist verbs, 36, 86.
Second declension, 8, 11, 20, 171.
Subjunctive, 61-64;
  The chart, 198, 199.
Subordinate clauses and phrases, types
  of construction, 205, 206.
Suffixes for substantives, adjectives,
  179, 180.
Superlatives, comparatives, 98, 99.

Syllables, ultima, penult (second
    syllable from the end of the word)
    and antepenult, 3.
Syntax charts, 191–220.
Syntax of the cases, 90–92.

Temporal clauses, 205, 206.
Tenses, 5, 6, 177.
Third declension, 37–40, 43, 100,
    172–174.
Two-ending third declension
    adjectives, 100.
Types of first, second and third
    declension forms and endings, 11,
    171–174.

Verb chart (tenses, usage, etc.),
    195–197.
Verbal prefixes and suffixes, 15, 16,
    168, 169.
Verb "to be," 33, 86.
Vocabulary, 226–247.
  Greek-English, 226–236.
  English-Greek, 237–247.
Voice, 5.
Vowels, 2.

Word formation, 181–184.